THE SACRED CHANGEMAKER'S GUIDE

BEYOND PROFIT

TO REIMAGINING BUSINESS AND LEADING

REGENERATIVE CHANGE

JAYNE WARRILOW

Praise For Beyond Profit

"Beyond Profit is a profound guide for leaders yearning to make business a force for good. Jayne Warrilow invites us to step beyond mere profit, embracing a regenerative approach that prioritizes purpose, people, and the planet. This book resonates with the wisdom of interconnectedness, offering a framework that is both practical and soul-stirring. A must-read for anyone seeking to lead with heart and transformative impact." -**Jerry Colonna, *Author of Reunion: Leadership and the Longing to Belong and Reboot: Leadership and the Art of Growing Up.***

"We all exist in energy fields we can't see, but we know when we are with people who live by a higher purpose than making money, who care about us when we buy from them, and who have a love for the planet we walk on. My financial profile consists of companies I trust and believe in the power of business as a force for positive change, and my financial worth keeps growing. How can you start on this path? *Beyond Profit* will take you on a journey to hear the call of your own sense of purpose and how to use it as your guiding light, even when the path is dark. Then, the book explores what it means to lead with purpose and create businesses that foster cultures of care and contribute to creating a world that works for all. I hope everyone reads Jane's book, *Beyond Profit*, so we can make a difference together." - **Dr. Marcia Reynolds, Founder of Covisioning and Author of Breakthrough Coaching**

"This book should be essential reading for everyone in business. It is beautifully written by a beautiful person, and weaves together timeless wisdom and practical insights to create a happier, sustainable future for us all." - **Dr Manoj Krishna, *Founder, HappierMe***

"There is only one thing worse than being a disappointment to your parents, and that is to be a disappointment to your grandchildren. In this carefully researched and beautifully written book, Jayne Warrilow explains how business leaders can avoid this tragic fate by reimagining the role and purpose of business in the 21st century. Using a broad range of sources and tools, the book takes the reader on a comprehensive journey from the mantra of profit to the mantra of purpose. Read it and feel an exciting new leadership calling emerge from within you.' - **Dr John Blakey**, *Author 'Force for Good - How to Thrive as a Purpose-Driven Leader*

"Beyond Profit is a brave invitation to reimagine business as a source of real, positive change. It calls us to step up with courage and take responsibility for the lasting impact we leave in our communities and the world. Jayne's compassionate wisdom and practical guidance equips conscious leaders to realign their values, build resilience, and foster a deep sense of purpose in their work. Beyond Profit inspires us to create businesses that genuinely care—for people, for the planet, and for the future, we're all part of building." - **Sarah Santacroce**, *Conscious Business Coach, Author of Marketing & Selling Like We're Human*

"In the book "Beyond Profit," Jayne Warrilow provides a practical guide to how to organize differently with a recognition of all stakeholders. This book provides a meaningful regenerative roadmap for the transformation of ourselves, our communities, and, as a result, our environment. The book is practical and positively impactful. A must-read for anyone in organizations. Indeed, we are all here to make a positive impact on the world. " **Catherine R. Bell, MBA**, *Founder The Awakened Company*

"We stand at the brink of profound change, both as leaders and as human beings. Jayne Warrilow's book, *Beyond Profit*, serves as an essential guide to navigating this transformation and forging an unprecedented path forward. It invites us to embrace the spaces in between, inspiring a new paradigm for leadership and personal growth. She encourages us to reimagine the future of business and ourselves."
Jennifer K. Hill, *CEO & Evolutionary Leader*

"Beyond Profit is a transformative read that challenges conventional notions of the traditional metric of "success" in business. Jayne eloquently advocates for innovative business models and regenerative practices that foster sustainability and community connections that not only lead to better global outcomes but are also better for you. As well as being a guide, it is a heartfelt call to action for conscious leadership, inspiring individuals to embrace their unique potential and contribute to a meaningful legacy for future generations." - **Tim Jones**, *That B Corp Bloke*

"With the fantastic Beyond Profit, Jayne Warrilow helps us shift the narrative about the purpose of work. It can be a place that is full of meaning, growth, and community." -**Scott Shute**, **Founder -** *Changing Work*, **Author of The Full Body Yes.**

"Beyond Profit deeply resonates. It echoes a powerful call to redefine success in ways that honor our interconnectedness with life, people, and purpose. The message reminds us that true transformation in business comes not from the relentless pursuit of profit but from a commitment to deeply connect with oneself and create meaningful value for both people and the planet. It invites us to step beyond transactional thinking and embrace a regenerative approach that heals, nurtures, and inspires, aligning our work with a higher purpose. This vision feels refreshing and essential in a world longing for real, lasting change." **Arnaud Saint-Paul,** *Heart Leadership*, **Tapuat**

"An awakening number of us are realizing, as Jayne Warrilow says in this book, that humanity as a whole needs to undergo 'a radical shift—from a profit-centric mindset to one that honors the sacredness of life, the interconnectedness of all beings, and our responsibility as stewards of the Earth.' Business looms large as a locus of this shift, and Jayne Warrilow identifies exactly what, in that important sector, the shift could and must! look like." - **Michael Nagler**, *Author, The Search for a Nonviolent Future and President, Metta Center for Nonviolence*

"Beyond Profit is a soulful companion for anyone wrestling with how to bring their deepest inner wisdom into the workplace. If you've ever felt torn between your spiritual journey and business demands, Jayne Warrilow shows you don't have to choose. This is your permission slip to merge both worlds and create something beautiful and profitable in the process." - **Leisa Peterson**, *Author of The Mindful Millionaire*

"Jayne Warrilow is a pioneer in defining sacred change-making in the world. In this book, she guides readers on the powerful link between inner transformation and outer impact, inspiring business leaders to break free from the status quo and create businesses that go 'Beyond Profit.'"- **Fiona English**, *Keynote Speaker & Thought Leader*

Contents

About the Author	X
Also by Jayne Warrilow	XI
Dedication	XIII
Foreword	XV
Prologue	XIX
Letter From The Author	
A Sacred Invitation	
Introduction	XXV
Birthing A New Era Of Business	
Why Business As Usual Is No Longer Enough	
The Sacred Changemaker Vision	
Inner Compass: Guiding Questions	

Part 1

1. The Leader Within — 3
    Coming Home
    The Inner Work Required to Lead with Purpose and Integrity
    Energy Management: Avoiding Burnout
    Inner Compass: Guiding Questions

2. A New Way Of Being — 37
    The Call to Awaken
    When Worlds Collide
    Inner Compass: Guiding Questions

3. Why Sacred Changemakers? — 67
    Towards a Working Definition

The Role of Changemakers in Modern Business
Creating a Movement: Engaging Others in Your Vision
Inner Compass: Guiding Questions

Part 2

4. Regenerative Leadership: Catalyzing Necessary Change   91
   Leadership as a Sacred Duty
   Becoming Regenerative
   Unleashing the Potential Energy of the Organization
   Developing a Sacred Changemaker Mindset
   Redefining Success: New Metrics for Measuring Business Success
   Purpose-Driven Profits: Aligning Business Operations with Your Purpose
   Building a Regenerative Culture
   Inner Compass: Guiding Questions

5. The Path to Transformation   143
   From Me to We: Expanding Consciousness in Business
   Inner Compass: Guiding Questions

6. From The Individual To The Collective   175
   The Power of Purpose
   Integrating Indigenous and Sacred Wisdom into Modern Business
   Learning from Nature: Embracing the Wisdom of Living Systems
   From Me to We in Action
   Inner Compass: Guiding Questions

Part 3

7. Transformational Business Models   211
   1. Buy-One-Give-One (B1G1) Model
   2. B-Corporations
   3. Social Enterprises
   Redefining Giving and Trust
   Community as the Way Forward

      Conscious Business Models: Balancing Purpose and Profit
      Creating a Regenerative Business
      Scaling with Integrity: Conscious Expansion in Business
      Tools and Strategies: How to Map Your Business Ecosystem
      Navigating Challenges: Techniques for Managing Business Fatigue
      Inner Compass: Guiding Questions

8. Conclusion: Now You Know What Will You Do?   241
      A Vision for the Future
      Legacy And Impact
      What is your Sacred Invitation?
      Understanding Your Core Values
      Will You Be A Good Ancestor?
      Inner Compass: Guiding Questions

Epilogue   257

Acknowledgements   262

Endnotes   265

Copyrights   269

About the Author

Jayne Warrilow is a global speaker, bestselling author, and renowned Business/Executive Coach devoted to empowering changemakers and purpose-driven leaders. She is the founder of Sacred Changemakers (SacredChangemakers.com), a transformative community, and podcast dedicated to elevating consciousness, reimagining business, and inspiring a positive impact in the world. Jayne's work sits at the powerful intersection of soul, business, and technology, where she is passionately building resources and community for changemakers.

Known as one of the world's most exclusive business coaches, her clients, including CEOs, senior executives, and thought leaders, are selected by invitation and referral only. Despite her high-profile clientele, Jayne's true mission is to support coaches, consultants, and changemakers in realizing their potential, leading regenerative change, and inspiring others to create businesses that align with their deepest values and the needs of the human soul.

As a thought leader, Jayne is a regular keynote speaker at international business and leadership conferences on the frameworks featured in her books, including Beyond Profit: A Sacred Changemakers Guide to Reimagining Business and Leading Regenerative Change; Coaches as the Changemakers for Humanity's Evolution and An Energy Awakening: Waking Up To The Journey Ahead.

Originally from England, Jayne has worked with leading organizations and visionary individuals across the United States, Europe, Asia, Australia, and Latin America. She now lives and works out of Columbus, Ohio, dedicated to supporting changemakers on their journeys to creating a better world. Contact Jayne via SacredChangemakers.com

Also by Jayne Warrilow

An Energy Awakening: Waking Up To The Journey Ahead

The Secret Language Of Resonance: The Incredible Truth About Life And Well-Being

The 10-Day Coaches MBA – The Small Business Book For Coaches Who Want To Play Bigger

The Profitable Coach: How To Double The Profits From Your Coaching Business And Make A Meaningful Impact In The World

The Evolving Coaching Business – Design The Canvas For Your Greatest Work And Re-Think Your Business To Deliver Meaningful Impact and Even Greater Profit.

Fully Booked – Make A Bigger Impact With Your Coaching

Empath Energy Cleanse – The Proven 21-Day Formula To Breakthrough Your Energy Blocks And Find Your Flow

Professional Coaches Evolve – Changing The Way Coaches Do Business

You Were Meant For Something More – Living Radical, Real & Resonant, Insightful Journeys, A Compilation by Authors In The Resonance Project

Dedication

To my clients—my greatest teachers,
whose wisdom has opened my heart and mind
in ways I could never have imagined.
To my coaching colleagues around the world,
who change lives, ease suffering, and make each day a little better
through their relentless commitment to this work.
And to the inspiring members of the Sacred Changemakers Inner Circle,
whose dedication and spirit remind me of why we do this—
together, in service of a brighter, more compassionate world.
This book is for you.

Foreword

By Steven Morris

Beneath the damp, dark forest floor, under ancient trees and decaying leaves, something timeless, universal, and primordial spreads. An invisible thrumming network of mycelium—the hidden architecture of life and nature—connects roots and trees across the world, quietly and persistently sustaining life. This threaded web carries wisdom through soil and shadow. In it flows a steady pulse of exchange and renewal that keeps the earth whole. Patient and relentless, there is a quiet yet undeniable truth in it—a reminder that strength lies in connection and that all growth happens in mutuality.

In *Beyond Profit*, Jayne Warrilow takes us into an unflinching practical yet sacred journey through the undercurrents of business, peeling back layers of polished presentations and market shares to reveal something deeper, something more alive and sustainable. Here, beneath the world of numbers and transactions, she reveals the delicate threads that bind us, beyond profit, to purpose, people, and planet.

She rightly states that business is more than an endless hunger for growth, more than a machine devouring resources to manufacture wealth. What if, she asks, it could be regenerative, like the mycelium? A living system pulsing with reciprocity, pushing through the darkness and into the light, where every part is connected, where every part matters.

This book is not a manual but an actionable call for a new way of seeing. *Beyond Profit* is a soul calling—your soul's calling—to see beyond the simple answers, the quick fix, the binary, and the easy extraction and instead listen to the resonance toward the patient rhythms of sustainability. Like the mycelium, Warrilow's vision is resilient, interwoven, persistent, and driven by a sense of attentiveness and care for the Universal Energy of the whole.

Every action from and on behalf of Universal life energy is transformative because the relationship between our soul and the world is reciprocal. As we work to heal the world of business, we heal each other and the earth. In turn, others heal us, and the earth heals us in a continuum of virtuous cycles.

Within the soul-filled pages that follow, Jayne offers us a business *way* that, instead of roaring through the world, might actually heal it and us—nourishing employees, communities, the planet, and yes, even the bottom line, but without sacrificing one for the other.

As I read *Beyond Profit*, I found my attention returning, again and again, to the mycelium, to the invisible dark and pulsing quiet beneath the forest floor, to the vital visibility of our everyday lives and work. In a society that worships the alters of speed, spectacle, and surface, mycelium reminds us that true power often lies unseen, in the hidden currents, in the spaces between. Warrilow asks us to bring this same depth to our work: to turn business into an act of love, to build connections that give without demanding, and to ask not only what we can take but what we might give.

All living things hold a sensual longing for communion with the attributes of life that are connected to the dynamic and Universal system. Our longing, in life and business, is to sustain and nourish that connection. Through that connection, we are furthering the evolution of consciousness, and through this book, you will deepen your business consciousness.

Imagine a business, she suggests, that grows not by conquest but by kinship, that moves forward not by accumulation but by integration, empathy, and shared purpose. A business that, like the forest, holds all things within its reach and recognizes that its own survival is interwoven with the survival of all around it. The Universe conspires to provide the necessary thread when we begin to weave. The threads within this book are not just ideas; they are sacred change-making material for those who've grown tired of the fractured, soulless grind of conventional commerce and who know that the future lies not in personal gain but in the strength of the collective.

Jayne Warrilow reminds us that the real measure of success is not in the red or the black ink but in the health of the network we tend. She asks us to look beyond the numbers, resist the myopic narrowness of profit-only, and instead embrace a business vision that regenerates and renews your business and everything it's connected to.

No, this is not a book to merely read and shelve. *Beyond Profit* is a soul-calling to action to live and breathe your business anew. It's a time-urgent invitation to look beneath the surface, to feel the pulse of something more significant, and to set out on a journey toward a business model rooted in resilience and reverence.

So open your heart and turn the pages with reverence. Step into the flow that awaits you. A sacred business journey is here for you to enter the river of joy constantly flowing in your direction. Here is your soul's invitation to answer the call of interconnection, take the next steps on a soul-growth healing journey, and see and know the full-spectrum beauty beneath the glittering façade of profit-only-driven enterprise.

Just as the mycelium nourishes the world's wilderness in ways we cannot see, so too does *Beyond Profit* offer the sustenance and vision needed to reimagine your business—as a beautiful, regenerative, sprawling ecosystem where every thread is sacred, every vibration felt, every soul touched, and every aspect thriving.

—Steven Morris

CEO, Matter Consulting, and best-selling author of *The Beautiful Business.*

Prologue

Letter From The Author

Today, we stand at the edge, at the brink of impending disaster.

We know we do.

We've done this to ourselves, which is a hard pill to swallow; what we decide to do next matters.

We could turn our heads away, close our eyes, keep breathing poisoned air, keep eating toxic food, and witness the extinction of those we love while continuing to take whatever we want from the Earth.

We could ignore the warning signs from extreme weather to mental illness, from mass extinction to water shortages, from the lack of political concern to our way of doing business that continues to take from the planet in the relentless pursuit of profit, regardless of the cost to life.

We could disregard the gnawing feeling in our souls, retreat from the edge, stay in our comfort zones, and allow ourselves to fall into the inevitable decline.

We could do that. And many of us will.

Others won't.

Some of us will refuse to accept the status quo. We will stand against the decline to inspire change that will shift our destiny in a different direction.

We know this is not the best we can do.

We can do better.

This is not how human life is meant to be.

This is not how business is meant to be.

And this is not the legacy we want to leave for future generations.

We're being invited to transcend our current ways of being and doing to write a new story for humanity. We are beginning to remember this story because it lies deep within our bones. It is emerging in the hearts of those of us who care.

We know it, we can feel it, and many of us long for it: a world where life is more joyful, family and relationships are prioritized above work, and business creates real value for all.

We have a duty to care for life, to live within it, and not to try to rule it.

But what will it take to turn away from all that is not working and step beyond the edge of our knowing?

It will take courage, faith, and love to overcome our fears.

It will take all of us to join hands and face the unknown together.

The required changes are more significant than any one of us, and they begin with each of us committing to our collective future.

The future begins with you.

We can do this.

Our grandchildren's lives depend upon it.

Thank you for joining me on this journey and for all you do to make our world a better place.

I hope somewhere along this sacred path, I get to look into your eyes, feel into your soul, and share a knowing glance as we remember each other and the work we came here to do,

With love and resonance,

Jayne xo

A Sacred Invitation

A number of decades ago, the change-makers arrived on the planet carrying the light. They arrived quietly, born to families around the world, destined to become torch-bearers for the evolution of humanity.

These humans are old souls, carrying with them the wisdom from many lifetimes, the courage of the ancient warrior spirit and the seeds of infinite potential. These souls have silently walked through the millennia, developing the energetic capacity to return to Earth at this time. They are here to facilitate a rebirth of the human spirit and embrace the deepest truths of their soul's resonance.

Born decades ago to be here right now, at this extraordinary time on Earth. These individuals are now awakening. The next evolutionary step for humanity is ready to be taken.

They are hearing their soul's calling to embody the space of deep transformation; to inspire, encourage and support others worldwide to raise their vibration and consciously shape our future for the next generation.

Emerging one by one from the lower vibrations of the physical realm, these conscious beings are walking barefoot upon the barren Earth. Grounded in the soil yet infused with a lightness of being that connects them to the sky, attuned with all that flows from the air above. They are unafraid to stand at the edges of what we believe is possible, and lead the way.

They have been learning how to recognize energy, and see the life force that permeates our world. They are mastering the invisible; to see beyond sight and hear beyond sound. They understand the interconnectivity of all things, the interwoven web of energy that holds us in delicate balance with life.

Each of these rare humans carry a karmic load, adorned with the collective wounds of humanity. They have been challenged, wounded, and broken open, to help them remember their spiritual path. They have walked within their own darkness, enduring hardship and pain. Yet despite their personal challenges, they have found their way to a new level of understanding that lies beyond fear. Their time has come to step into the light.

They know their path is one of profound self-healing, a lifetime of twists and turns that has inspired a depth of compassion and a resilience to create miracles when all hope is lost.

As these souls heal themselves, they spark a transformation so resonant, it creates a ripple effect of healing energy that transcends boundaries and borders, shatters the illusions of the modern world, igniting the collective soul of humanity.

These humans radiate with Universal Energy. With eyes, hearts and minds wide open, they are getting ready to bring forward their soul work to the world.

As we move through these challenging times, it is essential to remember that we are not here by accident. We have entered the world with the clear purpose of facilitating the changes that are needed during this time. We are among the most important people who have ever lived. We will determine whether humankind will grow or die, evolve or perish.

If you have been pulled into our vibrational web, **you are one of us.** Regardless of how unfulfilled your life may seem, regardless of how meager your self esteem, or how profit-poor your business, you are being called to consciousness by the necessity of our times.

We are being called to gather together, to become more than we ever thought we could be. We are being invited to step up and lead, to bring forward our gifts to help heal the world. We are here to guide ourselves and others towards the essential truths that lie deep within.

When we learn to listen closely, we can begin to attune our actions with our higher purpose and become exactly who we were meant to be.

We cannot remain paralyzed in the stuck vibrations of fear and disconnection from our souls; it is time we all became whole.

We have the capacity to create a world that is capable of preserving the integrity of all life. One that transcends modern-day business structures to inspire the human spirit. We are here to make a difference. We are the ones who will facilitate the evolution of humanity. Together, we will achieve more than any of us can dream.

The time is now.

You have a higher purpose and a soul mission. It's time to live the life you were meant to live. Your skills are needed. Let's show the world the power of our actions.

Your destiny is calling, and you must answer...

- *The Sacred Invitation is a channeled transmission from the Elders as received by Jayne in May 2019. It was the spark that catalyzed a new adventure, becoming a Sacred Changemaker.*

Introduction

> *"It's not the critic who counts, not the man who points out how the strong man stumbles or where the doer of deeds could have done them better. The credit belongs to the person who is in the arena. Whose face is marred with dust and sweat and blood; who strives valiantly ... who at best knows, in the end, the triumph of high achievement, and who at the worst, if he fails, at least fails while daring greatly ..."* T. Roosevelt[1]

To the visionaries, trailblazers, and changemakers leading the fundamental transformations our world needs, I want this book to be your guide. If you're a founder or business leader looking to succeed financially and elevate your presence to become the soul of your enterprise, you're in the right place. You may be a coach, consultant, or mentor who knows that profit and purpose can fuel each other, driving a more conscious way of doing business. You might also be that regenerative leader who sparks the human spirit and is committed to the inner journey that will turn you into the beacon the world is waiting for. If any of this resonates with you, I hope this book will serve as your map to creating a business—and a life—that's not just successful but deeply meaningful and fulfilling.

As an experienced business and executive coach, I've worked with CEOs, entrepreneurs, and changemakers as they navigate the ever-changing world of leadership and business. My journey has taken me from the corporate boardrooms of some of the most iconic brands to the deeply intimate spaces of personal transformation, helping people redefine success—beyond profit—to include the well-being of both people and the planet.

In 2004, after a life-changing battle with a terminal diagnosis and a transformative healing journey with a team of unconventional therapists, I emerged with a new sense of purpose. I became dedicated to mapping consciousness to business and leadership—a blend of ancient wisdom and modern innovation. This began my (now) body of work on resonance and the interconnectivity between all things. It felt like the missing link between my professional role as a strategic changemaker and my spiritual path. Integrating these different parts of me has genuinely enriched my work.

My experiences around the world have shaped my approach even further, allowing me to connect deeply with leaders from all walks of life to help them to shift their consciousness and acknowledge the inherent interconnectedness of people, systems, and fields of awareness. It is this shift in consciousness that gives us the capacity to change. I've also shared many insights through my podcast[2], where the voices of changemakers echo with a community hungry for a new era of business.

This new era is emerging now, as the old ways are not fit for today's challenges. This is true of many dimensions of our human lives that demand change. But what change have we been taught to bring forward in these times? Unfortunately, like so much of the business world, we tend to bring a siloed approach. Many changemakers tend to walk through a narrow door. They might be a coach, facilitator, or consultant when what is really needed is all of the above. To make matters worse, they may also have specialized in a particular genre of coaching or consulting, which means their contributions can feel too small for the complex changes our clients are facing.

What is needed today lies beyond profit, which is a metaphor for what we're doing in most things. Yes, our vision needs to move beyond profit in business, our leadership needs to move beyond our own self-centered interests, and our vision for change needs to move beyond the narrow definitions that have shaped and unconsciously limited the careers of so many changemakers.

The best changemakers in the world come from multiple disciplines. These are the edge walkers, those who walk between worlds and can find value in the in-between. These are the individuals who know that to inspire change is a leadership journey. And today's leaders understand that leadership goes beyond the individual, acknowledging the inherent interconnectedness of human and non-human forms of the ecosystems and fields of awareness we live within. Life and leadership are fundamentally relational. Our role is to release the intelligence and information already present within those relationships. This demands a shift in consciousness, and it demands resonance.

I have spent most of my career working with business leaders in coaching and consulting. I learned at coaching school not to be on my agenda when coaching but to create space for the client's agenda, and although this felt limiting to me, it worked well for a time. However, I soon felt confined by this practice, as did my clients, so we began to explore the space in-between. Not my agenda or my clients but what was emerging in and between us. That's when a deep shift took place in the room; instead of talking about competencies and outcomes, we began to notice the broader ecology, the systems we were both a part of that were also present, the desires and longing propelling us forward, the fears and shadows holding us back and what emerged as a co-created result was exponential. The outcomes were so much more than I could have defined as the coach and so much more than what the client could have defined; it felt like magic.

This approach demands a higher level of consciousness than what we're used to in life and business. It lies beyond the intellect, data, and evidence we have learned to trust. It demands a different type of trust: trust in yourself, others, and life itself. So, when we encourage change, we must embrace life as the third party in the room. We need to bring all of our influences into the room.

- *Where is the flow of your life naturally taking you?*
- *What wants expression through you?*
- *What is the change that's emerging in and around you that needs us*

to explore today?

I've noticed something exciting in my work as a coach; the truth is most of us know what we need in terms of growth and development, and life knows better than we do. And although most change is directed toward individual development, it is an illusion. Nothing changes all by itself. Not even you. That's why I wrote this book, because our approach to change needs to change.

When I look out into the world at all the challenges we're facing and rise in consciousness, I can begin to see the interconnectivity between them. The climate crisis, biodiversity issues, diversity, equity and inclusion, mental illness, and suicide—they all affect each other. The pattern that emerges is one of disconnection.

The climate issue is about being disconnected from the earth, and the impact we're creating; diversity, equity, and inclusion are how we've become disconnected from each other, and mental illness and suicide are a result of how we've become disconnected from ourselves. We've also got quantum science proving how we're all interconnected in a web of life; this is fact, not fiction.

- *Can you see how the worlds become interwoven?*
- *And what insights emerge when we consider seemingly disparate views and look at the relationship between them?*

The solution to the meta-crisis we now face lies in the interconnectivity between all things, and we can only understand, embody, and encourage this through learning to live at a higher level of consciousness. This was a key driver in me writing this book to guide your changemaking and leadership path.

At the heart of every founder and business leader lies a big question: Should you build a thriving, profitable enterprise, or should you serve the greater good? For-profit or not-for-profit? Traditionally, business has been defined in these clear-cut terms, with no middle ground. But things are shifting now. You may find yourself at a crossroads, torn between purpose and profit, wondering: Can I do both? The answer is yes. And that's also why I'm writing this book—to show you how.

This book is for those who believe in the power of business as a force for positive change but wrestle with the fear that following their heart might cost them their livelihood. It's for the visionary who dares to dream of a world where business ignites the human spirit and respects the planet, even when the future feels uncertain. It's for those of us who know that change is and always will be a core part of our lives, and it is time for us to evolve our consciousness so we can adapt to the world around us.

In these pages, you'll discover how to survive and thrive in this new era of business. You'll learn how to inspire change for good and integrate regenerative approaches and social responsibility into your company's core, so as your profits grow, your positive impact on the world also grows. It's not about choosing between making money and making a difference—it's about mastering how to do both together.

Together, we'll embark on a growth journey that begins in *Part 1*. The focus is on personal transformation as the essential foundation for inspiring the changes needed to move *beyond profit*. This journey starts on the inside by cultivating a deep sense of self-awareness, trust, and alignment, which form the basis of regenerative leadership. Here, you'll discover how to connect more deeply with yourself, awaken your soul, and expand your consciousness beyond the intellect.

We will explore the inner work required to lead with purpose and integrity, recognizing that leadership is not just about external achievements—it's about who you *become* as a leader. This inner journey will guide you through practical steps to deepen your self-awareness, manage your energy, and cultivate emotional mastery, all while expanding your capacity to create meaningful impact in the world.

In *Part 1*, you'll:

- Discover how the world shapes us as leaders and how to reclaim your inner power to lead from a place of authenticity.
- Learn practical techniques for quieting the mind, managing emo-

tions, and tapping into stillness through practices like meditation and reflection—tools that are vital for leading with clarity and presence.

- Understand the importance of self-compassion and energy management so you can avoid burnout and lead with resilience.

- Explore the deeper dimensions of resonance and alignment, learning to navigate the energies of mind, body, and spirit to create a more meaningful connection to your purpose.

- Begin the shift from *'me' to 'we'*—awakening to the collective well-being at the heart of sacred changemaking as you expand into the 8 dimensions of change.

By the end of *Part 1*, you will have laid the groundwork for becoming the changemaker you need to be—not just for your growth but to inspire and empower those around you. You'll be ready to expand beyond your individual goals and move into a new way of being, fully equipped to bring your vision into the world.

In *Part 2*, we shift from the inner work of personal transformation to exploring what it means to lead with purpose in today's evolving business landscape. This section invites you to expand your definition of success, embracing a regenerative approach where people, planet, and profit hold equal weight. As a conscious leader, you are called to drive financial performance and create a lasting positive impact on the world around you.

You'll be invited to reflect on who you truly want to become as a leader and the deeper purpose of your leadership. Together, we'll explore how ancient wisdom and modern innovation can work hand in hand to reimagine business practices that align with integrity, purpose, and regeneration. By learning from nature and embracing a living systems mindset, you'll discover how to create a thriving, sustainable ecosystem within your organization.

In *Part 2*, you'll:

- Discover how aligning your leadership with purpose can future-proof your business, ensuring its long-term success and resilience.

- Learn how to integrate indigenous and sacred wisdom into modern business practices, gaining insights from living systems and the natural world to guide your leadership.

- Explore regenerative leadership principles, focusing on building a culture of trust, crafting a narrative that inspires change, and developing a mindset that honors the sacred in both leadership and business.

- Redefine success with purpose-driven profits that align with your business's impact on people, communities, and the planet.

- Master practical strategies for catalyzing change within your organization by expanding consciousness, promoting diversity and inclusion, and fostering a culture of empathy and collaboration.

This journey through *Part 2* is an invitation to become a regenerative leader who nurtures both the people within your organization and the environment around you, leading a profitable and powerful business for good. As we embrace this conscious approach to leadership, we lay the foundation for a new era of business that honors ancient wisdom while embracing future innovations.

Finally, in *Part 3*, we pull everything together to focus on the larger vision: creating a better world through the transformative power of business. In this section, we will reimagine the pivotal role that companies can play in driving meaningful, co-created change for the global good. It's time to expand our view of leadership beyond traditional business metrics, looking instead at the regenerative impact we can have on society, ecosystems, and future generations.

Together, we'll explore how businesses can become catalysts for positive change, fostering cultures of hope and actively contributing to societal improvement. By embracing innovative models, you'll gain the tools to shape a business that serves not only profit but also the planet and its people.

In *Part 3*, you'll:

- Explore transformational business models like B Corporations and social enterprises that redefine the balance between purpose and profit.

- Learn how to create a regenerative business ecosystem that drives sustainable change while maintaining the integrity of your growth.

- Discover strategies to scale your business with purpose, ensuring your impact expands as your company thrives.

- Reflect on your leadership legacy and the values that will guide the impact you leave on the world, asking, *"Will you be a good ancestor?"*

This section provides a powerful blueprint for sustainable change, helping you expand your leadership into the role of a Sacred Changemaker. You'll gain insights into how to create a regenerative business that contributes to financial success and the betterment of society and the environment. As we conclude this journey, you'll see how resonant leadership, innovative business models, and a commitment to regenerative practices can leave a lasting legacy that harmonizes the needs of people, the planet, and profit.

As you read this book and absorb its wisdom, I hope you'll feel inspired and ready to redefine success for yourself. This isn't just about changing how we do business; it's an invitation to step into your highest potential to join a movement that sees business as a force for good where personal values align with global needs.

In the next section, "Birthing A New Era Of Business," I'll share part of my transformation journey. I'll share how a profound shift in my understanding of success reshaped my work and created Sacred Changemakers. I hope that sharing my story will light the way for you to pioneer your path in this new era of business and find your own story.

Birthing A New Era Of Business

> *"The cost of inaction is greater than the cost of action. Businesses that fail to address sustainability will not only lose their license to operate in society, but they will also miss out on the biggest opportunities of our time."* - Paul Polman[3]

What do you fear most in this life? What is your biggest fear? Right now, in this moment.

When I have asked myself that question at different times in my life, so many fears have risen to the surface, everything from not having enough money to being in so much pain that life becomes intolerable to some disaster happening to my children, and the list goes on…

But more recently, a new fear has begun to emerge. And it's not just about me but all of us.

A few days before Halloween in October 2019, I found myself in the Labor and Delivery suite of our local hospital as my daughter gave birth to her first baby and my first grandchild. I watched in absolute awe at the powerful force of childbirth and the marvel of a new human soul entering our world.

As I held this beautiful little soul in my arms for the first time, I felt overwhelming love. Tears welled up in my eyes, and everyone in the room was smiling. The joy was palpable.

From the outside in, everything looked exactly as it should, but for me, something else was going on internally, something I didn't yet understand. The joy I felt holding my granddaughter, Phoebe, was quickly replaced by a soul-deep, pervasive, and heavy sadness, and I had no idea why. It took me a few weeks leaning into this space on my meditation cushion to unpack the heavy emotions surrounding Phoebe's birth, and I was assisted in my understanding by a dream I had one night.

I dreamt that it was Phoebe's 21st birthday. When she turned to me, looked me straight in the eyes, and asked me what I had done with my life to help change the world for the better, I gulped, felt very uncomfortable, and then woke up in a mild sweat.

Reflecting on everything that had happened, I realized why I had felt so sad at her birth. This was not the world I wanted to bring her into. She's a girl who will grow to become a woman living in a man's world. She's also of mixed race, with her father from Peru and her mother from England.

When I look back on my career, I realize I have worked in many masculine-dominated environments, and not much has changed in the past 30 years. Most of the power is still held by men. It's true; I have inspired significant change and transformation for leaders all over the world. I've built multi-million dollar businesses for myself and my clients. I've changed corporate cultures for the better, and my clients tell me I have positively impacted many lives.

But is that enough? Not for me.

In the three decades I have been blessed to work as a coach and consultant, I can count on one hand the number of times I have expanded the conversation to include not only what the clients want and need but also what the world needs from them and their leadership.

Male and female inequality is just the tip of the iceberg when I consider all the challenges we face today. So much is rising to the surface and demanding our attention today. We're living through soul-defining times, a time of profound transformation for humans everywhere, and what we choose to do or not do will define the future for ourselves, our children, our grandchildren, and the generations to come.

This brings me to my greatest fear, the one that is newly emerging and calling me deeper onto my soul path - it is simply that I will not fulfill my soul purpose in this lifetime, to ease suffering and to help us all live in resonance with ourselves, each other, and all living things and to help others elevate human consciousness. My fear is that I won't step fully into my potential; I won't be able to look Phoebe in the eyes on her 21st birthday and say I did everything possible.

And let me say this is not my first calling to soul.

Hindsight is a beautiful thing; as I look back on my life's journey, I can see how there have been different times when my soul has stirred, I've heard its whispers and responded. There have been times when I've ignored my soul, which reminds me of my terminal diagnosis back in the early 2000s, which you may have read about in my earlier books, that put me firmly on my soul's path as I defied the doctors, after four years bed-ridden and in a wheelchair, to find a way to come back to life.[4]

This was the first level of my soul's integration into life and the beginning of my body of work integrating resonance into leadership. Now, I'm being called to fully embrace the soul as a guide for others, not just as individuals but also as a collective.

This also leads me to the *'we'* space and the fear that we won't fulfill our soul purpose and collectively step into our full human potential. It's time we all became whole again.

As I look at the world around me, I notice how we have lost our souls in many places, and this is particularly true in business. It's time for us to bring the soul back into our lives and businesses, to stop being who we think our industry needs us to be and become more of who we already are, to live into our spiritual truth in all its resonance. It's a soulful awakening, opening into a new way of doing business.

I believe business is the most significant lever for change we have in the modern world, and yet we're not harnessing its power to create change for good. In its current state, we're not allowing business to fulfill its soul-deep potential.

Honestly, I've always been afraid to speak about soul in business. It's simply not welcome in the logical, rational, masculine world that has defined business for many years. I believed that if I did open up a deeper soul conversation, I would lose all credibility, and I'm here to tell you the opposite is true.

The more I speak about the soul in business, the more I integrate the sheer power of the sacred into conversations. People nod their heads in agreement; I've even had CEOs of global organizations whisper that this is the direction they want to take their organization; they see this as the future of business.

I agree.

The pressure is mounting with the United Nations Sustainable Development Goals clearly defining our collective path to human survival over the next decade. With the disruption brought by the COVID-19 virus, we are all waking up to the truth of our interconnected global reality and piercing the illusion that we must sell our souls to the corporation to provide for our families.

We're all yearning for more meaning, more fulfillment, more soul.

I was reminded recently of the words of the Gnostic Gospel of Thomas :

> *"If you bring forth what is within you, what you bring forth will save you; if you do not bring forth what is within you, what you do not bring forward will destroy you."*

Think about that: if you don't listen to the whispers of your soul, it will destroy you.

This is your wake-up call.

Imagine for a moment you are standing at a crossroads in your professional journey. The well-trodden path beckons with its promise of familiar success, but it's fraught with tension and disillusionment.

There's an alternative route, one less defined, rippled with the whispers of intuition and the fragrance of a more sacred purpose—a path that demands more from you and, indeed, for you. Perhaps you've felt the stirrings of discontent, a gnawing sense that there is more to your work than revenue targets and market share. I have met many others like you: bright, ambitious souls yearning for soul-deep transformation. These kindred spirits unknowingly ignited the flames for me to write this book.

Your responsibility in life is to utterly, thoroughly, and completely embody your unique soul potential. You are meant to light up the world with your genius and design your work and leadership as a bridge to the people you are here to serve.

That's precisely what your work can do for you. We're talking about purpose and profits while making a meaningful difference in the world.

There's so much I can't wait to share with you because this is business and leadership from the inside out. Our journey together is NOT just about how you do your work; it's about you and your life.

It's about the magic of resonance which changes everything when you learn how to flow. It's about embracing uncertainty and leading change in more conscious ways. It's about the everyday practicalities of what is working in business today—a unique combination of energetics, soul-deep transformation, and proven business tools/strategies.

Are you ready?

It's time to begin...

The Call for Change

> *"The old story of business is about competition, conquest, and domination. The new story is about contribution, compassion, and interconnectedness."* - Charles Eisenstein.[5]

We're standing at the edge of a grand business renaissance, where the old maps no longer guide the pioneering spirit of today's business leaders and entrepreneurs. There's a growing realization that the traditional paths to business success aren't sustainable—or even fulfilling—anymore. This book is an invitation to step into a future where business becomes a force for good, deepening our approach to change in service of the collective well-being of both society and the planet.

This shift is characterized by the question:

Do you want to be the best leader IN the world?

OR

Do you want to be the best leader FOR the world?

It's just a small word change, but it makes all the difference to what your leadership is in service of. It speaks to the gap between where we are and where we need to be.

This journey begins with the understanding that business success goes far beyond financial statements—it's about the human experience and contributing to society. A value-first approach isn't just some idealistic dream; it's a necessary strategy for leaders and entrepreneurs who want to thrive in our changing world.

In many ways, this book is a call to action for those who feel compelled to bring meaning, purpose, and a real sense of making a difference to their work. It's for the changemakers, the dreamers, and ultimately, the leaders who can envision a business landscape where humanity, the environment, and integrity are just as important as profit. It's for the coaches, healers, and conscious humans who want to help others lead better lives.

Ultimately, I invite you to reimagine what success means for you to feel successful—not the generic version of success you've been told to strive for, but what it truly means for you, deep in your soul.

I want to challenge the age-old idea that financial gain is the ultimate marker of success and propose a new model in which our positive impact on the world becomes just as important. This new era of business requires a radical shift in mindset—from a mindset of scarcity and competition to one of abundance, collaboration, and regeneration.

As the business world evolves, more entrepreneurs and leaders are waking up to the fact that the old way of doing business—solely chasing profits—is outdated. Now, more than ever, there's a clear call for a value-first approach.

The businesses that will thrive in the future will be the ones that ground their operations and strategies in humanistic values and ethical frameworks. This shift is essential. Traditional capitalist models focusing solely on profit have shown their inherent limitations, especially regarding long-term sustainability. As Paul Pollman states

> *"The cost of inaction is greater than the cost of action. Businesses that fail to address sustainability will not only lose their license to operate in society, but they will also miss out on the biggest opportunities of our time."* [6]

We're also seeing this shift in action as today's customers are more discerning.[7] They demand transparency, authenticity, and a meaningful connection with the brands they support. This isn't just a passing trend—it's a significant shift in consumer consciousness. Businesses that recognize and adapt to this change will ride the wave rather than get swept away by it.

It's also a shift toward a more human workplace, embracing values like integrity, empathy, and sustainability into the core of business operations. It's about creating a culture prioritizing financial success and the well-being of employees, customers, and the planet.[8] It's about understanding that profit and doing good don't have to be at odds—aligning with higher human values can lead to even greater profits. A business that operates with a conscience becomes a magnet for like-minded consumers and talented employees who resonate with its values, boosting its appeal and competitive advantage.

The first step in making this shift from traditional to conscious business is redefining success. We must shift the beliefs that hold everything in place and keep us working in the same detrimental ways. Success is no longer just about the bottom line; it now includes a business's social and environmental impact.[9] These aspects can't be ignored if a company wants to survive and lead in this new business landscape. It's about co-creating a story where purpose-driven profits align with the well-being of society and the planet.

Another critical factor is recognizing the interconnectedness of all stakeholders. In this new era, relationships with stakeholders are no longer just transactional—they're relational and collaborative. Today's leadership requires adopting a holistic perspective that considers the ripple effects of decisions on the community and environment. Businesses can create shared value and build deeper loyalty by fostering this sense of connectedness.

Here's what we've learned:

- A purpose-driven strategy doesn't detract from focusing on financial health—it recontextualizes it.

- We need to design creative solutions that balance the triple bottom line with the understanding that when you aim for meaning, money follows.

- This approach also demands a commitment to continuous learning and adaptation—qualities that are essential for thriving, both now and in the challenges to come.

The momentum behind conscious business models isn't going unnoticed. From small start-ups to global corporations, we're seeing more and more stories of businesses thriving with this expanded approach. These companies have redefined what success looks like for them and, in doing so, are reshaping the markets they operate in. The positive impact is clear: It fosters both economic growth and meaningful societal progress.

Embracing The Paradigm of Purpose-Driven Business

The journey toward a value-first approach is both essential and deeply rewarding. It starts by challenging the status quo, imagining a business model where purpose stands shoulder to shoulder with profit, and having the courage to put that vision into action. As you read through these pages, I invite you to dive deeper into this paradigm shift—not as some idealistic dream but as a practical and actionable path to lasting success in the new business frontier.

Together, we'll explore the pillars that support this new way of doing business: integrating sacred and Indigenous wisdom with modern practices, embracing regenerative leadership, and unlocking the transformational power of purpose-driven work. These aren't just concepts—they're practical, actionable, and deeply relevant to today's challenges and opportunities.

Please think of this book as a roadmap for those of us ready to embark on this sacred journey *(and yes, I did say sacred).* In many ways, to follow this path is a soul journey. *Beyond Profit* is a soul calling. I aim to guide you through the nuances of this shift, offering insights, strategies, and real-world examples of how to align your business practices with your deepest values. Whether you're an entrepreneur just starting, a coach in a small business, or an executive in a multinational corporation, this book offers an innovative and profoundly human path forward.

For a long time, we've been told that profit—the bottom line—is the ultimate measure of success. But this profit-centric model, like an old tapestry, is beginning to show its frayed edges. Its limitations are becoming apparent, like the narrow beam of a lighthouse that can't fully light up the vast ocean of human experience and need. It's simply not sustainable in the long run. Companies that operate solely on this principle have seen employee morale drop, customer loyalty waver, and their contributions to society come into question.

The wave of change urging businesses to prioritize well-being, mental health and purpose is more than just a ripple—it's a powerful swell, transforming the landscape. Think of business as a living organism. Just like a tree needs healthy soil to grow, a company needs an environment where employees are engaged, customers are satisfied, and society thrives. When we focus on well-being, we nurture creativity, collaboration, and commitment, creating fertile ground for long-term success.

However, the transition to a new era of business isn't without its challenges. It requires courage, resilience, and an unwavering commitment to growth and learning. But the rewards—both personal and collective—are immense. By aligning your business with the principles in this book, you're not just choosing to succeed differently; you're becoming part of a global movement toward sustainability, equity, and meaningful impact.

You're becoming part of the solution the world needs right now.

This is the path to becoming a Sacred Changemaker—someone who aligns their personal growth and spiritual journey with their efforts to create positive change. Sacred Changemakers understand that true transformation, both within and outside in the world, are interconnected and driven by a deep sense of purpose, compassion, and a commitment to the greater good.

Sacred Changemakers take a holistic approach to change, recognizing that social, environmental, and spiritual healing are all part of the same continuum. We leverage our inner wisdom, values, and spirituality to inspire, lead, and co-create meaningful change, uplift communities, protect the environment, and create a more just, equitable, and harmonious world.

It's a sacred calling that goes beyond traditional activism or advocacy—it's about embodying real change in your daily life, relationships, and career, creating ripples of positive impact with every action and decision. Real change starts within, and it starts with you. When you embody these principles, your presence changes the world one conversation at a time.

This is the collective path toward a better future for all life.

As you turn each page, allow yourself to be inspired by what's possible. Let these words guide you as you transform your thinking about success, leadership, and the role of business in shaping a more resonant future for us all.

Let's explore this new era of business together, where we go beyond profit to discover our greatest potential for impact and fulfillment—and perhaps, in the process, become the most extraordinary, compassionate humans we know we can be.

Why Business As Usual Is No Longer Enough

We're facing unprecedented challenges testing the fabric of our global society, and the traditional business model—driven by the singular goal of profit maximization—is showing its limitations. With its hyper-focus on financial outcomes and profit for a few at the expense of people and the planet, it's becoming obvious this old way isn't viable anymore. There are many interconnected reasons for this, all pointing to the urgent need to embrace a new era of business. This journey isn't just essential in the business domain; it takes us deeper into understanding what it truly means to be human and helps us become more intentional about who we want to become.

Let's take a closer look:

Environmental Crisis: The most urgent reason to rethink how we live our lives and do business comes from the environment. Climate change, resource depletion, and biodiversity loss aren't distant concerns—they're immediate crises.[10] The old business model, which thrives on extracting from the Earth without concern, has driven countless species to extinction. We now know that how we've been doing business is a significant factor in accelerating climate change, making it clear that we need more sustainable and regenerative practices. *We've forgotten that as humans we are deeply interconnected with all of life.*

Mental Health and Well-Being: Conventional work culture treats people like machines with long hours, high stress, and relentless focus on productivity. This has led to a rise in workplace-related mental health issues like burnout, anxiety, and depression.[11] The pursuit of profit without considering the human cost has revealed how disconnected we are from our humanity and our need for balance, meaning, and connection. *We've lost ourselves in the constant drive for more.*

Social Inequalities: The old business paradigm has widened the gap between the wealthy and the poor, contributing to systemic inequalities.[12] By prioritizing profits over people, many businesses have missed the opportunity to foster inclusion, social justice, and equity. Today, there's a growing demand for businesses to be part of the solution rather than perpetuating the problem. *We've built systems that are unfair to many.*

Lost Sense of Purpose and Meaning: Many people feel deeply disengaged and disconnected from the purpose of their work. The traditional business model, with its narrow focus on financial success, leaves little room for meaningful contributions or personal fulfillment.[13] This has sparked a movement of professionals seeking work that provides a livelihood, aligns with their values, and allows them to contribute to something greater than themselves. *We've lost touch with our souls in the pursuit of efficiency.*

The Call for Resonant, Regenerative Leadership: The old leadership model—based on hierarchy, control, and power—is becoming outdated.[14] There's a growing desire for authentic, compassionate, and visionary leaders who can drive positive change. This shift reflects a broader hunger for a more human and soulful approach to business—one that values the intrinsic worth of every person. *We've forgotten that leadership is, at its core, a human experience.*

Technological and Social Evolution: As technology advances and the world becomes more interconnected, businesses face new challenges and opportunities. The old ways of doing things—built on competition and secrecy—give way to a model that values collaboration, transparency, and shared prosperity. The rapid rise of AI is also forcing us to reconsider what it truly means to be human. This technological evolution demands a rethink of business practices so we can harness technology for the common good. We've created artificial intelligence that can replicate many human actions, and now we're worried about being replaced. *We've not considered what it means to be human in the age of A.I.*

We need to ask ourselves: **What kind of future do we want?**

In short, the status quo isn't enough anymore. The challenges we face—environmental degradation, mental health crises, social inequalities, a yearning for purpose, and rapid technological change—demand that we radically reimagine who we are becoming and how we do business. This new era of business calls for weaving together individual achievement with our collective well-being, profitability with purpose, and sustainability with success.

To be clear, this isn't about ignoring profit to follow some idealistic vision. Profit is—and will likely remain—the fuel of modern life and business. But it's about integrating profit with values that make business a force for life, not something that undermines it at every turn.

As we stand at this crossroads, the path forward is clear. We must embrace a new paradigm that puts humanity, the planet, and the soul of business at the center. By doing so, we can transform today's challenges into tomorrow's opportunities and create a world where business is a powerful force for good.

This is the essence of the new era of business—a vision that goes beyond the usual conversations and enables leadership and business to become a force for meaningful change and positive impact.

Business is Changing

Think about this. Business is everywhere. We're completely immersed in it, so much so we rarely question it.

From your earliest memories to the moment you picked up this book, you've been surrounded by business—products, services, and marketing messages. You've learned to recognize billboards on the side of the road, logos in Facebook ads, and to spend your time and money responding to what businesses offer. Consumerism is everywhere. In many ways, I'd argue that business, even more than the natural world, is the landscape of our modern lives.

Everywhere we turn, a business thinks it can solve whatever problem we believe we have. And with technology on the rise, the noise from the marketplace is only getting louder and more pervasive. We've come to take business for granted because it's been woven into our lives for so long. We all have a business story shaped by our most recent experiences with it. Like fish, who don't notice the water they swim in, we often fail to see its invisible impact on us.

Unlike the fish, however, we're not entirely unaware. We know things are changing, and we probably sense that these changes are happening faster than ever, but they often feel external—out there in the world. What we don't always realize is how business is changing us. Our interactions with business shape how we view the world, our beliefs about what's possible, and even where we feel we belong.

Business influences us on a deeper level than we realize, and we can be sure it's shaping us. As business leaders, it's crucial to understand the power we hold—because we have the same influence with our businesses. And with that influence comes the responsibility to use it honestly and ethically.

It's time to be more intentional, not just about improving business, but about using business as a vehicle for the changes we want to see in the world. I've always believed that business is the most powerful lever for change and has the potential to be a real force for good. Yes, growing your business and serving the people you care about is essential, but what excites me most is that this idea—using business for good—is no longer just a nice to have. It's fast becoming a critical success factor for businesses everywhere.

That belief led me to research and ask a fundamental question: *What is business really for? What is its true purpose?* To find the answer, I spoke to many people and looked closely at the current business landscape to see what's becoming apparent today.

Here's what I found:

Business is in a relentless pursuit of more efficiency, clients, and profit. Looking back over the last thirty years, especially with my corporate clients, it feels like they all have the same one-word mission: MORE. This mission has become so ingrained that no one even questions this endless quest or the costs that come with it.

A key driver in business is improvement—getting better at what we do. This results in better service, better experiences, and better results for stakeholders.

Business is also a source of power. It shapes culture, creates connections, and builds status, credibility, and authority. It sustains lives through employment, offering opportunities for personal and professional growth. It can launch careers; for many, it's a path to something greater.

Whether we like it or not, we're all deeply immersed in business. As consumers and leaders, business impacts us on several levels. And it's important to realize that no matter your profession—whether you see yourself as a coach, changemaker, an entrepreneur, or something else—you're also a business leader.

But most of all, business is about change. You could even say that business **is** change. And I'm not just talking about the transformation industry. Business itself catalyzes change—whether it's a new TV, a wedding dress, a gadget, or a new home. Every time we engage with a business, something changes in our lives.

The truth is, we're all in the business of change. And each of us can create more change than we might realize. Our opportunity—and perhaps our responsibility—is to build a life and maybe even a career we can genuinely be proud of. A career that inspires change for ourselves, our clients, and our communities, creating a ripple effect of positive impact that benefits us all.

Expanding Our Approach to Change

> *"Change is hard. Change to something better is easy"* - Jakob Trollbäck, Designer of the United Nations SDG's and IDG's[15]

Change is everywhere, yet so often, it's not the kind that lasts. And if we're honest, we all know that "change" can be a mixed bag—some changes are hard, while others feel natural, almost like an expansion into something better. A colleague of mine, Jakob Trollbäck, who helped design the UN's Sustainable and Inner Development Goals, put it perfectly: *"Change is hard. Change to something better is easy."* When we see a change that's meaningful, one that we know will improve our lives or our world, there's often a feeling of ease, even excitement. This is the kind of change we're here to explore together: the regenerative, life-affirming change that becomes a force for good.

As someone who's worked nearly three decades in change—through consulting, coaching, training, and facilitation—I've witnessed the shifts people experience as they try to improve their lives, their work, and their impact. Yet, through all those years, I've come to realize that when we talk about "change," we rarely stop to define it. Instead, we assume everyone's on the same page and that they know what we mean. But as I've seen, and perhaps you've experienced too, we all approach and experience change a bit differently.

We live in a world where change is accelerating, mostly thanks to technology, which has outpaced our awareness. We're seeing this play out in society, where many of today's issues seem so daunting they're hard to believe. To make matters even more complex, our capacity to keep up with change has been stretched thin. It's as if human consciousness, our collective awareness, hasn't quite caught up to the speed of life today. This means we're living with a gap—a disconnect between the pace of change and our ability to process, integrate, and respond consciously to it.

Over the years, I've understood that, to bridge this gap, we need a more expansive approach to change—one that doesn't just address symptoms or quick fixes but embraces multiple dimensions, each with a vital role to play. These eight dimensions[16] emerged in my work; they come together as a whole, forming a powerful, interconnected framework that brings the full spectrum of change into focus. Each dimension offers a unique lens that, when combined, contributes to a more resilient, sustainable, and whole transformation.

When these dimensions work together, they create a kind of change that has the power to endure. This isn't about isolated solutions but about a holistic approach to transformation that roots itself in the core of who we are and what we believe while reaching outward to benefit the world around us. Each dimension has a purpose, and together, they form the foundation of a regenerative change that grows, sustains, and strengthens our collective future.

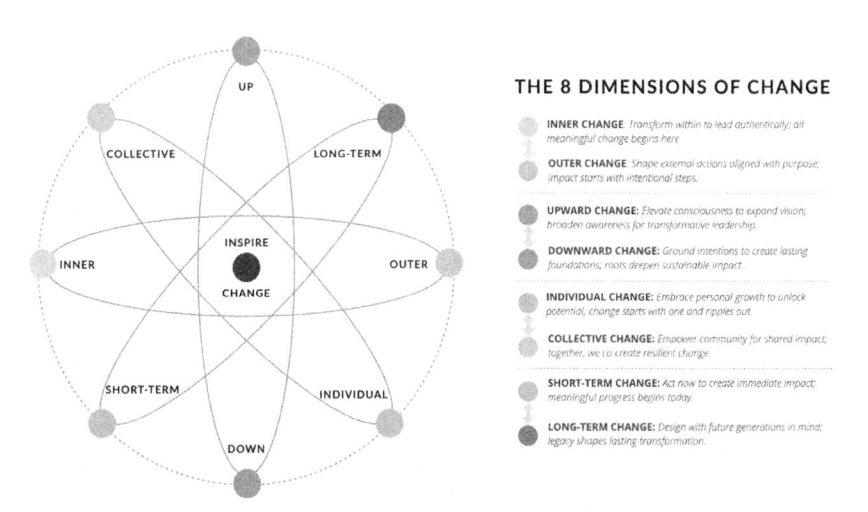

THE 8 DIMENSIONS OF CHANGE

INNER CHANGE: Transform within to lead authentically; all meaningful change begins here.

OUTER CHANGE: Shape external actions aligned with purpose; impact starts with intentional steps.

UPWARD CHANGE: Elevate consciousness to expand vision; broaden awareness for transformative leadership.

DOWNWARD CHANGE: Ground intentions to create lasting foundations; roots deepen sustainable impact.

INDIVIDUAL CHANGE: Embrace personal growth to unlock potential; change starts with one and ripples out.

COLLECTIVE CHANGE: Empower community for shared impact; together, we co-create resilient change.

SHORT-TERM CHANGE: Act now to create immediate impact; meaningful progress begins today.

LONG-TERM CHANGE: Design with future generations in mind; legacy shapes lasting transformation.

Expand your approach to change through the 8 dimensions

1. Inner Change

Inner change is where all lasting transformation begins. Without it, external changes often fall flat or don't last. When we change internally, we're transforming the beliefs, values, and identity markers that define who we are. This work happens at a deep level; it's about reshaping the core of how we see ourselves and what we believe we're capable of. Inner change addresses the often unconscious drivers of our actions and reactions, giving us the chance to step into a more empowered version of ourselves.

This dimension is the foundation of all change. If our identity and beliefs remain the same, any external shifts we make are unlikely to endure. Inner change is the essential first step that allows us to align with the other dimensions in a way that's genuine and sustainable.

2. External Change

External change is the outward expression of our growth, where ideas become actions, and intentions take form. It's what others see and what we measure—the tangible outcomes, habits, and behaviors that signal transformation. For decades, most change work has focused primarily on this dimension, often with tools like coaching, training, and organizational development. Yet, without the internal shift to support it, external change often fades.

External change is essential for bringing ideas into the world. It's where our intentions and insights turn into visible, measurable impact. But without the grounding of inner change, it remains only surface-level, disconnected from a deeper purpose. Together, inner and external change create a balanced, authentic transformation.

3. Upward Change

Upward change refers to the elevation of our consciousness, the kind of growth that allows us to see life from a wider, higher perspective. As we mature, our consciousness naturally expands; however, consciously choosing to develop this dimension is something unique. It's what allows us to understand the bigger picture, to move beyond our limited perspective, and to resonate with a larger, more expansive reality.

In my work, I call this "Full Spectrum Resonance," a way of understanding how we resonate with ourselves, with others, and with the world. As we grow upward, we're better able to engage with life from a place of greater awareness, which in turn influences all other dimensions. Upward change enables us to transcend old patterns and respond to challenges with wisdom, helping us integrate and balance every other type of change in a unified approach.

4. Downward Change

If upward change is about expansion, downward change is about grounding. It's the process of taking our highest visions and ideas and translating them into the physical world. This change anchors ideas into tangible reality, making the unseen seen. Often, this dimension involves doing our "shadow work"—exploring the parts of ourselves that hold unprocessed wounds or fears that keep us from manifesting our ideas.

Downward change is essential for making our insights actionable and lasting. It's the force that brings our ideas down to earth, giving them form and structure so they can impact our lives. By working with both upward and downward change, we ensure that transformation is both elevated in purpose and grounded in reality, creating a balance that is both visionary and practical.

5. Individual Change

In the Western world, individual change is often the primary focus. Self-help, education, and personal development all center on enhancing the individual, yet this is also where we can easily fall into the illusion of separateness. Although individual change is crucial, it doesn't happen in a vacuum. Our values, identities, and skills are all developed through our relationships with others.

Individual change is important because it empowers us to take responsibility for our growth. By understanding who we are and who we aspire to become, we can align our choices with our values and goals. However, it's equally important to remember that our individual growth is always interconnected with the people, places, and systems around us. Individual and collective change together remind us that our journey is both personal and relational, reflecting our capacity to grow alone and alongside others.

6. Collective Change

If individual change asks, "Who am I becoming?" collective change asks, "Who are we becoming together?" Today's global challenges demand that we expand our focus to include the well-being of the collective. Collective change involves recognizing the interconnected nature of our lives and understanding that our actions impact our communities and the entire planet. It's the dimension that reminds us of our responsibility to future generations.

Collective change encourages us to move beyond personal goals and toward shared solutions that create a better world for all. It's the dimension that helps us think about regenerative change, the kind that sustains itself and restores life. It calls us to contribute to a legacy that extends beyond our lifetime, making the world better for those who will follow. This dimension ensures that our work in the other areas doesn't remain isolated but expands outward in ways that benefit the larger community.

7. Short-Term Change

Short-term change has its own unique value; it's the quick response that often saves the day in emergencies. We're familiar with this from putting out "fires" in our personal or professional lives. Short-term change allows us to respond to immediate needs, even if it's not sustainable over time. It's where we find quick wins that serve a specific purpose in the here and now.

However, if we focus solely on short-term change, we risk creating solutions that don't last. Short-term changes can be powerful, but only when they're balanced with long-term thinking. Together, these dimensions provide a complete approach, allowing us to meet immediate demands without sacrificing our long-term vision.

8. Long-Term Change

Long-term change requires a broader perspective, one that looks beyond our immediate needs and into the future. Indigenous cultures often speak of "seven generations"—a commitment to consider the impact of actions on those who will come after us. In today's world, this kind of forward-thinking is rare, yet it's precisely what we need to build a sustainable future. Long-term change invites us to think about our legacy, the impact we'll leave behind, and the world we're shaping for future generations.

This dimension is essential for ensuring that our actions today align with the future we hope to create. Long-term change holds us accountable, inviting us to think not just about profit or growth but also about purpose and impact. It's the anchor that connects all the other dimensions, urging us to act for ourselves AND the well-being of all life.

When we look at these eight dimensions as a unified whole, we begin to see each one as part of a larger ecosystem, each playing a unique role in creating lasting change. Together, they give us a way to move beyond isolated, short-term efforts and into something far more meaningful—a holistic approach that regenerates, sustains, and truly enriches life.

By engaging all eight dimensions, we're able to create the kind of change that doesn't just put out fires or fix immediate issues but reshapes our future. It's change that aligns with our deepest values, drawing from our collective potential to build a world that reflects who we indeed are and what we stand for.

This approach invites us to go beyond business as usual and create a change that truly matters—a change that's alive, interconnected, and regenerative. It's the kind of transformation that breathes life back into our lives, our work, and our world. In embracing this, we're no longer just reacting to challenges; we're actively shaping the future, inspiring a movement that lights the way forward for humanity.

In doing so, we step into our power as changemakers—individuals and communities who are not only transforming lives but inspiring a whole new way of being. We're choosing to live with purpose, to lead with intention, and to co-create a future that holds promise for everyone. And that, I believe, is the kind of change that lasts.

The Sacred Changemaker Vision

In a world longing for transformation, we created Sacred Changemakers as a beacon of hope and a roadmap for a future where business can be a true force for good. At the heart of our vision is the belief that when aligned with purpose, sustainability, and community, business can uplift humanity and heal our planet. This vision calls for a radical shift—from a profit-centric mindset to one that honors the sacredness of life, the interconnectedness of all beings, and our responsibility as stewards of the Earth.

We're not alone in responding to this urgent need. This transformational shift is already in motion, driven by a growing consciousness among consumers and leaders alike. People are looking for more meaning in their lives, extending that quest into their work and the products and services they engage with.

At Sacred Changemakers, we transcend the old divide between profit and purpose, advocating for a model where both can coexist and strengthen each other. It's not about "either…or"; it's about "yes…and".

At the core of this vision is the idea of integrating a deeper, more meaningful purpose into the fabric of business itself. This purpose goes beyond the typical goal of financial gain and embraces a broader mission—creating a positive, lasting impact in the world. It encourages businesses to ask different questions: How can we increase the bottom line, contribute to the greater good, and craft a legacy that benefits future generations?

We now live in a purpose-driven economy, where consumers aren't just buying products—they're choosing to support companies that align with their values and contribute to the well-being of society and the planet.

We've evolved from the product economy of the 1970s through the product-and-service economy of the 1990s into an era sparked by digital technology and globalization. As information started flowing freely globally, consumers began to expect more from businesses. They started demanding purpose, which has paved the way for where we are today. We now live in an awakening economy, which accelerated into the mainstream post-lockdown. Business is now market-driven, and client-centricity is everything.

Gone are the days when large corporations decided what they would offer to passive consumers. Today's consumers are active, engaged, and empowered. Thanks to technology and social media, they have a voice, and they're using it.

We're witnessing the rise of an entirely new era of business. The collective trauma we all experienced during the COVID-19 pandemic has led to a fundamental shift in consumer attitudes. Experts believe these changes in behavior are here to stay.

> Dr. Manto Gotsi from the University of London said, *"I think the pandemic has been like a midlife crisis for us all. It brought to the surface all the anxiety we had before, but our fast-paced lives didn't give us time to deal with it. As consumers, it gave us time to research and learn about the brands we interact with. Before Covid-19, people might not have known much about Jeff Bezos. Now, they can tell you five facts about him, how Amazon treats its employees, and the challenges in the global supply chain. Consumers are becoming experts and sharing what they learn with their friends and family."*[17]

As a result, we're seeing more ethical and human priorities rise to the surface. This shift is evident in the growing demand for ethical, sustainable, and socially responsible brands. Consumers are voting with their wallets, supporting businesses committed to more than profit alone. This shift in behavior is pushing companies to reexamine their missions, operations, and impact on the world.

At the same time, the market is responding to these evolving expectations with innovation and adaptability. Entrepreneurs and established businesses recognize the competitive advantage and long-term benefits of aligning with purpose, sustainability, and community values.

This alignment isn't just about reducing risks or complying with regulations—it's about seizing the opportunity to lead in a new market where meaning, authenticity, and impact are the key differentiators.

Companies that embrace this Sacred Changemaker vision drive growth and profitability. They also build deeper connections with customers, employees, and stakeholders. This shared search for meaning and integrity in business creates a positive cycle, propelling this movement forward and embedding it more deeply into the fabric of the global economy.

Purpose Beyond Profit

For the data lovers out there, here are some stats:[18]

- 95% of employees believe businesses should benefit **all** stakeholders, not just shareholders.
- 92% of employees are more likely to recommend their employer if they work for a company with a real, embodied purpose.
- 86% are more likely to work for a company that stands up for environmental and social issues.
- 85% of millennials believe making a positive difference in the world is more important than professional recognition.
- 80% of consumers see the world as entirely digital.
- 79% of consumers say they'd be more loyal to a purpose-driven

company.

- 77% feel a stronger emotional connection to companies with purpose.
- 73% would even defend a purpose-driven company if people spoke badly about it.
- 68% of employees don't think businesses do enough to instill a sense of purpose in their work culture.
- 67% believe that purpose-driven companies care more about them.
- 65% of Millennial and Gen Z consumers want to join businesses with activist communities.

And it's not just about existing businesses. The pandemic sparked a new wave of entrepreneurs. In the third quarter of 2021 alone, 1.5 million new business applications were filed in the U.S.—double the number from pre-pandemic levels. Europe has seen similar growth.

Just take a moment to consider how high these figures are. These are significant shifts.

The awakening economy is expected to hit a tipping point by 2025 when over 75% of the job market will be millennials driving these changes.[19] You've probably noticed how consumers are speaking out on social media, taking a stand for various issues, and waking up to their personal role in humanity's evolution. It's impacting every industry, driving massive shifts as people demand more purpose and meaning in their individual and collective lives.

This is changing everything—how people buy, why they buy, and even whether they choose to buy at all. We need to align our businesses with these new expectations of our awakening clients. If you're leading a business today, even a small one like a coaching or consulting business, you can't afford to ignore this trend.

I explain it to my clients like this: If your business were a car, it would be racing down the track at 100mph, and you wouldn't even be behind the wheel—your clients would be.

In the broader marketplace, we're witnessing a shift as business leaders around the world scramble to awaken themselves, their supply chains, and their company cultures to keep up with new trends like impact investing, transparency, conscious leadership, and the growing demand for meaning behind their products and services.

In many ways, this is a grassroots movement fueled by the Great Resignation[20], as employees choose not to return to the office, actively seeking new ways of working. Alongside that is the quieter yet equally pervasive trend of "Quiet Quitting," where employees do the bare minimum, clocking in for a paycheck without genuinely engaging in their work. This silent epidemic is growing, and it shows us that most employees are disengaged at work. I've heard many leaders describe it as the perfect storm.

Is this the best we can do in business? I certainly hope not.

Because of these shifts, there will be winners and losers. If clients are driving this awakening economy, we must respond or risk failing to align our businesses with what the market now demands.

This evolution toward purpose-driven business models marks a profound transformation in the corporate world, where profit is naturally intertwined with purpose. It's a recognition that businesses have the potential to be powerful agents of change, capable of addressing the world's most pressing challenges while also achieving financial success. By embedding purpose into their strategy, operations, and culture, businesses can enrich their soul, build deeper connections with their stakeholders, and unlock new levels of engagement and loyalty.

We now know that customers, employees, and investors are increasingly drawn to companies that stand for something greater than just profit. They want to support, work for, and invest in organizations that offer quality products and services and demonstrate a commitment to ethical practices, social responsibility, and environmental stewardship. When values align, it creates a powerful resonance, attracting like-minded individuals and building a community united by shared principles and aspirations.

In this new paradigm, the question is no longer whether businesses can afford to integrate purpose with profit—it's whether they can afford not to.

Integrating purpose and profit isn't a trade-off—it's a powerful combination that drives innovation, sustainability, and resilience. The good news is that businesses embracing this holistic approach find that doing good and doing well aren't mutually exclusive. In fact, they reinforce each other.

This is the essence of building better businesses for a better world: realizing that businesses succeed financially and contribute to happier employees, a flourishing society, and a healthier planet when businesses operate as a force for good.

Sustainability as a Foundation

For us, sustainability goes far beyond being a buzzword or a box to check—it's a foundational principle, the bedrock on which the future of business is built. It's about recognizing our profound responsibility to the planet and future generations, weaving environmental stewardship into every level of business operations. From responsibly sourcing materials to reducing carbon footprints and embracing circular economy principles, sustainability isn't just one aspect of business—it's central to redefining what success means in the modern world.

However, this is merely the starting point of a much-needed journey toward even more ambitious goals. As we navigate the complexities of today's global landscape, it's clear that merely practicing sustainability is the minimum response in an era that demands we race toward restorative and regenerative models. These approaches go beyond maintaining the status quo—they aim to actively improve and rejuvenate the ecosystems and communities we affect. The urgency of this transition is highlighted by the slow progress toward the United Nations Sustainable Development Goals (UN SDGs).[21] With the 2030 deadline fast approaching, it's clear we're not on track to meet these critical benchmarks. This shortfall has sparked the rise of Integrated Development Goals (IDGs)[22], representing a shift toward a more holistic view of our global challenges. It's a recognition that shaming or confrontational tactics won't motivate the business transformation we need.

We now realize that the path forward requires an inward journey for business leaders—a fundamental shift in the beliefs, values, and metrics that drive business decisions. Business isn't something happening "out there"; like all meaningful change, it begins within the hearts and minds of people who care. It starts with leaders who dare to inspire a new way of being at work, to show more compassion, and to embrace the humanity in every person they touch.

Shifting the business landscape means we, as leaders, must take a long, hard look in the mirror at what it means to be human and make conscious choices about who we are and who we want to become. It's about becoming better humans who live better lives so we can be compassionate leaders who have earned the right to make decisions that impact us all.

By moving beyond the old divide of profit versus purpose and embracing a model that integrates both, businesses can bring humanity back into the workplace and become a force for good. This shift invites us to adopt new beliefs, encourage new practices, and evolve the core mindset with which we approach business—recognizing the power of companies to inspire and drive meaningful change through people.

In this context, sustainability becomes part of a broader, more ambitious strategy that includes restorative and regenerative efforts, accelerating progress toward the United Nations Sustainable Development Goals.

By embracing this larger vision, businesses can contribute to the planet's health in broader, more impactful ways—building resilience, fostering innovation, and ensuring long-term viability. This shift toward practices that not only sustain but enhance our world will create the changes needed for a better future.

This evolution toward sustainability, restorative, and regenerative approaches is at the core of the Sacred Changemaker vision. Here, a business's success is measured not only by its financial achievements but also by its positive impact on the lives of all stakeholders and on the world.

Fostering Community And Connectivity

At the heart of our vision is a simple truth often overlooked in traditional business models: business is inherently human, relational, and interconnected. It thrives on mutual respect and collaboration. This perspective challenges the prevailing focus on hyper-individualism and instead advocates for a model that emphasizes 'power with' rather than 'power over.'

It's a call to move beyond competitive isolation and embrace a more collective approach that harnesses the strength of our interconnectedness for the greater good. Businesses are not isolated islands of self-interest but vibrant ecosystems that thrive through collaboration, inclusivity, and mutual support.

Creating workplaces that honor diversity, equity, and belonging is just the beginning. This vision extends to businesses engaging with the broader community, recognizing the importance of listening, learning, and co-creating solutions to shared challenges. It's about understanding that every individual—whether they're an employee, customer, or community member—plays a vital role in organizational success and, in turn, contributes to a more just and sustainable world.

By prioritizing relationships and connectivity, businesses can transform the workplace into a community and collective empowerment space. This requires a fundamental shift in how we view leadership. Leadership is not just about driving the organization toward its strategic goals; it's about creating an environment where people feel safe, valued, and truly part of the mission. In this sense, leadership is about fostering a sense of belonging. It's about empowering employees to bring their whole selves to work, knowing their contributions are seen and valued.

> Jerry Colonna writes in his book *Reunion*: "Each of us has a responsibility to live up to the true meaning of leadership. The full measure of a leader is more than a return on investment. It's more than the anxious need to constantly prove our worth by measuring our lives in what we've dominated or the toys we've collected. One true measure of a leader is the number of people who feel safe enough to belong."[23]

This relational approach to business acknowledges that employee well-being is not an afterthought—it's central to organizational success. A culture of belonging and mutual respect drives innovation, resilience, and a shared commitment to the organization's goals. When people feel supported and connected to a larger purpose, they're more engaged, productive, and motivated to contribute to the organization's success and the well-being of the broader community.

By embracing this interconnected model, businesses can become powerful agents of change, tapping into their employee's collective energy, creativity, and commitment to tackle complex challenges and make a lasting, positive impact.

The Sacred Changemaker vision redefines what it means to succeed in business, shifting the focus from individual achievement to collective flourishing. It's a vision for change that helps build a more inclusive, equitable, and sustainable society—through business.

This holistic approach addresses the urgent challenges of our time and unlocks new opportunities for growth, innovation, and competitive advantage. When leaders integrate purpose, sustainability, and community into their core model, they profoundly transform the business's role.

They move beyond being mere economic entities to becoming positive forces that contribute to the well-being of society and the planet.

Purpose-driven brands attract loyal customers and talented employees. Sustainable practices reduce waste and increase efficiency. Community-oriented businesses build trust and resilience, which can only be good for all of us.

In essence, the Sacred Changemaker vision[24] offers a new narrative for business—one where success is measured by a profitable bottom line and its positive impact on the world. On a larger scale, it invites us to reimagine the role of business in society, not as part of the problem but as a vital part of the solution.

As we embrace this vision, we naturally rise into a new era of business characterized by deeper meaning, reverence for life, and a commitment to the well-being of all. I want to invite you to consider this vision for yourself. It's more than a call to action; it's an invitation to step into your potential and become part of a transformational movement that completely redefines business success. *Doesn't that feel like a worthwhile intention for your life and leadership?*

Inner Compass: Guiding Questions

This *Inner Compass: Guiding Questions* section invites you to reflect deeply on the ideas presented in the previous section. It's a time to bridge the gap between the book, your life, and leadership. These questions help you explore your beliefs, values, and aspirations as you begin your journey toward conscious leadership and regenerative business. Take time to ponder these, as they will guide you in aligning your purpose with the greater good.

- **What does "birthing a new era of business" mean to you?** How do you see yourself contributing to this shift in your work and leadership?

- **The Call for Change:** In what ways do you feel the world is calling for change right now? How do these global challenges resonate with your personal and professional life?

- **Purpose-Driven Business:** How aligned is your current business or leadership role with the idea of purpose beyond profit? What steps can you take to better integrate purpose into your daily work?

- **Why Business As Usual Is No Longer Enough:** Reflect on the traditional ways of doing business in your industry. What "business as usual" elements are holding back progress in your field, and how can you shift them?

- **The Sacred Changemaker Vision:** What does being a Sacred Changemaker mean to you personally? How can you embody this vision in your business practices and leadership style?

- **Sustainability as a Foundation:** How does sustainability factor into your current business operations or leadership? Where can you improve or innovate to create more sustainable outcomes for people and the planet?

- **Fostering Community and Connectivity:** How well are you promoting a sense of community within your organization or network? What actions can you take to strengthen connections and encourage collaboration for collective impact?

- **Purpose Beyond Profit:** What would embracing a purpose beyond profit mean for your business or leadership? How might this shift influence your decision-making, culture, and long-term success?

Part 1
THE INNER JOURNEY - Becoming Who You Need To Be

1
The Leader Within

"We don't have to wait for some grand utopian future. The future is an infinite succession of presents, and to live now as we think human beings should live, in defiance of all that is bad around us is itself a marvelous victory." - Howard Zin, historian.[1]

We are at the dawn of a new era of leadership that requires us to rethink what it means to lead and, more importantly, what it means to be human. The traditional leadership models, with their focus on profits, efficiency, and rigid hierarchies, are no longer enough to meet the challenges of our time. Today's world demands something more profound, authentic, and aligned with all life's interconnectedness. This is where sacred change-making comes in—it's not just a new way to lead but a profound inner journey of becoming who you need to be to create the change the world desperately needs.

At the heart of this shift is the recognition that leadership begins within. The journey of the sacred changemaker is a leadership journey that invites you to awaken to your potential, heal the inner wounds that have held you back, and embody the values and purpose that align with your highest truth. Becoming a leader in this new era isn't about titles or positions—it's about mastery of the self. It's about learning to lead from a place of authenticity, compassion, and presence.

You might not even think of yourself as a leader. It may not be a word you use to describe yourself, and yet, whether you recognize it or not, you still lead—your life, your decisions, your actions, and your relationships.

Leadership isn't just for those with titles or positions of authority. It's something we all do, every single day.

I was once speaking at a global leadership conference in Washington, D.C., to a room full of executives and changemakers from around the world. At the start of my talk, I asked the audience, "How many of you consider yourselves to be leaders?" Out of hundreds of people, only about 25% raised their hands. These were individuals holding leadership roles in organizations, yet many of them didn't see themselves as true leaders. Then, I asked a second question: "How many of you consider yourselves *global* leaders?" Only two hands remained raised.

This was a striking moment for me. Even in a room full of people with leadership titles, most felt like leadership was something others did—something bigger than themselves. But the truth is, we are all leaders, whether we carry a title or not. We lead our own lives, our families, our communities, and our businesses. And in times like these, when leadership is critical to navigate the challenges ahead, it's important to recognize that each of us has the potential and responsibility to lead. Leadership is not reserved for the few; it's a role we all play, consciously or unconsciously, every day.

Why is this so important now?

We are living in times where profound transformation is needed. The systems and structures that have governed business and society for generations are no longer sustainable. People are searching for deeper meaning, purpose, and connection—both in their personal lives and work. Leaders who can tap into this deeper current of change within their lives and align their leadership with values like sustainability, compassion, and collective well-being will not only thrive in this new landscape—they will help shape it.

This chapter invites you to explore the leader within. It's a call to become fully human—to move beyond the roles and masks that society has handed you and embrace your true self. Through practices like meditation, reflection, and emotional mastery, you'll begin to cultivate the inner stillness and resilience needed to navigate this new era of leadership.

You'll also discover the power of self-compassion as an essential tool for leading yourself and others with integrity, empathy, and care.

Finally, you'll learn how to manage your energy—not just your time—to show up as your most present and empowered self. In a world that often glorifies hustle and burnout, learning to protect and nurture your energy is an act of radical leadership. It reminds you that to truly lead others, you must first be able to lead yourself.

This is the path to mastery. Sacred changemaking isn't just about external change—it's about the inner transformation that enables you to live and lead with purpose, clarity, and impact. By developing the leader within, you become the change-maker that today's world calls for—a leader who is grounded, conscious, and deeply committed to creating a more just, compassionate, and sustainable future.

Coming Home

Andrew came to me for coaching at a pivotal moment in his life. On the surface, he had everything a successful leader could want—status, financial success, and a thriving business. From the outside, he looked hugely successful, yet despite all his achievements, Andrew felt deeply challenged. Behind the confident exterior, he admitted that he was struggling. "I feel like I'm just going through the motions," he told me. "I'm not connected to any of this anymore."

He confessed to feeling burned out and unfulfilled, as if he had been wearing a mask for years, performing the role of a leader without any real sense of who he was underneath it all. He had never intended to become a CEO, but it was the dream his father held for him, and Andrew had never questioned it. His pursuit of success had led him far from himself, and now, he wasn't sure how to find his way back. What Andrew needed wasn't more success or external validation. He was seeking to reconnect with his soul, his core self, to regain his humanity. He needed to come home to himself. He just didn't know it yet.

As we worked together, it became clear that Andrew's leadership journey wasn't just about managing people or achieving new milestones—it was about learning to lead from a place of authenticity and inner alignment. It was about becoming human again—reclaiming the parts of himself that had long been buried beneath the pressures of leadership and success.

This journey to reconnect with his true self transformed how he led his business. Andrew began to see that leading wasn't just about driving results but about relationships, inspiring trust, empathy, and connection. He started to lead with presence and integrity, listening to his inner voice rather than the constant demands of the external world. Through self-reflection and compassion, he began to peel back the layers of expectation and pressure, allowing himself to be more human in his leadership. And the results were profound—not only did his sense of fulfillment return, but his team responded with greater engagement, loyalty, and respect.

This is the journey of the Sacred Changemaker—a leadership journey that starts from the inside out. When discussing leadership in this new era, we're not just talking about external achievements or titles. We're talking about leading ourselves first—embracing our humanity, strengths, vulnerabilities, and values. And in many ways the context is irrelevant. Yes, Andrew was the CEO of an international business but the same applies in many different contexts; from conscious parenting the next generation to taking a stand for what matters most in our lives. It's all about leadership.

For Andrew, this meant understanding that authentic leadership required him to step away from the performance of leadership and embrace the truth of who he was at his core. He realized that being human—leading with empathy, compassion, and presence—was the most powerful way to lead. As he made this shift, he didn't just become a better leader—he became more fully himself and found more joy and meaning in his work. He felt connected to something larger than himself and began to make an impact far beyond what he thought possible.

This transformation is what becoming human is all about. It's a return to ourselves, a shedding of the roles and masks that society has handed us, and a journey into our most authentic selves. As leaders in this new era, we are called to lead from this place of truth—to lead with our hearts as much as our heads, to embrace the power of vulnerability, and to create space for others to do the same.

This path is not just about external change but inner transformation. It's about recognizing that our humanity—our capacity to connect, care, and be present—is our greatest strength as leaders. When we embrace this truth, we create the conditions for real, meaningful change in our organizations, communities, and the world.

Throughout my career, I have been fortunate to guide leaders from all over the world—senior executives at the highest levels of global leadership, innovative entrepreneurs in Silicon Valley, coaches, and changemakers dedicated to improving the lives of others. What stands out from my experiences is not just the opportunity to witness their growth and success but also the chance to peer beneath the surface and see what drives personal fulfillment, lasting change, and effective leadership.

Over the years, I've learned that leadership is not simply an external event. It's not just about strategy, profitability, or managing teams. It's about who you are—your values, beliefs, and the stories you tell yourself. It's easy to focus on external results, like revenue, market share, or business growth. Still, the truth is that leadership is profoundly shaped by internal factors that are often ignored in traditional leadership development.

When I examine the state of leadership today, I see that many leaders operate from unhealed stories. These stories can be rooted in past experiences, cultural expectations, or societal pressures. They create limiting beliefs and can lead to trauma and toxicity in the workplace. The way we lead is often a reflection of how we have been shaped by the world—by the systems we've been a part of, the education we've received, and the environments we've navigated.

Yet, healing is not often discussed in the world of business. In boardrooms, we discuss leadership competencies, strategy, and outcomes, but we rarely discuss the importance of understanding who we are at our core—our beliefs, behaviors and traumas—and how these invisible factors shape how we lead. Without this understanding, we remain stuck in old patterns, repeating the same mistakes, creating systems and environments disconnected from our own truth.

In my work, I've seen many people split leadership off from the person. They see leadership as an external set of behaviors or competencies to be mastered. But leadership is not just something we do—it's something we are. Leadership comes from a hidden reality within us. It is an intimate expression of our values, principles, life experiences, and soul essence. The leader and the person are the same.

As we learn to master our personal growth, we also step onto the path of mastery in leadership. This journey is not about perfecting a skill or achieving external accolades—it's about becoming more of who we indeed are. It's about aligning our inner development with our outer leadership to lead from a place of integrity and authenticity.

So, what does leadership mastery mean?

For many, it's seen as the mastery of external skills—the ability to influence, be a dynamic speaker, craft strategic visions, or consistently deliver bottom-line results. However, true mastery is not just an external process. Mastery is an ongoing internal journey—continually expanding who we are and what we are capable of, both in life and in leadership.

Unfortunately, our traditional education and development systems have focused heavily on the external aspects of leadership. We're taught what to do but not how to be. We're trained to achieve but not to understand the deeper nature of what we are achieving and why. We learn facts and strategies but rarely explore the nature of leadership as a process of becoming through inner transformation.

I remember learning this distinction between inner and outer growth earlier in my career when my mentor told me a story about a professor who walked into a graduate class holding a glass of water. He spoke about leadership development, explaining how we often treat learning as a process of horizontal development—where we bring in an empty glass of water, and the teacher fills it with information, tools, and resources so the students leave with full glasses. But over the past decade, things have changed; there's been a slow shift toward inner or vertical development. Instead of just filling up our glasses, we're being asked to expand the size of our glass to grow our capacity for understanding and insight. Now, students leave the room with buckets of water, representing our inner growth. This is how we can expand our human potential.

Despite this shift, many organizations still operate under the old model—measuring success purely by external achievements like revenue, product breakthroughs, or market share. These are important, but they are not the whole story. The real question is: Where do these external results come from? Is focusing solely on external achievements enough to sustain long-term success? Or are we missing the human dynamics beneath the surface that support actual, lasting performance?

As I've worked with leaders worldwide, I've found that leadership challenges are often internal, even though they manifest as external issues. It's not just about what someone does—it's about who they believe they are and what they think is possible. Their decisions, leadership style, and ability to inspire others are shaped by their inner world—their emotions, sense of meaning, and understanding of themselves.

This is true not only for senior leaders but also for people at all levels of an organization. Leadership is not confined to those with titles. It exists at every level and can be expressed in countless ways—through ideas, systems, people, or innovation. What defines successful leadership is the ability to connect with others, influence, inspire, and create lasting value.

Leadership is inherently relational.

In this context, mastering leadership means more than achieving external success. It means making a conscious difference in our lives and the lives of others. It means unleashing our full potential—mind, body, and spirit—so that we can create value not just for ourselves but also for everyone we touch. Leadership, then, becomes not only a process of external success but also a journey of inner mastery.

As you progress in your leadership journey, remember that it's not only about leading from the inside out. It's also about balancing the energetic exchange between the inner and the outer. We live in a constant dynamic flow—between ourselves and others, our internal beliefs and the external world, and the "I" and the "We." Mastering this balance is critical.

This is the foundation of leadership in this new era—the journey of coming home to ourselves and becoming human. The path invites us to lead from the inside out, from a place of deep integrity and alignment with our highest purpose.

As we embrace the journey of becoming more fully human and leading from the inside out, it's essential to reflect on how we got here—to understand how the world has shaped our beliefs about leadership and influenced how we lead. While the journey of self-awareness and inner growth is crucial, it's also true that our external environment—our upbringing, education, career experiences, and societal norms—has a powerful impact on how we see ourselves as leaders.

This next section explores how the world, with all its complexities, shapes us. It reveals how the external systems we've been a part of have influenced our inner world, and how reclaiming our power requires both deep reflection and the courage to challenge the old ways of thinking about leadership.

How the World Shapes Us as Leaders

Our external world plays a significant role in shaping us. Leadership is not just a matter of personal development—it's also about how we interact with, respond to, and are shaped by the world around us.

The world influences us from the moment we are born, constantly shaping our beliefs, behaviors, and understanding of who we are. The environments we move through, the systems we are part of, and the expectations placed upon us, all contribute to the person and the leader we become.

While it is true that leadership mastery requires deep inner work, we cannot separate ourselves from the world that shapes us. Our beliefs, habits, and patterns are heavily influenced by societal norms, cultural conditioning, and personal experiences. So, to fully understand leadership from the inside out, we must also understand how the external world has shaped us, often in ways we are not even aware of.

Knowing ourselves is understanding our fundamental nature as biological/energetic organisms who received specific stories we came to hold as true. As people with unique genetic and energetic endowments and histories, alongside the inevitable accumulation of our individual deep histories and every choice we have ever made. We are who we are today because of the lessons we have learned *(or not)* and what we have experienced throughout our lives.

Think about that for a moment.

Who you are today is the direct result of every choice you have ever made, AND who you will be in the future will be shaped by the choices you make now. By becoming conscious of how we became who we are, we can awaken to the unfolding story of our lives and see ourselves within the bigger picture of the developmental framework.

We can become conscious of our personal development, enter into it, and become more present to the influences shaping us moment by moment. We can actively participate in becoming co-creators of our own lives.

We are born with the natural impulse to grow and develop; no one needs to teach us this. We know at a deeper level that this is what we are meant to do. We have a natural impulse to experiment with creativity and to express ourselves fully as human beings. Watch any young children at play to see this in action. It is true for them, and it was true for you way back in your early childhood. Our bodies also have a natural orienting mechanism that guides us toward pleasure and away from pain.

As a consequence, we begin to form patterns of behavior that constrict our fullest expression as human beings. We can start to see that we are the products of all our experiences; we are conditioned by the world around us.

> As the poet David Whyte says, *"We shape ourselves to fit this world, and by the world, we are shaped again."*[2]

Over time, these patterns become embedded as habits, and our particular accumulation of habits then forms the foundation of our personality. The nature of habit is that we no longer need to think about them; they are automatic and invisible and become just part of who we are. Our habits are stored within our energy field, in our bodies' very shape and complex neurological wiring. They are triggered by events and people around us, which justify our behaviors in our internal stories. It's all very rational, and of course, it all makes perfect sense.

You can see how easily we limit our world—and, in truth, we're just limiting our way of being. The world is still out there, but we no longer see or relate to it in the same open way. We've learned to engage with life in ways that help us get what we want and avoid what we don't want, shaping our experience through sensations, emotions, stories, and interpretations that construct meaning and justify our habits.

In this way, we realize that our habits are default practices and unconscious mechanisms that restrict how we see, interpret, and act in the world. We don't see things as they are; we see them as we *think* they are. And there's a subtle difference.

As we grow from childhood to adulthood, we go through learning, socialization, and development, differentiating ourselves from others to form our unique identity. This identity is how we know ourselves. It's what we hold as true about who we are. For example, you might see yourself as a great parent, a reliable friend, or a powerful coach. When you go out into the world with that identity, you unconsciously seek experiences that reinforce your self-view, strengthening your sense of self.

We often create circumstances that support the identity we're trying to build. This allows the healthy development of our ego and helps us feel capable, valuable, and accepted in the world. We're not always aware we're doing this—it happens naturally. And there are positive aspects to it. When we discover our strengths, we build on them, improving at what we already do well.

But at the same time, our identity can limit us. In a real sense, it becomes a self-fulfilling prophecy. Our identity ensures survival by alerting us to threats or anything that doesn't match our view of who we are. We have sophisticated psychological defenses that protect our ego and shield us from too much negative information that doesn't align with our self-image.

In this way, we can find ourselves living in a mind-made prison. The natural ups and downs of life can either fuel our personal growth or push us deeper into fear and limitation. Without realizing it, we retreat from life—step by step—until one day, we wake up to find that our world has become so small it's barely recognizable. We've lost the flexibility to respond to what life throws at us.

Even though we develop our identity honestly and our habits through years of hard work, adaptation, and self-preservation, there comes a time when we realize we've outgrown certain aspects of ourselves. Circumstances have changed, and those old habits and beliefs no longer support who we've become.

At various points in our lives, our growth requires us to transcend ourselves. We need the agility to let go of old ways of being that no longer serve us and step into new possibilities. Most of us reach a moment when the way we've been doing things doesn't work anymore. We come to a threshold—a choice: Do we embrace change, or do we keep living with the discomfort of staying the same?

This is the moment to focus on personal transformation. It's time to shift the assumptions and stories that form the foundation of our lives, make conscious decisions, expand our potential, and reorient ourselves in life and work.

Our world needs optimistic, resourceful, authentic, resilient, and committed changemakers. We must first learn to develop these capacities within ourselves, and then we can bring a greater understanding to those we want to help transform.

Humans can't help but evolve; we've been doing it for millions of years worldwide, and as individuals, we have grown massively since birth. We think we don't like change, but the truth is we are all changing every minute at a biological level.

Change is a constant in our lives, albeit this natural development takes place relatively slowly. Why? Our primal biological needs for self-preservation, adaptation, and conformity tend to form habits rather than accelerate the development of ways of being that are responsive to our environment.

We are primal creatures, and this runs very deep into our ways of being. This means we default to the ways that have helped us survive for millions of years, even if those ways are not as relevant to our circumstances today.

Awakening our energy and accelerating the development of others requires understanding how we became shaped into the people we are. We must clarify our shared assumptions about how humans grow, change, and develop because our work rests on these assumptions.

And lots of questions arise for me, these are just a few;

- How did we become the person we are today?
- What is it that holds our personality and behaviors in place?

- How do we go beyond the habits and beliefs we hold at an identity level to travel beneath the surface into the subtle energy structures to create ourselves anew?

These are big questions that many of our greatest human minds have explored in various fields, from philosophy to psychology, neuroscience to genetic biology. It is foundational to our work that we understand how humans develop, form personalities, change, and resist change, including ourselves.

Now is the time to create a new way of being—not just for yourself but for all of us. The shift begins internally, but as you'll see later in the book, many collective changes are also encouraging us to grow.

The Inner Work Required to Lead with Purpose and Integrity

In today's business landscape, it's rare to encounter an organization embodying a soulful approach to its operations. Amid the relentless drive for more, we often overlook the human element—the dedicated individuals navigating high-pressure environments at the core of every growing business. Many of our challenges stem from widespread neglect of our inner selves and the values that truly matter.

This constant quest for external business success can lead to a disconnection that not only diminishes individual fulfillment but also limits the ability of businesses to act as agents of positive change. It's clear that achieving genuine success and fostering an environment ripe for leadership and innovation requires us to prioritize personal growth. Without addressing this foundational aspect, efforts to advance and innovate can fall short, missing the larger potential of what leaders can achieve when they operate with a fully engaged and soulfully invested workforce.

Great humans make great leaders, and cultivating our inner selves is paramount.

The focus on business as an external entity, separate from our personal growth and well-being, needs a radical shift. It begins with the realization that who we are—our values, beliefs, and the energy we embody—directly impacts how we show up to life and business. Every interaction, decision, and leadership moment is infused with the essence of our being, carrying the potential to either uplift or detract from the collective well-being. Our actions make a difference, and it's within our power to decide the kind of difference we want to make.

This understanding compels us to look inward, to engage in the deep, often challenging work of self-exploration and healing. It's a soul-deep calling to acknowledge and nurture our values, align our actions with our higher purpose, and consciously create the conditions for our success and those around us.

By focusing on personal transformation first, we lay the groundwork for change.

Embarking on this multidimensional journey of personal transformation requires courage, commitment, and a willingness to embrace vulnerability. This path leads to becoming a Sacred Changemaker, one who understands that leadership is an inside-out process. By cultivating our inner selves, we enhance our capacity to lead ourselves and others purposefully and contribute to a broader cultural shift toward sustainability, compassion, and integrity in business.

The Inner Journey: Practical Steps to Begin

For many leaders, the idea of an inner journey can feel abstract or confusing. It's easy to focus on external actions—making decisions, solving problems, and driving results—but when it comes to going within, I've had countless leaders tell me, *"I don't know what that means."* Yet, the inner journey is the key to becoming the kind of leader who can navigate today's complex, fast-changing world. It's the process of getting to know yourself deeply—understanding your thoughts, emotions, and behaviors and learning how to lead from a place of clarity, presence, and authenticity.

So, how do you begin this journey inward?

Here are some practical steps to help you cultivate the foundations of your inner journey.

1. Start with Mindfulness

Mindfulness is simply paying attention to the present moment without judgment. It sounds simple, but it can be surprisingly difficult to achieve in our fast-paced lives. We're often so caught up in our thoughts—worrying about the future, rehashing the past—that we lose connection with the here and now.

As a leader, cultivating mindfulness allows you to become more present in every aspect of your work and life. It helps you listen more deeply, respond rather than react, and lead with greater clarity and intention. Mindfulness is the first step in the inner journey because it teaches you how to slow down and observe what is happening within you.

Here's a simple way to start:

- Set aside five minutes in your day to sit quietly and focus on your breathing.

- As you breathe, notice the sensations of the air moving in and out of your body.

- If your mind wanders, gently bring your focus back to your breath. There's no need to judge or analyze your thoughts—observe them and return to the present.

This practice of mindfulness can help you become more aware of your thoughts, feelings, and sensations. Over time, you'll notice patterns in your thinking and behavior that you might not have been conscious of before. This is the foundation of self-awareness.

2. Cultivate Self-Awareness

While mindfulness helps you be present in the moment, self-awareness is about developing a deeper understanding of your internal world—your thoughts, emotions, and motivations. Self-aware people know their strengths, weaknesses, and blind spots. They understand how their feelings and behaviors impact others and can manage themselves with greater skill and effectiveness.

To cultivate self-awareness, ask yourself:

- **What are my automatic thoughts?** Pay attention to the habitual ways you think—about yourself, your team, and your work. Are these thoughts empowering or limiting you?

- **How do I feel in different situations?** Emotions provide valuable insights. Notice when you feel frustrated, anxious, or energized, and try to understand the source of those feelings.

- **How do I typically respond under stress?** Observe your reactions in stressful moments. Do you retreat, become defensive, or act impulsively? Reflect on whether these responses align with the leader you want to be.

A practical self-awareness exercise:

- At the end of each day, take a few moments to reflect on how you showed up as a leader.

- Ask yourself: What went well? What didn't?

- Write down any observations, paying attention to your thoughts and emotional responses throughout the day.

This simple exercise will help you develop the habit of self-reflection, allowing you to identify patterns and make conscious adjustments to your leadership style.

3. Listening to Your Inner Dialogue

A big part of the inner journey is learning to tune in to conversations in your mind. We all have an inner voice that narrates our experiences, and this voice has a significant impact on how we feel and act. What stories are you telling yourself? Are they stories of confidence and growth or stories of limitation and doubt?

Begin paying attention to your inner dialogue:

- Notice when your inner voice is critical or negative.

- Challenge the assumptions behind these thoughts. For example, if you think, "I'll never get this right," ask yourself, "Is that really true? Or is this just a temporary challenge?"

- Practice reframing negative thoughts into more empowering ones. Instead of "I can't handle this," try "This is tough, but I'm capable of figuring it out."

Learning to listen to your inner dialogue with curiosity and compassion helps you gain control over your mindset and emotions, empowering you to make better decisions and respond to challenges with resilience.

4. Creating Space for Reflection

Reflection is an essential part of the inner journey. In our busy lives, it's easy to rush from one task to the next without pausing to reflect on what we've learned or how we've grown. But without reflection, it's hard to truly understand ourselves.

To create space for reflection, try this:

- Schedule regular time—even 10 minutes a week—to reflect on your experiences. Use this time to think about what went well, what challenges you faced, and what you can learn from them.

- Reflect on how your inner state (thoughts, emotions, energy levels) affected your decisions and interactions.

- Consider how you can show up as a more present and authentic leader in the future.

Reflection helps you become more intentional about your growth and development, allowing you to course-correct and align more fully with your values and vision.

5. Integrating the Inner Journey into Leadership

Once you cultivate mindfulness and self-awareness, the next step is learning to integrate this inner work into your leadership. This means leading from a place of authenticity, where your actions and decisions are aligned with your values and inner truth. It's not about perfection but about leading with a greater sense of purpose, presence, and integrity.

To integrate this inner work into your leadership, ask yourself:

- **How can I bring more presence into my daily interactions?** Whether in a meeting, making a decision, or simply having a conversation, practice being fully present.

- **How can I lead with more compassion and understanding?** As you become more aware of your emotions and inner dialogue, extend that awareness to those around you.

By bringing your **inner awareness into your outer actions**, you create a more grounded, compassionate, and effective leadership style that inspires others and fosters a culture of authenticity and growth.

This is the start of the inner journey—becoming more mindful, self-aware, and intentional in your leadership. As you move forward, this foundation of presence and awareness will help you explore mindful practices like meditation, reflection, and emotional mastery, which we'll discuss next.

Exploring Inner Stillness: Meditation, Reflection, and Emotional Mastery

In today's fast-paced world, inner stillness can feel elusive. Many leaders feel like they're constantly in motion—juggling decisions, managing teams, and responding to crises—without ever pausing and catching their breath. But inner stillness is one of the most powerful tools you can cultivate as a leader. It allows you to step out of the chaos, ground yourself, and respond to the world from a place of calm clarity.

In this section, we'll explore three practices that can help you access this stillness: meditation, reflection, and emotional mastery. These practices aren't about escaping from the pressures of leadership but about helping you navigate them with greater presence, insight, and resilience.

Meditation: The Practice of Presence

Meditation is one of the most effective ways to access inner stillness. It's a practice that helps you quiet the mind and connect with the present moment, even amid a busy day. For leaders, meditation isn't about tuning out or becoming passive—it's about cultivating the mental clarity and emotional stability needed to make better decisions and lead from a place of wisdom.

The beauty of meditation is that it trains you to observe your thoughts and emotions without being consumed by them. This can be incredibly powerful in moments of stress or uncertainty, where your ability to stay centered directly impacts the outcomes of your leadership.

Here's a simple meditation practice to get started:

- Find a quiet space where you won't be interrupted, even if just for 5-10 minutes.

- Sit comfortably with your back straight and your hands resting on your lap.

- Close your eyes and take a few deep breaths, letting go of any tension in your body.

- Begin to focus on your breath—notice the sensation of the air as it enters and exits your body.

- If your mind starts to wander (which it will), simply notice the thought and gently bring your focus back to your breath. There's no need to force anything—just observe.

- As you continue to breathe, allow yourself to settle into the stillness that naturally arises when you stop trying to control or solve anything.

Meditation is a skill that develops over time. At first, it might feel challenging to quiet your mind, but with regular practice, you'll find that moments of stillness come more easily, helping you carry that sense of calm into your daily leadership.

Meditation, like any skill, takes practice. It's not about getting it perfect but about showing up consistently. If you're new to meditation or seeking guidance, the **Headspace app*** is a great place to start. It offers easy-to-follow meditation practices designed to help you reduce stress, improve focus, and cultivate inner calm—all with the guidance of experienced teachers. Over time, you'll find connecting with that inner stillness easier, even when distracted or busy.

Reflection: Cultivating Inner Insight

While meditation helps you connect to the present moment, reflection is about looking inward and examining your experiences. As leaders, it's easy to get caught up in the cycle of action—solving problems, setting goals, driving results—but without reflection, we lose the opportunity to learn from those experiences.

Reflection allows you to step back from your busyness and gain a deeper understanding of your thoughts, behaviors, and emotions. It helps you recognize patterns in your leadership, identify areas for growth, and make more intentional choices in the future.

A simple self-reflective practice:

- At the end of each day or week, find a quiet space to reflect without distractions.

- Ask yourself a few guiding questions:

    - What went well? What didn't?

    - How did I show up as a leader today?

    - What emotions surfaced, and how did they influence my actions?

    - What can I learn from this experience that will help me grow?

- Write down your insights in a journal. Writing helps solidify your reflections and gives you something to look back on as you continue your journey.

Reflection is essential for personal and leadership development. It allows you to be more aware of how your inner world is influencing your outer actions, helping you make more conscious, aligned decisions.

Developing the habit of reflection takes practice, especially when it comes to creating time and space for it in your busy schedule. The **Insight Timer app**[3] is a helpful tool for guided reflections and mindfulness practices. With thousands of free resources and guided sessions, Insight Timer supports deepening your self-awareness and creating meaningful insights. Regular use of this app can help you make reflection a natural part of your daily or weekly routine.

Leading with Emotional Intelligence

As leaders, our ability to navigate emotions—both our own and those of others—is critical. Yet, many leaders feel uncomfortable or unprepared to deal with the complex range of emotions that arise in leadership. Emotional mastery is not about suppressing emotions or controlling them with sheer willpower—it's about learning to recognize, understand, and work with emotions in a way that enhances your leadership.

Emotions are powerful messengers. They give us valuable information about ourselves and our situations. However, emotions can also be overwhelming, clouding our judgment or driving us to react impulsively. Developing emotional mastery allows you to respond rather than react, bringing greater wisdom and empathy to your leadership.

Here are a few steps to begin cultivating emotional mastery:

- **Pause and observe**: When you feel a strong emotion—frustration, anxiety, or excitement—take a moment to pause. Instead of immediately acting on the emotion, observe it. What is the emotion telling you? What triggered it?

- **Name the emotion**: Naming your emotion can help you create distance between yourself and the feeling. Instead of saying, "I am angry," try saying, "I'm noticing anger." This simple shift helps you remember that you are not your emotions—they are temporary experiences that you can work with.

- **Check your narrative**: Emotions are often fueled by the stories we tell ourselves. If you're feeling stressed or upset, ask yourself, "What story am I telling myself right now?" Challenge whether that story is based on facts or assumptions. This process can help you shift from a reactive state to a more thoughtful, grounded response.

- **Practice empathy**: Emotional mastery isn't just about managing your own emotions—it's about understanding the feelings of others. Practice putting yourself in the shoes of your team members, colleagues, or clients. What might they be feeling? How can you respond with greater compassion and understanding?

Developing emotional mastery takes time, but it's a critical part of leading with emotional intelligence. It allows you to create a more emotionally aware and resilient culture within your team, where emotions are acknowledged, understood, and worked through rather than suppressed or ignored.

Building emotional mastery requires ongoing practice, particularly when learning to work with your emotions and navigate the feelings of others. The **HappierMe app**[4] is a fantastic resource for strengthening emotional intelligence and supporting mental health. It offers tools and exercises to help you manage stress, develop greater emotional awareness, and cultivate a positive mindset. Using this app regularly will help you grow your emotional intelligence and resilience over time.

Integrating Stillness into Leadership

"When the storm rages and the winds howl, there is always calm in the eye of the storm. Seek that stillness in your heart and mind, and you will find the peace you need to weather the storm." - Proverb

Inner stillness doesn't mean withdrawing from the world or avoiding difficult situations. It's about cultivating a calm, clear space within yourself to lead with clarity and purpose. Whether through meditation, reflection, or emotional mastery, these practices help you stay grounded in the face of challenges, allowing you to lead with greater presence and insight.

In leadership, finding stillness allows you to pause and observe—becoming the witness of your impulses. Rather than reacting immediately to stress or pressure, you create a moment of space between stimulus and response. In this space, true leadership emerges—the ability to respond with intentionality, grounded in awareness, rather than reacting unconsciously out of habit or fear. This shift allows you to access a more conscious and reflective part of yourself, which can make all the difference in high-stakes situations.

By getting curious in this space, you can ask yourself: *What am I feeling? What's driving my impulse to react?* This curiosity helps break the automatic chain of reaction, allowing you to choose how you want to respond. With self-awareness, you can navigate difficult emotions, manage your energy, and make decisions with greater wisdom and clarity.

As you regularly practice stillness, you stand in the calm, still center at the eye of the storm while the chaos of life swirls around you. This cultivates emotional resilience and strength, essential for navigating leadership's inevitable ups and downs. By leading from this place of stillness, you inspire those around you to bring more presence and calm into their lives and work, creating a ripple effect that can transform your leadership, team, and organization.

Next, we'll explore the role of self-compassion, an often overlooked but vital element of effective leadership. Self-compassion enhances your well-being and strengthens your ability to lead with empathy and resilience, qualities that are more important now than ever before.

The Role Of Self-Compassion

"If your compassion does not include yourself, it is incomplete."
— Jack Kornfield, Buddhist teacher and author.[5]

Leadership often calls for resilience, strength, and an unwavering commitment to the goals at hand. But what many leaders forget in their pursuit of high performance is the importance of self-compassion—the ability to be kind to yourself in moments of struggle or failure. We are often our harshest critics, expecting ourselves to rise to every challenge without faltering. Yet, compassionate leadership starts from within.

Self-compassion doesn't mean letting ourselves off the hook or lowering standards. Instead, it means recognizing that we, like everyone else, are human. We will make mistakes, face setbacks, and encounter moments where things don't go as planned. In those moments, self-compassion becomes essential. It allows us to acknowledge our imperfections without judgment and move forward with a sense of care rather than self-criticism.

As leaders, many of us feel an almost constant pressure to perform flawlessly—to have all the answers, never show weakness, and push through adversity without hesitation. We believe that our value lies in our ability to keep moving forward no matter the challenge, and any display of vulnerability may be perceived as a weakness. Yet, this perfectionist mindset, while typical, is profoundly unsustainable. It wears us down emotionally and physically and creates a ripple effect, setting an impossible standard for others to follow.

In today's fast-paced, ever-changing business environment, leaders without self-compassion are at higher risk of burnout. The unrelenting drive to succeed, combined with a lack of inner kindness, leads to exhaustion, disengagement, and, eventually, a performance breakdown. I have seen how, over time, leaders who are hard on themselves—and those around them—cultivate a culture where mistakes are punished and failure is feared. In such environments, employees are less likely to take risks, creativity is stifled, and innovation grinds to a halt. This is why so many high-pressure organizations struggle with retention and morale—the relentless demand for perfection becomes toxic.

But the truth is, no leader can succeed without failure, setbacks, or difficult moments. What separates those who thrive under pressure from those who burn out isn't their ability to avoid failure but their capacity to recover from it. This is where self-compassion plays a vital role.

Self-compassion gives you the emotional resilience needed to keep going when things get tough. It allows you to recognize that you are human, and being human means sometimes falling short of your expectations. Instead of criticizing yourself for every misstep, self-compassion teaches you to embrace failure as a learning opportunity—a chance to grow, adapt, and become even stronger. By treating yourself with the same kindness and understanding you would offer a friend, you create a space for yourself to bounce back from challenges rather than being paralyzed by them and getting stuck.

As a leader, self-compassion transforms the environment and the energy field you create for your team. When you are compassionate with yourself, you naturally extend that compassion to those around you. You show your team that it's okay to make mistakes and that learning and growth come from imperfection. This shift in mindset fosters a culture of support rather than perfectionism, where those around you feel safe to take risks, explore new ideas, and innovate without fear of harsh judgment.

In a culture driven by self-compassion, leaders and teams are more likely to bounce back from setbacks, collaborate more effectively, and maintain higher morale and engagement levels. This not only boosts productivity but also ensures that people feel valued for who they are, not just what they achieve; in contrast to environments where perfectionism rules, self-compassionate cultures breed trust, collaboration, and creativity.

And, when you model self-compassion, you teach others to care for their own well-being. This is critical in avoiding burnout across the organization. Leaders who demonstrate kindness toward themselves, especially in times of stress, encourage their teams to do the same. Instead of pushing through exhaustion or silencing their own needs, team members feel empowered to set healthy boundaries, take time to recharge, and approach challenges with a more balanced mindset. In this way, self-compassion becomes a key ingredient for long-term sustainability and success, both for leaders and the people they serve.

Self-compassion is not a weakness—it's a powerful strength. It is the foundation of resilient leadership, enabling you to endure and grow from challenges. It ensures that your leadership is rooted in authenticity, where kindness toward yourself and others becomes a source of empowerment, creating a healthier, more productive, and more fulfilling environment.

When you embrace self-compassion, you are not only caring for your well-being—you are leading by example. You are showing others that humanity and high performance can coexist and that the most successful leaders lead with both heart and head.

The Practice of Self-Compassion

Self-compassion, like mindfulness, is a practice that can be cultivated over time. It begins with self-awareness—recognizing the moments when we are being harsh or overly critical of ourselves. Once we become aware of those moments, we can choose to respond differently.

Here are three practical steps to integrate self-compassion into your leadership:

1. **Acknowledge Your Pain or Struggle:** When facing a challenge or setback, take a moment to recognize your emotions without judgment. Instead of trying to push through or ignore the discomfort, simply acknowledge that this is a difficult moment. Say to yourself, "This is hard right now, and that's okay."

2. **Treat Yourself as You Would a Friend:** Imagine how you would respond if a close friend or colleague were going through the same struggle. You likely wouldn't berate them or tell them to "toughen up." Instead, you'd offer understanding and support. Now, offer that same kindness to yourself. Remind yourself that everyone experiences challenges, and you are no different.

3. **Reframe Your Self-Talk:** Notice your inner dialogue when things don't go as planned. Are you blaming yourself? Are you catastrophizing the situation? Gently shift that internal conversation toward more compassionate language. Instead of saying, "I'm not good enough," try saying, "I'm learning, and that's okay." This simple shift in perspective can have a profound impact on your emotional well-being.

Research has shown that practicing self-compassion can increase resilience, emotional intelligence, and overall well-being. Leaders who practice self-compassion tend to have stronger relationships with their teams because they are more open, approachable, and empathetic. By being kind to themselves, they can extend that kindness to others, fostering a more supportive and trusting work environment.

Self-compassion also allows leaders to learn from mistakes without falling into a cycle of self-blame. Instead of seeing failure as a reflection of personal inadequacy, self-compassionate leaders view it as an opportunity for growth. This mindset shift helps them approach challenges with a growth mindset, which is critical for innovation and long-term success.

As you begin to integrate self-compassion into your leadership, remember that it's a practice, not a one-time shift. It requires regular attention and a willingness to be vulnerable with yourself.

By practicing self-compassion, you not only strengthen your own resilience and well-being but also cultivate a leadership style that inspires others to lead with care, empathy, and authenticity. In the next section, we'll explore energy management and how to avoid burnout by nurturing your own well-being and creating a sustainable foundation for long-term leadership success.

Energy Management: Avoiding Burnout

In our culture of constant activity and high expectations, burnout has become a common experience. We often treat time as our most valuable resource, meticulously managing our schedules to squeeze the most productivity out of every day. But time isn't the only resource that matters—our energy is equally important, if not more so. Without the right energy to match our tasks, no amount of time management will keep us from becoming exhausted or disengaged.

Burnout doesn't happen overnight. It's the gradual result of depleted energy, where the constant demands on our time, attention, and emotional capacity exceed what we are able to replenish. Leaders often face a unique kind of burnout because their responsibilities require not only managing their own energy but also supporting their teams through challenges. Over time, the stress of juggling multiple responsibilities and making high-stakes decisions without adequate recovery can lead to emotional, mental, and physical exhaustion.

Energy management is about prioritizing your personal well-being so that you can sustain the energy needed to lead effectively over the long term. It's about ensuring that you have the reserves to face challenges, make thoughtful decisions, and bring your best self to your work. Rather than just focusing on how much time you spend on tasks, energy management encourages you to pay attention to the quality of energy you bring to each moment.

Recognizing the Signs of Burnout

The first step in energy management is recognizing the early signs of burnout before it becomes overwhelming. Burnout often manifests in subtle ways long before we reach the point of emotional collapse. Here are some common signs that your energy is being depleted:

- **Chronic fatigue:** Feeling constantly tired, even after a whole night's sleep

- **Decreased motivation:** Finding it hard to muster the energy or enthusiasm for tasks that you once enjoyed

- **Irritability or frustration:** Becoming more easily frustrated or irritable with colleagues, family, or yourself

- **Difficulty concentrating:** Struggling to focus or make decisions

- **Physical symptoms:** Frequent headaches, muscle tension, or digestive issues

- **Emotional withdrawal:** Feeling detached or disconnected from your work or the people around you

These early indicators are signals from your body and mind that your energy reserves are running low. Ignoring these signs can lead to more severe consequences, including chronic stress, illness, and complete burnout. To avoid this, you need to take a proactive approach to protecting and restoring your energy.

Practical Steps for Managing Your Energy

Managing your energy requires a multi-faceted approach that addresses your physical well-being and emotional and mental energy. Here are some practical steps to help you maintain your energy levels and avoid burnout:

1. **Prioritize Rest and Recovery -** Rest is not a luxury—it's a necessity. High-performing leaders understand that recovery is as important as effort. This doesn't just mean getting enough sleep (though that's critical); it also means creating moments of stillness throughout the day to recharge. Whether it's taking short breaks between meetings or scheduling downtime in your calendar, make rest a non-negotiable part of your routine.

2. **Set Boundaries -** In today's hyper-connected world, it's easy to feel like you're always "on." To protect your energy, it's essential to set clear boundaries between work and rest. This could mean establishing specific times when you're unavailable for calls or emails, or creating a morning routine that helps you start your

day grounded and focused. Setting boundaries allows you to be fully present when you're working and fully recharged when you're not.

3. **Move Your Body -** Physical activity is one of the best ways to replenish your energy. Regular movement—whether it's a walk, yoga, or a workout—helps reduce stress, increase circulation, and boost mental clarity. Exercise improves your physical health and gives you a mental break, allowing your mind to reset and your energy to renew.

4. **Manage Your Emotional Energy -** Emotional energy is just as vital as physical energy. Pay attention to the emotional toll your work is taking. Are you dealing with unresolved conflicts, carrying the weight of others' expectations, or feeling emotionally drained by certain tasks? Taking time to process your emotions—whether through journaling, talking to a trusted colleague, or seeking professional support—can help prevent emotional exhaustion.

5. **Engage in Activities That Energize You -** Energy management isn't just about avoiding depletion; it's also about finding ways to replenish. Think about what activities bring you joy or help you feel recharged. This could be a creative hobby, spending time in nature, or connecting with loved ones. These activities fill your energy reserves, allowing you to approach your work with renewed focus and passion.

Creating an Energy Management Plan

Energy management isn't something you do once and forget—it's a daily practice that requires ongoing attention. It's helpful to create a personal energy management plan to maintain your energy levels and avoid burnout. Here's a simple approach to start:

1. **Track Your Energy:** For one week, take note of when you feel most energized and when your energy dips. Pay attention to the tasks, times of day, or interactions that drain or replenish your energy.

2. **Identify Energy Drainers:** Once you're aware of the things that deplete your energy, look for ways to either minimize them or balance them with more energizing activities.

3. **Build in Recovery Time:** Be intentional about scheduling time for recovery, whether that's daily meditation, taking a walk, or simply unplugging from technology for a few hours.

4. **Adjust as Needed**: Life and work are dynamic, so your energy management plan must be flexible. Review what's working regularly and make adjustments as necessary to keep yourself balanced and energized.

Energy management is a vital skill for leaders who want to sustain their well-being and avoid burnout. By proactively protecting and renewing your energy, you can lead with greater resilience, clarity, and purpose over the long term.

In the next chapter, we will explore the deeper nuances of energy, resonance, and the resonance codes, further expanding your understanding of how to harness your inner resources for personal and collective transformation.

Inner Compass: Guiding Questions

This section is designed to guide you through thoughtful reflection on your inner journey, personal growth, and well-being. As you explore each topic in this chapter, these questions will help you deepen your self-awareness and align your leadership approach with your inner values and energy. Take time to engage with these questions and apply them to your experiences.

- **How do you define leadership in today's world?** Reflect on how your personal experiences have shaped your view of leadership. Do you see yourself embracing a new, more conscious approach to leadership?

- **How has the world shaped you as a leader?** Reflect on societal, cultural, and personal influences that have impacted your leadership style. Are you adopting beliefs or behaviors that no longer serve you or align with your true purpose?

- **What does the inner journey mean to you?** As you reflect on mindfulness and self-awareness, how do you integrate these practices into your daily leadership? What inner work still needs your attention?

- **How do you currently engage in practices of inner stillness—such as meditation, reflection, or emotional mastery?** What practices have been effective for you in calming your mind and grounding your leadership presence? How can you expand these practices to serve you better?

- **In what ways can you practice self-compassion as a leader?** Think about how you treat yourself in moments of stress or difficulty. Do you offer yourself kindness and understanding, or are you more critical of yourself? How can self-compassion enhance your resilience and leadership?

- **How are you managing your energy in both your personal and professional life?** Consider the balance between your mission and your well-being. Are there areas where you're overextending yourself, and how can you adjust your energy management to prevent burnout?

- **How can you model emotional resilience and energy management for your team?** Reflect on the importance of leading by example. In what ways can you demonstrate the value of well-being and self-care in your leadership while maintaining effectiveness in your mission-driven work?

1. **What practical steps can you take to begin your inner jour-

ney? Think about the tools and practices—whether mindfulness, self-reflection, or emotional awareness—that resonate with you. What small, consistent actions can you take to cultivate inner growth?

2
A New Way Of Being

"Nothing is as infectious as energy. It affects your prosperity, your relationships, and your health and well-being. Everyone knows when you're not resonant - do you?" — Jayne Warrilow[1]

Outer change begins within. As we've explored, who you *become* shapes everything around you—your work, your relationships, your health, and your impact on the world. Whether you're aware of it or not, the energy you are radiates outward and affects everything in your life.

As the quote suggests, energy is an invisible force that drives our lives. It's the undercurrent of every thought, decision, and action, influencing how we show up in the world. When our energy is aligned and resonant, everything flows with ease and clarity. But when we're out of resonance, we experience personal and professional friction, challenges, and disconnection.

This is why who you *become* matters. True transformation isn't just about changing external circumstances; it's about shifting your inner state of being. It's about becoming aware of the energy you're emitting and learning to harness its power consciously. When you do this, you unlock the potential to transform your life and the world around you.

Throughout this chapter, we'll explore the concept of resonance and how these Resonance Codes, which represent different levels of consciousness, can deepen our understanding of who we are and how we show up in the world. We'll look at how discovering your "home frequency" can illuminate personal challenges and strengths and how embracing these energies can help you overcome barriers to personal fulfillment.

But it doesn't stop there. True transformation doesn't just stay within; it ripples out into our work, relationships, and, ultimately, the world around us. We'll dive into how aligning your inner work with your outer actions can lead to genuine change—whether redefining what success means for you or integrating your personal growth into your business practices. We'll also outline practical strategies you can implement as a leader.

This chapter calls for a shift from focusing solely on personal success to embracing a broader vision of collective well-being, environmental stewardship, and social equity. We'll explore how the Resonance Codes can guide not just your personal journey, but also how you lead and grow in your leadership. We'll look at practical ways to bring these higher levels of consciousness into everyday actions, turning your leadership into a force for good that serves a greater purpose.

So, as we consider a new way of being, remember: it always seems impossible until it's done. But with each step we take, guided by the wisdom of the Resonance Codes, we move closer to creating a life—and a world—that aligns with who we are at our core.

The Call to Awaken

We are beginning this journey of awakening to resonance right here, right now. This call to awaken is already alive within you. It's a call to enhance your life, relationships, and ultimately, your work - it's all about you, expanding who you know yourself to be—a journey into the Self and the world around you

It's about the whole of you: your dreams and aspirations, your hopes for the future, your intentions, your feelings, your thoughts, your relationships, your wisdom, and ultimately, your beliefs and ideas about what matters most to you, of what it means to live a seriously fulfilling life.

You see, the trouble is somewhere in our evolution. In our history, we've been brainwashed, and we've forgotten our true nature. For the past three hundred years, scientists have influenced our thinking, persuading us to believe in a clockwork, mechanical Universe in which life emerged as a "random accident". We were told we exist as isolated cogs in a mundane world machine, leading brief, meaningless lives while battling against nature's harsh and often brutal realities. Whatever thinking didn't fit this worldview was dismissed—consciousness, feelings, thoughts, intuition, creativity, energy, and even our life force itself.

In this so-called modern age, we have managed to deprive ourselves of our fundamental nature, humanity, and instinctive connection to living in alignment with our souls. We have been taught to view the world as purely physical, to know something when we see it, not before.

But that is changing.

Our vision of reality is now transforming so profoundly it is shattering the foundation of our knowledge about ourselves and the world around us. Many of us are awakening. We are taking an evolutionary leap forward, a quantum leap in consciousness, a leap towards what we know to be true at a deeper level of our being.

We are rediscovering our interconnectedness with others, leaping away from knowledge and towards our inner wisdom and power, increasing our awareness of other dimensions of reality, and discovering the simple truth that, scientifically speaking, life is not as we thought.

The world does not exist "out there" as we have fondly imagined.

When we look closer at "solid objects," we don't see tiny separate particles, as Newtonian physics would have us believe, but rather a dynamic and interlocking web of energy fields. The physical world seems to have disappeared before our very eyes, suggesting a superficial appearance amounting to nothing more than an illusion. This quantum revolution takes us to the learning edges of our reality and encourages us to look beyond.

At the same time, humanity is reaching a turning point, a threshold where we find that the way we live doesn't work as well anymore. We are on the threshold of an evolutionary leap as the global pace of change is accelerating at an extraordinary pace, calling each of us to redefine our relationship with the world.

Things are not as they seem, neither are we.

What is more, science is playing a critical part in this shift. Quantum physics has shown that consciousness plays a crucial role in physical reality. There are no passive observers, as we once thought; everyone participates in the matrix of life, whether conscious or not. Reality emerges directly with our thoughts and beliefs, molding itself around us in complex and indescribable ways.

And this changes everything.

The new biology is just as startling, showing how our beliefs affect our physiology at a cellular level. People, animals, and even crystals are now known to have the ability to communicate in *"telepathic ways."* Truths that would have been dismissed as science fiction or just plain impossible only a few years ago are emerging.

The old worldview is not wrong; it is just severely limiting. It deprives us of the magical energy of life, the inexplicable, and the miraculous. It removes a more profound sense of meaning, altering and distorting our vision and potential.

However, it's not always an easy transition to navigate this level of transformation. As we shift from a physical to a metaphysical reality, we move from matter to energy, from an inert, passive universe to an evolving, conscious universe. The truth is we are taking a profound journey that takes us beyond the limitations of time and space to explore the inner realms and stretch the boundaries of our consciousness. It invites us to reach beyond our human potential towards the spiritual, the unseen subtle energies that swirl within us and around us in every moment of our lives.

This chapter will be your guide to propel you forward on your life path and take you beyond your sense of individual identity and into the world of energy, where you can begin to consider yourself an integrated system of energy continuously changing, forming, and reforming in every moment. To discover the fundamental truth - that there is nothing static about you.

You don't just have energy; you ARE energy.

Pause for a moment and let that sink in.

Our journey is about understanding what you want to create through life and business to fulfill your highest potential. It is about activating your life through the attunement of your energy to manifest what your soul desires. It is about stepping back and embracing a more expansive view of life. It is about seeing your life within a global and even a universal context, not just within the constraints of your current situation.

This book is about life, and that begins with YOU.

The changes we inspire are not solely about doing. It's not just about you doing something differently to change how your life and leadership look from the outside looking in.

It's about coming home to yourself at your very core.

It is about finding the courage to let go of who you think you should be and to be who you already are. It's about becoming all you can be as a human, changemaker, and business leader at every level of existence.

As we journey together, we will consider some core questions, some choices you have in your work, about whether you feel called to this emerging evolutionary work, to embrace a profound level of transformation, and to ask yourself who you need to become to participate.

You see, business is no longer transactional. Your customers want to know what you stand for in this world, and others will pick this up before you even say a word because you are communicating this and other things through your energetic field.

You may think I write only words here, but words have energy. Allow the energy from my words to enter into your experience, to gently swim around in your energy field. Don't distance yourself by analyzing what you read; instead, feel the meaning rippling through you, settling into the depths of your intelligence so that you enter into an active dialogue with the content rather than passively absorbing what is offered. Let the content engage with the whole of you at a new depth of meaning, like a cloud can point you to sense the vast potential of the sky.

Simply open your mind to possibility. Along the way, I'll hold the intention for you and keep reminding you of the infinite potential that awaits you. Feel into your energy, notice what comes up as you read this, and begin to know yourself at a deeper level of awareness. I will hold the energetic space for you to explore until you're ready and willing to hold it for yourself.

The truth is that being fully awake is your natural human state; it's not something you need to learn. It's just a matter of clearing away the negative, stuck energy that is clouding your view. Your primary instinct is to reconnect with your soul, your natural flow of energy, and your birthright. It's not a question of whether you will or not; it's only a matter of when.

And if you're not ready by the end of this book, that's okay, too. I think of this book as merely planting seeds. It may not be your time just yet. But if it is, I ask you to go out into the world, shine your light, and share your message.

Share your wisdom and spread positive energy wherever you go. The world needs more people who have come alive to inspire and awaken others who are just waiting in the hope of a better future.

So, we will begin this journey of awakening to the power of your energy and using your life force to activate your life. We will take it one step at a time. Please honor the rhythm of your own body and set the pace that feels comfortable for you. I want you to take time to process, recharge, and renew.

When you become aware of your energy, you know at a core level that your understanding will emerge in the right rhythm and timing; there is no need to push or force your thinking into a space that's too small. If you encounter thoughts that don't move, don't worry. It's just a sign that you are at a profound threshold of personal growth. Just breathe and relax, and the energy flow will find you.

When Worlds Collide

I remember a few years ago, I was brought in to work with a senior executive team at a Silicon Valley start-up that was facing some serious challenges. They were a highly talented group of individuals, but despite their expertise, the team was underperforming. Their communication had broken down, and tensions were running high. What was once a highly collaborative, innovative environment had become toxic, with each member seemingly defending their own position rather than working together toward a common goal.

As we sat in the training room, the air was thick with tension. The team members were talking, but it felt more like a battle than a conversation. Each one was quick to point out the failures of the others. Every suggestion was met with defensiveness, every question with a retort. But beneath the surface of these conflicts, I could see that they weren't just about professional disagreements—something deeper was at play.

The root of their conflict wasn't incompetence or even unwillingness to collaborate. What struck me was that they were all speaking different languages—not literally, but energetically. They were using the same words, but their meanings were completely misaligned. They each had a vastly different way of seeing the world, interpreting their roles, and understanding success. It was as if they were living in different worlds, and these worlds were clashing in the room.

As I observed their interactions, it became clear to me that each of them was operating from a different level of consciousness. Some of them were deeply practical and focused on survival, concerned primarily with tangible outcomes and deadlines. Others were more emotionally driven, seeking deeper meaning and connection in their work, frustrated that no one seemed to care about the people behind the projects. Still others were visionaries, pushing for innovation and growth, dreaming of possibilities but disconnected from the present realities that the rest of the team was struggling with.

Because they were at such different levels of consciousness, they literally couldn't understand each other. It wasn't that they weren't trying—it's that their perspectives were so fundamentally different that they were talking past each other. One person's priority was another's blind spot. Their differing values, beliefs, and ways of processing the world were creating invisible barriers between them.

The conflict wasn't just about disagreements over tasks; it was rooted in a profound disconnect between their levels of consciousness. This disconnect affected every aspect of their work. Projects were delayed, decision-making was slow, and creativity had come to a halt. They were stuck in a loop of miscommunication and misunderstanding, which was eroding trust within the team.

At that moment, it became clear to me that this team didn't need more technical skills or even better communication strategies. What they needed was a new way of seeing themselves and each other. I introduced the idea that they were each operating at different levels of consciousness—different ways of understanding themselves, their work, and their place in the world.

When I explained this, you could see their initial skepticism. "What does consciousness have to do with coding and deadlines?" someone asked. But as I walked them through the concept, something clicked. They started to see that they had been talking in circles, not because they didn't care, but because they had fundamentally different ways of approaching problems and interpreting success.

I explained that each of them had a home frequency—a resonance where they naturally operated. When we come from different levels of consciousness, we see and interact with the world in profoundly different ways. For some, their primary drive was survival—getting the job done and hitting deadlines. For others, it was about connection and meaning—understanding how their work impacted the greater good. Still others were focused on growth, innovation, and pushing the boundaries of what was possible.

Once they understood this, they could understand how their ability to resonate with themselves and each other affected their interactions. How it affected the quality of their connections, conversations and relationships. More importantly, they started to understand each other better. They could now recognize why one person was always so fixated on the bottom line while another seemed more concerned with the team's emotional well-being. They weren't just clashing personalities—they were embodying different levels of consciousness, and once that became clear, they could start bridging the gap.

Over the next few sessions, we worked on raising the group's collective consciousness. As they began to understand their resonance codes, they learned how to communicate across their differences. They became more aware of where they operated from and how that influenced their behavior. As they developed this awareness, the energy in the room began to shift.

Instead of fighting or defending their positions, they started listening to each other—really listening. They began to appreciate the diversity of perspectives within the team, understanding that while they each saw the world differently, those differences could be complementary. Their conflicts weren't obstacles anymore; they became opportunities for deeper collaboration.

By the end of our work together, the team was functioning in a state of coherence. They were on the same page—not because they all saw the world the same way, but because they understood each other's perspectives. They had developed a shared language that honored the diversity of consciousness within the team while allowing them to operate in alignment with a collective goal.difference and The transformation in their performance was remarkable. Projects that had been stalled for months were suddenly moving forward, and the team's morale had skyrocketed.

Reflecting on this experience, I realized how many of the challenges we face—whether in teams, organizations, or society—are really problems of consciousness. We often think conflict arises from differences in opinion, but more often than not, it's about different levels of awareness. We live in different worlds, shaped by our individual perspectives, beliefs, and values.

When we raise our consciousness, we begin to see the bigger picture. We no longer need to be taught how to respect each other or honor life, because it becomes obvious. As we elevate our vibration, we naturally become more empathetic, understanding, and connected to the people and the world around us. The problems that once seemed insurmountable start to dissolve because they were never really about the surface issues—they were about our capacity to see and understand each other at a deeper level.

Introducing the Resonance Codes

The Resonance Codes are a map of consciousness, a system that helps you understand your unique energetic blueprint—the resonance that supports you most in your life right now, known as your *home frequency*. This home frequency is where you feel most aligned and alive, drawing the energy you need to recharge and show up fully in your relationships, career, and personal growth.

But here's the thing: we're not fixed beings. We move through different energies every day, shifting as life ebbs and flows. Your *home frequency* is just one of the nine Resonance Codes in this system, and while it's the place that grounds you the most, you also use all the codes in different moments of your life.

Life isn't static, and neither are we.

Think of them as signposts on the path to your highest potential. They help you understand where you are on your journey and how to move forward with clarity and intention.

For example, imagine a day when you're feeling completely overwhelmed—maybe you're dealing with a big deadline or family pressures. You might find yourself pulled into lower frequencies, like **Resonance Code 1** *(survival and grounding)*, where you focus on just getting through the day. But then, later in the evening, during a quiet moment of reflection or meditation, you may rise into **Resonance Code 5** *(truth and expression)*, where you reconnect with your deeper self, speaking your truth and finding clarity.

There is no better or worse code. The power of Full Spectrum Resonance is in recognizing which code serves you best in the moment. Each code represents a unique energy that can help you navigate life more effectively. It's about being flexible, about knowing when to ground yourself in the foundational energies and when to rise into the higher, more spiritual frequencies.

By becoming familiar with all nine Resonance Codes, you learn to recognize the energy you're in, the energy of those around you, and how to shift between these frequencies to optimize your life.

While your home frequency is the place that gives you the most energy and helps you feel aligned, Full Spectrum Resonance is about the full range of energies available to you. It's important to know that even though your home frequency supports you most right now, it doesn't mean it's where you'll always be. Life is a journey, and we are constantly evolving.

These codes are not about progressing linearly from one level to the next. Instead, they're a holistic framework that allows us to recognize the dynamic nature of our consciousness. You might resonate more strongly with one code right now, but that doesn't mean you're confined to it. It's simply the energetic frequency where you feel most at home, your "home frequency," understanding this can reveal a lot about your strengths, challenges, and the areas in your life that might need more attention.

The beauty of the Resonance Codes lies in their ability to illuminate the unseen aspects of our inner world. They help us see beyond the surface-level goals and aspirations, diving deeper into the motivations, beliefs, and patterns that shape our lives. By tuning into these different frequencies, we can better understand who we are at our core and how we can align our actions with our true essence.

Each code offers insights into a particular stage of personal evolution, from grounding and survival to the expansive realms of spiritual mastery and collective consciousness. They help us navigate the complexities of life with greater awareness and purpose, supporting us as we strive to live in alignment with our highest potential. Whether we want to grow personally, lead more authentically, or make a meaningful impact, the Resonance Codes provide guidance to stay true to ourselves and our journey.

Within the Full Spectrum Resonance system, the nine Resonance Codes are organized into three overarching levels of consciousness. These levels help us understand where we are in our personal journey and what kinds of energies we are resonating with:

1. **Foundational Levels (Resonance Codes 0-2)**: This is the world of mis-information. These are the grounding codes, where you are learning to feel safe, secure, and stable in both your internal and external world. At these levels, the focus is on survival, healing, and building a strong foundation. People in these codes often live with a more practical, action-oriented mindset, focus-

ing on the here and now, on concrete realities. This is where you establish your sense of self, your place in the world, and your ability to meet your basic needs.

2. **Transformational Levels (Resonance Codes 3-5)**: This is the world of work, love and prosperity, shifting at the higher levels to the world of mind, intellect and imagination. These codes are about learning to transform the self by moving beyond the ego. Here, you're working with emotional and intellectual growth, learning to trust yourself, speak your truth, and lead with integrity and compassion. At these levels, you begin to shift from an 'me' consciousness to a 'We' consciousness, recognizing your impact on others and starting to serve something greater than yourself. These codes represent the middle ground between the physical and spiritual realms.

3. **Transcendental Levels (Resonance Codes 6-8)**: This is the world of the sacred realms and enlightenment. At these higher frequencies, the focus shifts from transforming the self to transcending it. This is where you connect deeply with the sacred, embody wisdom, and live in service to the whole of life. These are expansive energies that bring you into unitive resonance with the spiritual, guiding you to live in harmony with all of existence.

Knowing where you are situated in the 3 broader levels of consciousness can give you a root of understanding before shifting to focus on your individual resonance code.

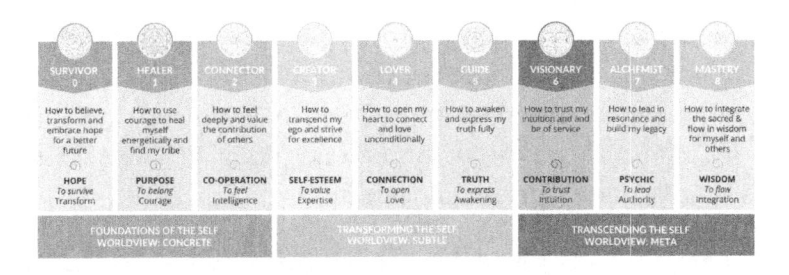

SURVIVOR 0	HEALER 1	CONNECTOR 2	CREATOR 3	LOVER 4	GUIDE 5	VISIONARY 6	ALCHEMIST 7	MASTERY 8
How to believe, transform and embrace hope for a better future	How to use courage to heal myself energetically and find my tribe	How to feel deeply and value the contribution of others	How to transcend my ego and strive for excellence	How to open my heart to connect and love unconditionally	How to awaken and express my truth fully	How to trust my intuition and be of service	How to lead in resonance and build my legacy	How to integrate the sacred & flow in wisdom for myself and others
HOPE To survive Transform	PURPOSE To belong Courage	CO-OPERATION To feel Intelligence	SELF-ESTEEM To value Expertise	CONNECTION To open Love	TRUTH To express Awakening	CONTRIBUTION To trust Intuition	PSYCHIC To lead Authority	WISDOM To flow Integration
FOUNDATIONS OF THE SELF WORLDVIEW: CONCRETE			TRANSFORMING THE SELF WORLDVIEW: SUBTLE			TRANSCENDING THE SELF WORLDVIEW: META		

The Resonance Codes Framework

The Resonance Codes represent nine unique levels of consciousness, each one offering a different lens through which we can view our personal growth and spiritual evolution. Imagine them as a spectrum of energies that reflect the various stages of our inner journey, from the foundational aspects of survival and purpose to the more expansive realms of wisdom and universal connection.

1. **Resonance Code 0: The Shadow Code of the Survivor** This is where it all begins—the grounding energy of survival. It's about feeling safe, secure, and having your basic needs met. At this level, the focus is on overcoming fear and moving from a place of survival to hope. It's the foundation upon which everything else is built, helping us transform the challenges of life into opportunities for growth.

2. **Resonance Code 1: The Identity Code of the Healer:** At this level, we start to explore our place in the world. It's about understanding our purpose and finding where we belong. This level is tied to our physical existence and our basic human needs—think security, relationships, and health. It's about anchoring ourselves in our truth and beginning the journey of discovering who we are.

3. **Resonance Code 2: The Social Code of the Connector** At this level, the energy shifts to connection and creativity. It's about our emotional relationships, our passions, and how we express ourselves in the world. Personal growth here means moving beyond personal desires and embracing a deeper sense of connection with others.

4. **Resonance Code 3: The Success Code of the Creator** This is where we find our personal power. It's about confidence, self-esteem, and taking responsibility for our lives. Challenges at this level often revolve around overcoming self-doubt and stepping into our true power. It's about recognizing our own worth and standing firmly in our authenticity.

5. **Resonance Code 4: The Edgewalker Code of the Lover** The heart of the matter—literally. This level is all about love, not just

for others but for ourselves as well. It's about giving and receiving love freely and learning to open ourselves up to deeper connections. This is where we cultivate compassion, both for ourselves and for the world around us.

6. **Resonance Code 5: The Soul Code of the Guide** Here, we find our voice. It's about speaking our truth and being authentically who we are. This level is about honesty and integrity in our communication, whether it's with others or ourselves. It's the bridge between our inner world and how we express that to the outer world.

7. **Resonance Code 6: The Spirit Code of the Visionary** Now, we start to look beyond the physical and into the spiritual. This level is about vision, intuition, and seeing beyond what's right in front of us. It's about trusting our inner guidance and using that to make decisions that align with our higher purpose.

8. **Resonance Code 7: The Wisdom Code of the Alchemist** At this level, we're looking at the bigger picture—our legacy and the impact we want to have on the world. It's about mastery, not just of a skill but of ourselves. It's about leading with purpose and understanding that our actions have a ripple effect on the collective.

9. **Resonance Code 8: The Unity Code of the Master** This is the highest level of resonance, where we transcend the individual and connect with the universal. It's about integrating all the wisdom we've gathered along the way and living in harmony with the greater whole. It's about serving something bigger than ourselves and embracing the sacredness of all life.

Each of these codes is a driver for transformation, helping you grow not only in your personal life but also in your ability to connect with others and align with the sacred. These energies guide you toward a deeper, more meaningful way of living, a more profound connection to yourself, your life and your relationship with the sacred.

I also want you to understand that each code reflects a different reality and a unique energetic vibration. It can help you to realize how we're all living in very different realities depending on our home frequency code. each of the nine Resonance Codes represents a distinct energy, and together they form a full spectrum of consciousness. These codes are not isolated from one another. In fact, they are deeply interconnected, and part of your personal growth involves learning how to integrate these energies into your daily life.

While we talk about the codes in terms of growth, with each level representing a higher vibration of consciousness, life isn't a linear journey. You don't live in just one code at all times. You might move between several codes throughout your day, depending on the situations you face, your mood, or the energy of those around you. We call this full spectrum resonance.

For example, in moments of creative flow, you might be in **Resonance Code 3** as the Creator, tapping into your personal power. But later, when engaging with others, you might shift into **Resonance Code 4** as the Lover, connecting with compassion and empathy. Similarly, in stressful situations, you might find yourself resonating with the lower codes, such as **Resonance Code 0** or **Resonance Code 1**, focusing on survival or grounding.

The goal of Full Spectrum Resonance is to help you recognize these shifts and become more intentional about which code you embody in any given moment. This flexibility is key to optimizing your energy and thriving in different contexts, from personal relationships to professional challenges.

Together the resonance codes offer a fluid system that encourages you to master all the codes, knowing that each one serves a unique purpose. The more conscious you become of how these codes operate in your life, the more empowered you are to navigate life's challenges with ease and grace.

Understanding the entire system has profound benefits, not only for your personal growth but also for the collective consciousness of humanity.

On a personal level, this system allows you to deepen your self-awareness by recognizing your *home frequency*—the code that resonates most strongly for you right now—and understanding how to work with the other Resonance Codes to support your growth. By learning to move between codes consciously, you enhance your ability to navigate life's challenges, build stronger relationships, and align with your highest purpose.

Navigating Your Home Frequency

Each of us has a unique *"home frequency"*—the Resonance Code that feels most natural and comfortable at this point in our lives. It's the energy that resonates most strongly within us, shaping how we see the world and how we respond to it. Identifying your home frequency can be a powerful tool for self-understanding, illuminating your strengths and the personal challenges you may face.

Think of your home frequency as your energetic comfort zone. It's where you naturally thrive, but it's also where you might encounter familiar patterns that keep you stuck. For example, if your home frequency is Resonance Code 3 *(Power & Self-Esteem)*, you might struggle with self-doubt or the fear of stepping into your true power. Recognizing this can help you see where to focus your growth and what might be holding you back.

On the flip side, understanding your home frequency can highlight your natural strengths and gifts. It can show you where you shine and how to use these qualities to advance your path. If you're resonating with Resonance Code 5 *(Expression & Truth)*, for instance, you might have a strong ability to communicate authentically and inspire others with your words. Knowing this allows you to lean into your strengths and use them as a foundation for your growth.

The key is not to see your home frequency as a limitation but as a starting point. It's where you are now, not where you'll always be. By understanding your current resonance, you can work consciously with the energies at play, using them to overcome personal barriers and step more fully into your potential.

You can learn how to identify your home frequency and discover how these codes can be powerful tools for overcoming personal barriers and embodying your true potential. This is where your energetic awakening begins—by understanding the energies that shape your inner world and how they influence everything you do.

To determine your home frequency and gain personalized insights into what this means for your growth and transformation, you can take The Resonance Codes profiling tool. Simply scan the QR code below and visit the link to access and start your journey of self-discovery.

Use this QR code to discover your Resonance Code...

Remember, your home frequency is just one piece of the puzzle. It's a guide to help you navigate your inner world and see how it influences your outer reality. Identifying your home frequency is just the beginning. Once you know where you resonate most, you can see how the patterns and energies associated with that frequency are shaping your life. This awareness is a powerful tool for overcoming personal barriers because it allows you to face your limitations head-on and transform them into opportunities for growth.

Each Resonance Code comes with its own set of challenges. These barriers can hold us back, whether they show up as fear, doubt, insecurity, or resistance to change. But the beauty of the Resonance Codes is that they don't just highlight these challenges—they offer a way through them. By embracing the lessons each level presents, we can transcend the limitations keeping us stuck.

Let's say, for example, your home frequency is Resonance Code 4 *(Love & Compassion)*. You might find it challenging to set boundaries, often giving too much of yourself to others and struggling to receive love in return. This pattern can lead to burnout or a sense of being unfulfilled in your relationships. By recognizing this, you can start to work consciously with the energy of Code 4, learning to balance giving and receiving and ultimately cultivating a more conscious sense of self-love and compassion.

Or you resonate with Resonance Code 2 *(Connection & Creation)*, where the challenge might be expressing your emotions authentically. You could feel overwhelmed by your sensitivity or have difficulty letting go of past emotional wounds. Embracing this level means accepting your emotional nature and finding healthy ways to express and channel your feelings, transforming your sensitivity into a powerful source of creativity and connection.

Overcoming these barriers isn't always easy, but it's deeply rewarding. As you work with the energies of your home frequency, you begin to see that the very things you once saw as limitations are opportunities to step into greater mastery. You learn to navigate these challenges not by avoiding them but by moving through them with awareness and intention.

This is what inner mastery looks like—understanding the energies that shape your inner world and consciously choosing how you respond to them. It's about turning the obstacles into stepping stones, each bringing you closer to your true self and highest potential. And as you grow in this way, you naturally begin to experience more personal fulfillment. You start to see that the journey isn't just about overcoming obstacles; it's about embracing the fullness of who you are, with all your strengths and imperfections, and using that as a foundation for everything you do.

So, as you explore the Resonance Codes and work with your home frequency, remember that every challenge is an invitation. It's an opportunity to break through the limitations of the past and step into a new way of being—one that is aligned, authentic, and truly fulfilling.

Alignment of Mind, Body, and Spirit

Transformation isn't just about changing how we think or what we believe. It's about bringing every part of ourselves—mind, body, and spirit—into alignment. This alignment allows us to truly embody the change we want to see, connecting our inner resonance with our external actions. When these three elements are in harmony, we move through life with a sense of ease and purpose, and our impact on the world becomes more authentic and powerful.

Achieving this kind of alignment requires us to be fully present in each moment, aware of our thoughts, emotions, and physical sensations, and understanding how they all influence each other. It's recognizing that our mind can shape our perception, our body can store emotions and memories, and our spirit holds the deeper truths of who we are. Integrating these aspects creates a solid foundation for personal growth, allowing us to show up more fully in all areas of our lives.

However, alignment is more than just an internal process. It's about how we bring this inner harmony into the world around us. It's about acting from a place of integrity, where what we say and do is in sync with who we are. This is where the Resonance Codes become practical tools for everyday living. They help us understand the qualities we need to embody at each level of consciousness and how to integrate these qualities into our daily actions.

For example, suppose you're working with Resonance Code 5 *(Expression & Truth)*. In that case, alignment might look like speaking your truth even when it's uncomfortable or creating space for honest conversations in your relationships. It's about communicating authentically and ensuring your words match your inner values. This alignment creates a ripple effect, encouraging others to do the same and fostering more meaningful connections.

On the other hand, if your journey is currently focused on Resonance Code 1 *(Purpose & Belonging)*, alignment could mean grounding yourself in your sense of purpose and creating a life that supports your well-being. It's about ensuring that your work, relationships, and environment reflect what truly matters to you. When aligned in this way, you feel more at home in your life, and your actions naturally resonate with those around you.

Embodying these qualities isn't always easy. It requires us to be mindful and intentional, especially when life throws challenges our way. But as we practice, we start to notice a shift. Our actions begin to reflect our highest potential, and we move through life with a sense of coherence and flow. This is where true transformation happens—when who we are on the inside matches how we show up in the world.

This inner embodiment leads to effective and conscious leadership. It's not about having all the answers or never making mistakes. It's about being honest, willing to grow, and inspiring others to do the same. When we align our mind, body, and spirit, we become leaders who lead by example and create change through what we do and who we are.

As you continue your journey with the Resonance Codes, pay attention to where you feel aligned and where you don't. Notice the areas of your life that feel out of sync and explore what might need to shift internally. This is the path to embodying your highest potential—becoming the person you need to be to create the impact you're here to make. Because when you're aligned, everything you do is infused with the power of your true self, and that's where real change begins.

From Inner Transformation to Outer Impact

As we've explored, understanding and embodying the Resonance Codes is a personal journey. It's about aligning your inner world—thoughts, emotions, and beliefs—with your identity. But transformation doesn't stop there. Inner work is the foundation, yet the real magic happens when we bring that inner alignment into the outer world, especially in how we lead our lives and do business.

As we rise to the higher frequencies, we shift beyond the ego and self-centric perspective to embrace the collective. This is where we move from "me" to "we." It's the point where personal growth translates into collective impact and where our internal shifts begin to influence the larger systems we're a part of.

This alignment between inner and outer worlds is essential because what we cultivate within ourselves inevitably ripples out, shaping how we interact with others and our decisions. The journey of transformation is both an inward and outward path. Internally, it's about discovering who we are at our core and aligning our actions with our true selves. Externally, it's about using that alignment to create businesses and communities that reflect higher consciousness—places where inclusion, collaboration, and ethical decision-making are not just values on a wall but lived experiences.

This shift from inner to outer transformation is crucial for leaders that want to thrive in today's complex and interconnected world. We understand that the health and well-being of our businesses depend on the health and well-being of the people and communities they touch. It's about understanding that our success is tied to something bigger than ourselves.

The Resonance Roadmap

After years of working closely with a wide array of clients—from entrepreneurs to global leaders—and witnessing the dynamic shifts within the modern business landscape, I've developed the **Resonance Roadmap**. This model has proven profoundly impactful, especially when trust is diminishing in the business world, and connection feels more elusive than ever. The framework emerged from a realization that authenticity and meaningful impact are not just desirable traits for success but foundational elements for leaders who want to foster authentic, enduring connections with their customers and communities. The **Resonance Roadmap** offers a structured, actionable approach to cultivating trust-based relationships far beyond traditional business strategies.

At the heart of this roadmap is an undeniable truth: **business is inherently relational**.

It's a dynamic living system shaped by the interplay between people, technology, and the environment. The mistake I have seen many leaders make is believing that business success is merely about *doing*—about executing the right strategies or following a prescribed formula. But resonance—true, lasting success—doesn't come from simply *"doing"*; it emerges from *"being"* in alignment with who you are and how that shapes everything you do.

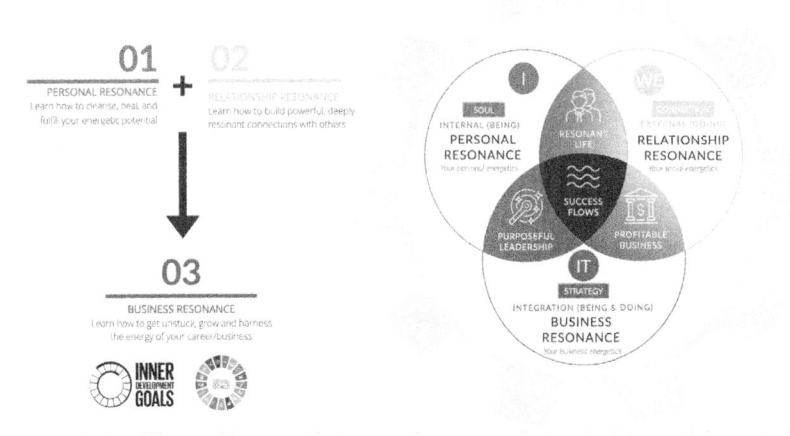

THE RESONANCE ROADMAP

The Resonance Roadmap

The Resonance Roadmap invites leaders to recognize and embrace the human element in business. It challenges the conventional view that companies thrive purely through tasks, productivity, and systems. Instead, it fosters personal connection, authentic self-expression, and alignment with a higher purpose.

It's about creating an environment where every individual—leader, employee, or customer—feels seen, heard, and valued. Everything changes when we stop treating business relationships as transactions and view them as living connections. Tasks flow more easily, decisions become more apparent, and success follows naturally.

This understanding transforms how we approach leadership, shifting the focus from transactional efficiency to cultivating more meaningful connections with ourselves and others. It's not just about getting work done; it's about creating a resonance within your organization where people thrive, trust is built, and success becomes a shared experience. Through the Resonance Roadmap, leaders are empowered to shift their focus to what truly matters—human relationships, authenticity, and purpose-driven clarity—creating lasting value for their businesses and the communities they serve.

The Three Pillars of Resonance

1. **Personal Resonance *('I' Space):*** The journey toward resonance begins within, with personal resonance. This is the space where leaders are invited to deepen their relationship with themselves—not just at a surface level but beyond the ego and personality, diving into the depths of their soul. It's about connecting to your higher purpose, that divine spark within that fuels your life and business. Personal resonance is a process of cleansing, healing, and fulfilling your inner world, cultivating the wisdom that allows you to truly embody your purpose.

    At the core of personal resonance is the ability to trust yourself. This is where clarity and confidence are born, particularly when it comes to making pivotal decisions in your business. When you embrace who you are *being* and *becoming*, you naturally begin to resonate on a higher level. It's an inner journey requiring you to do the work to heal, reconnect with your soul, and step into both your physical and energetic potential. Only when this alignment happens can you fully express your true self in both life and business.

2. **Relationship Resonance *('We' Space):*** Once personal resonance is cultivated, it's time to expand into the relational space—the "we." Relationship resonance is about forming meaningful, trust-filled connections with others. This isn't just about making connections; it's about attuning to others on a deeper level, showing up with openness, empathy, and a genuine desire to nurture those relationships.

   Building relationship resonance is vital to standing out in today's crowded market. The ability to inspire trust in others without asking for anything in return is a powerful force in business. This is how you communicate your value in a way that resonates—so that it goes beyond transactions. It's about showing people you care, building lasting connections, and maintaining an energy that keeps your relationships strong. When you can embody this level of resonance, people naturally trust you, and that trust leads to loyalty, visibility, and, ultimately, growth.

3. **Business Resonance *(Integration):*** The third pillar is where personal and relationship resonance intersects with strategic business execution. Here, you develop *business resonance*—the energetic and operational alignment of your business with your values and purpose. Every business, regardless of its size, must be nurtured as a separate entity with its energy, mission, and strategy.

   Your business resonance is about more than just making money; it's about showing that your business exists for a purpose greater than profit alone. It's about creating systems, products, and services that reflect your core values and make it easy for others to do business with you. When people see that your business is aligned with its stated purpose, they are more likely to say yes to working with you because they feel the resonance, care, and trust embedded into every part of your operation.

The Magical Convergence: When these three pillars—personal, relationship, and business resonance—align, something magical happens.

You experience a flow that eliminates the need for constant hustle and stress. The clarity and ease from this alignment create a natural momentum that drives your business forward, not just in financial success but in making a significant impact in the world.

Self-trust is the foundation of everything, and when you cultivate it at a soul-deep level, it frees you from imposter syndrome and allows you to show up fully as your true self. Others sense authenticity and trust you, effortlessly generating word-of-mouth marketing, referrals, and clients aligned with your mission.

Inspiring trust in others creates a ripple effect. Clients become ambassadors, spreading the word and bringing new opportunities your way. Business becomes less stressful, not because you're hustling harder but because you're attracting the right people to you. As trust deepens in your community, loyalty follows, and clients stick around and elevate your business by sharing their positive experiences with others.

When you build trust into the very heart of your business, it develops an energetic presence in the marketplace. It becomes a beacon—a lighthouse—shining brightly, attracting people who resonate with your values and purpose. You're no longer chasing clients; they're coming to you, drawn by the clarity of your mission and the strength of your presence.

Can you imagine the power of developing these three resonance levels at such a deep level? You'd not only be showing up fully for your life and business, but you'd also be effortlessly attracting clients, earning more, and creating a lasting impact in the world. This is the pathway to soul-aligned success.

Let's reflect on how resonance naturally leads to deeper inquiry. As you cultivate personal, relational, and business resonance, trust becomes the bedrock on which everything else is built. Trust in yourself, trust in your relationships, and trust in your business operations form the foundation of a business that thrives in profitability and creating genuine, lasting impact.

Guiding Questions for Trust:

- **How do I trust myself?** This question invites you to turn inward and examine your self-confidence, alignment with your values, and higher purpose. Building personal resonance begins here—grounding yourself in the truth of who you are, allowing you to make decisions with clarity and conviction. Trusting yourself is about honoring your intuition, embracing your journey, and standing confidently in your purpose.

- **How do I inspire trust in others?** Trust is the cornerstone of authentic relationships in business or personal life. How are you showing up in your connections with others? Are you being transparent, genuine, and supportive? Inspiring trust requires cultivating relational resonance—fostering an environment where others feel seen, heard, and valued. This deepens the bonds of loyalty and creates communities built on mutual respect and shared purpose.

- **How do I create a trusted business?** Building a trusted business means operating with integrity and ensuring that your business practices align with your mission and values. It's about creating an experience for your clients and customers that feels honest, reliable, and deeply connected to the impact you wish to make. Trust in business extends beyond transactions—it's about leaving a lasting, positive impression that resonates with those you serve.

The Resonance Roadmap offers a strategy—AND it's an intimate, transformational journey towards cultivating a business that connects with your audience, embodies authentic values, and creates meaningful impact. By navigating the interconnected spaces of "I," "we," and the broader business ecosystem, you, as a leader, are empowered to build a resonant, thriving business in today's dynamic world.

As we continue on this transformative path, leadership plays a pivotal role. The responsibility of guiding a business toward resonance and sustainability rests squarely on the shoulders of those at the helm. In the next section, we'll explore how leadership is not just a role but a profound calling that requires vision, empathy, and the courage to lead in alignment with a higher purpose.

This brings us to the essence of leading with resonance, where trust is cultivated at every level, and businesses thrive through authentic, purpose-driven leadership.

Inner Compass: Guiding Questions

As you journey through this chapter, these guiding questions will help you reflect on your own process of awakening and alignment. By diving deeper into your resonance, purpose, and transformation, you will explore how to align your inner work with the outer impact you wish to create.

- **What does the call to awaken mean to you?** Reflect on your personal experience of awakening—whether in your leadership, personal growth, or relationships. How are you responding to the inner call to live more consciously?

- **How do you navigate conflict when worlds collide?** Think about times when you've experienced conflict or misalignment with others. Could these moments be rooted in differences in consciousness, values, or perspectives? How can you shift your approach to create understanding and coherence?

- **What is your home frequency, and how does it guide your actions?** As you explore the concept of resonance codes, reflect on the frequency that feels most natural to you. How does this home frequency shape your thoughts, decisions, and interactions with the world?

- **How aligned are your mind, body, and spirit in your day-to-day life?** Consider how well your mental, emotional, and physical selves are integrated. Are there areas where you feel disconnected, and what practices can help you align these aspects of yourself?

- **What inner transformations have led to tangible outer impact?** Reflect on how your personal growth has influenced your external actions and leadership. How can you deepen this connection between your inner work and the outer changes you want to create in the world?

- **What does purpose mean to you beyond branding?** Reflect on your understanding of purpose—not just as a marketing tool but as the core driver of your leadership and business. How aligned is your purpose with the impact you want to create?

- **How aligned are you with the Resonance Roadmap?** Consider how the Resonance Roadmap can help you navigate personal and organizational alignment. Are there areas where you're out of sync with your values or your team? How can you create greater coherence between your inner purpose and external actions?

- **How do you cultivate trust within your organization and community?** Reflect on how you build trust with your team, clients, and partners. What steps can you take to deepen trust and ensure it is at the foundation of your relationships and leadership?

3
Why Sacred Changemakers?

"We must move beyond our human-centered notions of the world and begin to see ourselves as part of a sacred community of life." - Thomas Berry.

Expanding our role as change practitioners invites us to look deeper within ourselves. We must reflect on who we are becoming and how our work is evolving to meet the challenges of our time. It's about helping others succeed and aligning our professional practices with a higher purpose.

So, consider this:

- Who are you becoming as a change practitioner?
- What do you want to achieve with your work?
- How would your life and business transform if you treated them as sacred?

These questions guide us toward awakening the changemaker within—a fundamentally spiritual process. The word "spirit" comes from the Latin *spiritus*, meaning breath or life force. This life force is always within us, yearning to be expressed fully and authentically through our actions and intentions.

This journey is about connecting with the source of your true power and creating a life, career or business that expresses your soul's deepest desires. It's a collaborative process of awakening, breaking free from the mind's limiting beliefs and emotions, and embracing the full potential of who you are.

Awakening is more than a mental realization; it's a profound inner experience where you begin to recognize the immense potential that lies within you. It's about acknowledging that you can do so much more than you've ever believed—radiant, powerful, and brilliant beyond measure.

This awakening is a journey into your essence, where you connect deeply with your heart and soul. It's a moment of revelation, a shift in consciousness where you align with your authentic self, embracing the boundless energy and light that is your birthright. And although it can be easy, it can also bring challenges.

Here's the thing: mind and emotions do not easily surrender to spirit, especially in today's modern world. Getting caught in the constant push and pull between the mind, emotions, and spirit is too easy, leaving us feeling stuck or overwhelmed. This inner conflict can cloud our sense of clarity and purpose, making it difficult to navigate life's challenges.

Although life presents us with countless opportunities for awakening and growth, we often forget this amidst our daily struggles. Life is a series of awakenings, yet this is easy to forget. It is why embracing any change process can be so powerful; it helps us reconnect with our true selves, aligning our minds, hearts, and spirits to facilitate lasting change.

An awakening is realizing you are not who you think you are.

Awakening is more than just a moment of clarity; it's a profound shift in your sense of self and how you engage with the world. It's realizing that the limitations you once believed in were self-imposed and that your true essence is far more powerful, radiant, and brilliant than you ever allowed yourself to believe. This awakening is a call to release the part of you that has been hidden, longing to express its fullest potential.

Many clients experience this as a deep, inner yearning—a sense that they can no longer ignore the desire for a more meaningful, authentic life. They recognize that the life they've been living doesn't fully reflect their deepest values, aspirations, or potential. They feel ready to make a shift, prepared to break free from the constraints that have held them back. *But what about you?*

- Do you feel that same inner calling?

- Are you ready to step into a more expansive version of yourself that aligns with your highest truth and purpose?

- Can you see the benefits of expanding your current approach to change?

If you are, the invitation is to keep moving forward, even if doubt and fear arise. These emotions are natural companions on the journey of transformation. Trust in your inner guidance, and know that every step you take, no matter how small, leads you closer to the life you are meant to live. Embrace the awakening within you, and let it guide you toward a more authentic, fulfilling, and purposeful existence.

This awakening is part of a broader shift happening worldwide. As old ways of living and working feel increasingly misaligned, there is a growing awareness that the challenges we face cannot be solved by individual ambition or short-term success alone. What is now required is a new kind of leadership that integrates inner transformation with collective responsibility.

This is the path of a Sacred Changemaker.

Towards a Working Definition

A *"Sacred Changemaker"* is a transformational force in life and business. Sacred Changemakers integrate deeper, holistic, and often spiritual elements into their actions to foster profound personal and societal impact.

They recognize the interconnectedness of all life and actively contribute to creating a more harmonious and sustainable world.

Unlike conventional leaders who may focus primarily on tangible achievements, Sacred Changemakers embrace a broader vision. They balance personal growth with collective well-being, weaving together life's spiritual, emotional, and physical dimensions with their professional endeavors. This integrated approach encourages a systemic perspective, aligning personal ambitions with the broader needs of society. It's about moving from self-interest to service, guiding us toward a balanced and inclusive way of living.

Sacred Changemakers understand that real change begins within. To create a meaningful impact, we must heal our inner stories, shift limiting beliefs, and become more self-aware. This journey requires us to align our thoughts, decisions, and actions with our highest values and purpose. It invites us to step into a higher resonance, where what we think, feel, and do reflect the change we wish to see in the world.

This path is not easy. It calls for courage, humility, and a willingness to embrace personal transformation and collective responsibility. It challenges us to move beyond familiar ways of being and expand into a more authentic version of ourselves—one aligned with the well-being of others and the planet. As we rise to meet this invitation, we naturally begin to inspire others to do the same, creating a ripple effect that can reshape the systems and structures around us.

Sacred Changemakers recognize that how we live, lead, and do business must evolve. We are being called to embody leadership that not only achieves results but also elevates consciousness—inviting others into a shared journey of growth and contribution. This is leadership that integrates purpose with profit, balancing inner fulfillment with outer impact to create lasting change.

At its core, this is a shift from *'Me' to 'We'*—from focusing on individual achievement to embracing the collective well-being of humanity and the planet.

It is an invitation to lead from resonance—aligning with a frequency of purpose and connection that ripples outward, shaping organizations, communities, and the world. To shift conversations with our clients or employees from 'me' to 'we' to help them understand who they are becoming matters as much as what they do—because every action, decision, and behavior reflects a hidden truth about who they are and what they stand for. This is how we expand our approach to change to support the changes the world needs.

This is a critical distinction. Consider your work around change.

- Reflecting on how you inspire change in others, do you inspire individual change or also consider collective needs?

- How do you inspire your clients or employees in the direction of the 'we'?

Remember, it's not an *'either....or'* conversation but a *'yes...and'*.

To walk this path is to answer the call of our times. It is a call to become more than we thought we could be, not just for ourselves but for the world we are creating together. Sacred Changemakers know that the time for this shift is now—and that the future of business, leadership, and society depends on those willing to lead the way.

The Challenge of the Sacred

> *"We like the word changemaker, but sacred? I don't think you can go into business saying that, no one will listen."* – (How my colleagues responded to the name of my new business!)

When I first started Sacred Changemakers, many of my colleagues said they liked the word *'changemakers'* but felt uneasy about the word *'sacred.'* They thought it implied religion or spiritual dogma. It doesn't, not to me anyway. What I intended then, and what I stand by now, is a reclamation of the word *'sacred'* back into mainstream conversation. It doesn't represent any religious ideology—it's about expanding our purpose to think of change as a sacred calling.

I have to admit, the word felt edgy for me, too. I worried that using it might undermine my credibility or authority. *Would leaders and CEOs dismiss it as too soft or spiritual?* What I've found is that the opposite has happened. When I speak to business leaders about sacredness, they lean in. They listen more closely, often whispering their agreement—because they know, deep down, that business has lost its soul. They see how we've stripped business of its deeper meaning in pursuit of profit. There is a hunger for something more—for a way to reconnect leadership and business practices with values, purpose, and a sense of honor.

I have to laugh when I think back to the early days—every time I typed *'Sacred Changemakers'* into my computer, the spell checker would automatically change it to *'Scared Changemakers.'* Honestly, that's not entirely wrong *(and it did make me smile!)*. The sacred can initially feel scary—as it calls us out of our comfort zones. It invites us to see life, business, and leadership through a lens of reverence that demands more from us. It asks us to honor the interconnectedness of all things and hold ourselves accountable for what we achieve and how we achieve it.

Many of us have subjective ideas about religion, which can make the word *'sacred'* feel heavy or loaded. That's not what it means here. In this context, sacredness is about respect, honor, and intention—recognizing that all life has intrinsic value. It's the understanding that human life, relationships, and business can be sacred when approached with care and purpose.

Sacred Changemaking is not just about change for its own sake. It's about recognizing that the work we do—whether in business, leadership, or life—is part of a larger, interconnected whole. Change takes on a different weight and meaning when we see it as sacred. It becomes more than just action—it becomes purpose-driven, conscious, and deeply aligned with the well-being of others and the planet.

To embrace this more expansive kind of change, is to step into a higher level of responsibility and resonance. It's not only about personal growth or business success—it's about creating impact that reflects our highest values. It asks us to honor what matters most in every context, including the marketplace. When treated as sacred, business becomes a vehicle for healing, connection, and meaningful contribution.

This is why Sacred Changemaking is essential. It's not just change—it's *sacred change* that holds a larger intention beyond individual benefits. It calls us to move beyond the transactional mindset and lead with purpose, care, and reverence. This is the shift that so many leaders quietly crave—a way to restore meaning to their work and reconnect with what truly matters. And this is the invitation I extend to you: to embrace the sacred in your work, leadership, and life, to step fully into the changemaker you are called to be.

The 'sacred' aspect of being a Sacred Changemaker is about reconnecting with life's deep, inherent value and all its expressions. It involves seeing beyond the material and recognizing a deeper presence in all things. It differentiates you in the marketplace, as your customers are attracted to your deeper sense of purpose, which sets you apart from your competitors in several key ways:

This approach sets them apart from others in several key ways:

1. **Holistic Approach:** Sacred changemakers recognize that true transformation requires seeing beyond isolated goals and skills. We understand that personal and professional achievements are intertwined with spiritual, emotional, and physical well-being. It's about transcending conventional goal-setting and weaving together the different facets of life to create a balanced, inclusive, and harmonious way of life.

For example, when coaching, I don't just focus on what my clients want; I ask them to consider what the world needs from them. This perspective shift encourages them to reflect on the bigger picture and align their actions with what is necessary for collective well-being. By nurturing every aspect of our being; we can actively contribute to a more harmonious and sustainable world.

2. **Emphasis on Spiritual Growth:** As Sacred Changemakers, we strongly emphasize spiritual growth and personal transformation. This journey isn't just about introspection; it's about awakening our soul connection and aligning our lives with our deepest values and purpose. I've witnessed many times how this inner exploration can lead to a profound sense of authenticity and fulfillment. When we nurture this awareness, we uncover a sense of meaning that ripples out, touching others and elevating the collective consciousness. It's this resonance that leads to valuable, purpose-driven change.

3. **Focus on Inner Wisdom:** True transformation begins within, and I've seen how this process unfolds in countless individuals. As Sacred Changemakers, we guide people to connect deeply with their inner wisdom and intuition. It's about more than just self-discovery; it's about shifting beliefs, healing personal wounds, and cultivating an inherent understanding that our inner state is reflected in the world around us, creating a ripple effect of impact.

By embracing energetic resonance, we lead conversations that foster inclusivity and navigate conflict with empathy, utilizing practices like nonviolent communication. A critical aspect of this work is awareness of "othering"—the unconscious act of separating ourselves from those who are different. This awareness helps us remain present, connected, and compassionate, ensuring that any change we inspire is profound and authentic. We set the stage for genuine, inclusive change by dismantling barriers and embracing our shared humanity.

This focus on internal guidance enables us to act from a place of genuine understanding and compassion, creating a foundation for lasting transformation that resonates beyond the individual, touching the lives of others and elevating the collective consciousness.

4. **Commitment to Ethical Practices:** As Sacred Changemakers, our commitment to ethical, sustainable, and regenerative practices is unwavering. We advocate for decisions that harmonize profitability with

ethical and ecological responsibility, understanding that true success must benefit all stakeholders, including our planet. In a world where trust in business and leaders is notably low, we prioritize building trust through honesty and transparency, beginning with trusting ourselves. I've seen firsthand how this foundational trust inspires confidence in others and fosters a culture of integrity within business life.

By demonstrating that leadership and business can thrive on principles of integrity and sustainability, we set ourselves apart in today's marketplace. We prove that success and ethical practices are not mutually exclusive but complementary paths to positively impacting society and the environment. This commitment is more than just a business strategy; it's a way of life that reflects our dedication to leaving the world better than we found it.

For us, it's about the complete picture; achieving financial goals whilst also contributing to a regenerative future that upholds the dignity of all life. We aim to embody a new kind of leadership, one that is guided by empathy, integrity, and purpose, showing that businesses can be forces for good, creating value that extends beyond profit margins to benefit the whole.

5. **Creating Positive Social Impact:** As Sacred Changemakers, we strive to extend our impact beyond individual transformation, aligning our practices with broader social, environmental, and spiritual goals. We challenge the traditional divide between for-profit and non-profit models, illustrating that businesses can thrive through purpose-driven profits. By guiding others to contribute meaningfully to their communities and the world, we showcase how adding value and being a force for good are essential elements of contemporary success.

I've seen how integrating purpose and profit can catalyze profound shifts in people and organizations. This is more than a strategy; it's a reimagining of business itself, where success is measured in financial terms and in our positive impact on society and the planet. We are called to break down the false polarity between profit and purpose, demonstrating that businesses can flourish by embedding social responsibility into their core strategy and transforming the marketplace into a platform for meaningful change.

This alignment of values is not just a trend but a necessary evolution in how we approach business. As we all search for more meaning and fulfillment, it becomes clear that true success involves contributing to the well-being of all. By embedding social responsibility we help others less fortunate than ourselves. This is how we turn business into a force for good, reshaping the future in ways that honor the sacredness of life.

6. **Use of Diverse Modalities:** Sacred changemakers embrace various change tools and techniques, such as coaching, NLP, systems thinking, mindfulness, meditation, energy work, bringing together many different practices, seamlessly integrating these into their work. This eclectic approach bridges the gap between business, spirituality, and technology, breaking away from conventional methods and reclaiming the sacred in life and business.

This commitment to diverse modalities fosters an atmosphere of innovation and creativity, inviting leaders and individuals to explore both the depth and breadth of their potential. Combining ancient wisdom with modern innovation creates fertile ground for transformation, cultivating a balanced and holistic view of success that honors the sacred while embracing technological advancement.

We prove that leadership can be reimagined at this unique intersection, where purpose, progress, and planetary well-being coexist. This shift in perspective encourages a new kind of leadership that's deeply aligned with inner wisdom and external innovation, signaling a profound change in how we approach business, personal growth, and the future.

7. **Emphasis on Regenerative Leadership:** This naturally follows from our commitment to holistic change. As Sacred Changemakers, we champion regenerative leadership that transcends traditional profit-driven motives by integrating them with a conscious business ethos inspired by nature's wisdom. We understand that profitability and purpose can coexist, and true abundance comes from balancing economic success with ecological and social well-being.

Leaders are encouraged to apply these principles by regenerating ecosystems, their organizations, and personal well-being. This approach emphasizes resilience, interconnectivity, and sustainable growth, aligning business practices with nature's capacity for renewal.

Regenerative leadership is about more than immediate achievements; it's a commitment to a long-term legacy rooted in empathy, integrity, and purpose. We advocate for environments that nurture personal and professional growth, inspiring leaders to contribute to a sustainable and abundant future. This transforms the pursuit of success into a holistic mission, where business becomes a steward of societal and environmental health, embodying the true essence of regenerative leadership.

8. **Focus on Sustainable Transformation:** We also aim for sustainable and long-lasting transformation rather than the usual short-term solutions. We help others make changes that are deeply rooted in their values and sustainable over time. By channeling the wisdom of indigenous traditions, which advocate for considering the impact of decisions on seven generations ahead, we foster a vision of lasting change and, where appropriate, with value beyond our lifetime. This approach involves breaking free from habitual patterns, embracing a journey of lifelong learning, and acknowledging the constant evolution inherent in life.

Sacred changemakers cultivate an open, growth-oriented mindset fueled by curiosity and recognizing that no single approach fits all situations. Instead, we get creative and provide tailored solutions that resonate with individual values, ensuring that the transformation is profound and lasts.

In essence, a sacred changemaker is an individual who blends traditional methods with more holistic and often spiritual practices, aiming to bring about profound personal growth and positive societal change.

With a deeper understanding of what it means to be a Sacred Changemaker, we now focus on the critical role these individuals play in modern life and business. In a world marked by rapid change, complexity, and uncertainty, Sacred Changemakers serve as beacons of hope and agents of change. They bring a unique blend of spiritual insight, ethical leadership, and innovative action to address the most pressing challenges of our time.

Let's explore how this influential role manifests across various domains, from personal development to organizational change, and how it can inspire a new paradigm for business and society.

The Role of Changemakers in Modern Business

In today's marketplace, sacred changemakers are transforming the very essence of business by integrating purpose and profit. This isn't just a theoretical shift; it's a profoundly personal journey many of us have felt called to take. We understand that true success extends beyond financial metrics—it's about making a tangible, positive impact on society and the planet. As mentioned earlier, being a changemaker isn't just about one's actions; it's about embodying the sacred essence of life in every decision and action. It's a call to stand at the intersection of individual potential and collective well-being, becoming a conduit for the change we wish to see.

I've seen firsthand how this approach changes the game for individuals and organizations. It's not just about doing business differently; it's about being in business differently. It's about bringing our whole selves into our work to be and become more human—our values, hopes, and desire to contribute meaningfully to the world. It's not merely about the 'what' of business, but the 'how' and 'why'—a commitment to reclaiming the sacred in modern life and integrating it into our professional endeavors.

Take companies like Ecosia, Patagonia, and Seventh Generation. They're not just brands but living embodiments of what happens when purpose meets action.

Case Studies: Embodying Sacred Changemaking Principles

Ecosia exemplifies how businesses can integrate purpose into their profit mechanisms. As a search engine that donates 80% of its profits to tree-planting initiatives, Ecosia has planted millions of trees worldwide. Every search becomes an act of environmental stewardship, directly engaging users to combat deforestation. Ecosia's transparent business model and clear social impact resonate with an audience increasingly looking to align their daily actions with their values, proving that even a search engine can drive global environmental change.

Patagonia is renowned not just for its high-quality outdoor apparel but also for its unwavering commitment to environmental sustainability. The company donates 1% of sales to environmental causes and has been a vocal advocate for public land preservation and sustainable agriculture. Patagonia's "Don't Buy This Jacket" campaign, encouraging customers to consider the environmental impact of their purchases, epitomizes the company's ethos of conscious consumerism. This stance has built a loyal customer base that values the brand's integrity and mission as much as its products.

Seventh Generation, rooted in the Iroquois philosophy of considering the impact on seven generations to come, is a leader in sustainable and ethical consumer goods. The company's commitment to creating eco-friendly cleaning products matches its corporate responsibility, transparency, and advocacy. Seventh Generation's focus on long-term ecological health over short-term profits has set a new standard in the industry, proving that businesses can be profitable while prioritizing the health of people and the planet.

These case studies illustrate that redefining business success isn't just about adopting new practices; it's about embracing a purpose that aligns with broader societal and environmental goals. Companies like Ecosia, Patagonia, and Seventh Generation are not just participating in the market—they are reshaping it, proving that purpose-driven profits are not only possible but essential for the future of business. Their actions inspire other companies to consider contributing to a more sustainable and equitable world, paving the way for a new era of purposeful and profitable business practices.

Consider how these companies exemplify the principles of sacred changemaking: they honor the interconnectedness of life, embrace the need for change, and actively engage in creating a positive impact.

Ecosia's mission to fund reforestation projects through its search engine is a powerful reminder that even digital businesses can plant seeds—literally and figuratively—that grow into something beautiful and lasting. Patagonia's unwavering commitment to environmental activism, from donating profits to challenging the status quo, inspires us to ask: *How can my business stand for something bigger than itself?* The Seventh Generation's dedication to considering the impact of its products on future generations shows us that every decision, no matter how small, matters.

They remind us that sacred changemaking is about more than just changing what we do; it's about changing who we are and how we show up in the world. It's about creating businesses that feel like a natural extension of our highest aspirations and deepest values, businesses that not only survive but thrive by serving the greater good.

Embodying the Sacred in Business and Beyond

For sacred changemakers, business is not just a vehicle for profit; it's a powerful platform for meaningful change. Embracing the sacred in our work means seeing every aspect of business as an opportunity to create a positive impact and align with a higher purpose.

We see this in companies that move beyond conventional practices, adopting holistic approaches that honor people, profit, and the planet. These businesses recognize that every decision, from supply chain management to customer relations, has the potential to resonate with a more expansive truth. For example, organizations like Patagonia demonstrate that sustainability can be a core business strategy, not just a side project.

On a personal level, embodying the sacred means making choices that reflect who we are and what we stand for. It's about integrating our values into everyday actions through mindful leadership, ethical decision-making, or fostering a culture of compassion and inclusion within our teams.

This approach requires courage and a willingness to disrupt the status quo, challenging the traditional boundaries between profit and purpose. It invites us to reimagine success, not just as a financial achievement but as the ability to create a lasting, positive legacy in the world.

Ultimately, embodying the sacred in business and beyond means committing to a path where our actions—large and small—are infused with intention and meaning. It's about contributing to a world where businesses serve as stewards of social and environmental well-being and individuals live and lead authentically and purposefully. This lies at the heart of sacred changemaking, a call to align our inner values with our outer actions to create resonance, transforming our businesses and the world around us.

Essential Skills for Changemakers

Certain skills are critical in the journey towards becoming a Sacred Changemaker in today's fast-evolving business landscape. Strategic thinking, digital proficiency, and coaching skills are three essential skills that facilitate effective leadership and empower individuals and organizations to navigate the complexities of modern business dynamics. This section breaks down these critical skills and offers practical advice on cultivating them effectively.

Strategic Thinking

Strategic thinking is not just about corporate planning; it's a vital skill that enables leaders to foresee, plan for, and shape the future. It involves understanding the broader impacts of decisions, anticipating potential challenges and opportunities, and positioning the organization in alignment with long-term goals.

1. **Cultivate a Forward-Looking Mindset:** Encourage continuous learning and curiosity about industry trends, emerging technolo-

gies, and global market shifts. Regularly scheduled strategic review sessions help keep this perspective fresh and relevant.

2. **Scenario Planning:** Regularly engage in scenario planning exercises that challenge your team to envision future states and develop strategies to address these potentialities. This helps build a proactive rather than reactive approach to change.

3. **Foster Creative Problem-Solving:** Promote a culture that rewards innovative thinking. Encourage team members to think outside the box and explore unconventional solutions to problems. Techniques like design thinking workshops can facilitate this process.

Digital Proficiency

In an era where technology permeates all aspects of business, digital proficiency is not just advantageous—it's essential. This skill ensures leaders and their teams can effectively use digital tools to enhance business operations, engage with stakeholders, and drive innovation.

1. **Continuous Digital Learning:** Implement training programs that keep pace with the latest digital trends and tools. This could include workshops, online courses, or hands-on training sessions that help staff stay current with new technologies, and begin to integrate AI in ethical ways.

2. **Leverage Digital Tools:** Utilize digital tools to streamline operations, improve communication, and enhance data analysis capabilities. Tools such as project management software, CRM systems, and advanced analytics platforms can significantly increase efficiency and insights.

3. **Digital Security Awareness:** As reliance on digital technologies increases, so does the risk of cyber threats. Training in digital security best practices is crucial to protect sensitive information and maintain trust with clients and partners.

Coaching Skills for Powerful Conversations

Coaching skills empower leaders to inspire and facilitate change in others through effective communication. These skills are critical for engaging teams, guiding developmental conversations, and fostering an environment of continuous improvement and personal growth.

1. **Active Listening:** Develop the ability to listen actively and empathetically to understand the motivations, thoughts, and feelings of others. This builds trust and openness in conversations.

2. **Asking Powerful Questions:** Ask questions that challenge assumptions, provoke thought, and inspire greater self-awareness and insight. Questions should be open-ended and designed to encourage deeper reflection.

3. **Feedback Delivery:** Enhance skills in giving constructive feedback that motivates and supports learning rather than defensiveness. Effective feedback is specific, timely, and focused on behaviors rather than personal attributes.

4. **Empowering Others:** Instead of being prescriptive, focus on conversations that help individuals discover solutions for themselves. This will encourage ownership and accountability for personal and professional growth.

By developing strategic thinking, digital proficiency, and coaching skills, changemakers can enhance their ability to lead effectively in the modern business world. These skills enable leaders to navigate the complexities of today's global market with foresight, adaptability, and the ability to inspire change in others, ensuring their organizations are prepared to face future challenges and positioned to seize opportunities that drive meaningful change.

Creating a Movement: Engaging Others in Your Vision

The journey to becoming a Sacred Changemaker unfolds into a broader narrative when that transformation reaches beyond the individual, engaging a community in a shared vision and mission. This evolution from self to society underscores the potential of expanding your life's impact, embracing the art and science of building a business and a movement.

As we've navigated the 8 Dimensions of Change, The Resonance Codes, and the Resonance Roadmap, we've seen the importance of inspiring trust in others—trust that becomes the bedrock of any movement. A community of like-minded individuals and businesses, collectively driven by a purpose more significant than any single entity, harnesses the power of the community to amplify impact and catalyze profound, positive societal change.

Thanks to the accessibility of online platforms, creating a community around your brand is easier today than ever before. These communities can flourish online or offline, supporting vibrant communities of change. The essence of creating a movement lies in inspiring others with words and leading by example through action. It's about demonstrating what it means to live by your values, creating a ripple effect that encourages others to do the same. It all comes down to embodied resonance.

In the context of a Sacred Changemaker, a community has the potential to become a vibrant ecosystem where trust is paramount. Trust is cultivated through consistent, authentic engagement and by highlighting the impact of collective efforts. It is within this community space—whether forged online through social media and forums or built through face-to-face interactions—that the true potential of a movement is realized. Here, you will find conversations become human, transcending commercial interests, becoming social and in ways that can meaningfully address societal challenges.

The power of the collective cannot be overstated. It provides a foundation of support, a crucible for innovation, and a force for disruption. Grassroots movements, in particular, showcase the potential of community-driven initiatives to challenge the status quo and instigate change.

These movements are built on the shared commitment of their members to a cause greater than themselves, fueled by the belief that together, they can create a better future.

Thus, becoming a Sacred Changemaker involves more than personal growth; it requires cultivating a community through bringing together like minded people. This is where trust and support are nurtured, ideas flourish, and movements are born. It is where the collective power of individuals and businesses can come together to support, innovate, and disrupt for the greater good.

Recognize the transformational power of the collective, understand your role as a guide, and leverage that power to create lasting, positive change in the world. If you feel inspired to start a movement around the changes you would like to see in the world, here are a few practical strategies that can get you moving in the right direction, helping to inspire community around a common purpose:

- **Articulate Your Vision Clearly**: The first step in creating a movement is to communicate your vision in a clear, compelling manner. Your vision should resonate personally with potential followers, making them feel part of something larger than themselves. Use storytelling to convey the why behind your mission, making it relatable and inspiring.

- **Foster Shared Values**: A movement is built on a foundation of shared values. Identify and articulate the core values that underpin your vision, and seek out individuals and businesses that align with these values. This shared ethos becomes the glue that binds the community together, driving collective action towards common goals.

- **Leverage Effective Communication Channels**: Use various communication channels to reach your audience where they are. From social media to community forums and newsletters to public speaking engagements, the key is maintaining a consistent, authentic message that speaks to the heart of your mission.

- **Encourage Collaboration and Co-Creation**: Empower your

community members to take active roles in the movement by encouraging collaboration and co-creation. Create platforms where ideas can be shared, projects can be developed collaboratively, and successes can be celebrated collectively. This enriches the movement and fosters a sense of ownership and commitment among its members.

- **Provide Clear Calls to Action**: To mobilize your community, provide clear, actionable steps they can take to contribute to the movement. Participating in campaigns, volunteering, or spreading the word makes it easy for people to get involved and make a difference.

- **Cultivate a Sense of Belonging**: A strong movement is one where every member feels they belong. Cultivate this sense by recognizing contributions, celebrating diversity, and creating inclusive spaces where all voices are heard and valued.

- **Measure and Share Impact**: Regularly measure your movement's impact and share its achievements with your community. This will demonstrate the tangible difference your collective efforts make, motivating and inspiring continued engagement and commitment.

- **Be Adaptable and Responsive**: Finally, be prepared to adapt and evolve your strategies in response to feedback from your community and changes in the external environment. A dynamic and responsive movement is more likely to sustain its momentum and achieve its long-term goals.

Creating a movement is more than rallying people to a cause; it's about inspiring a collective shift toward a more conscious, purpose-driven way of life. By engaging others in your vision and building a community united by shared values and goals, you can turn individual transformation into a powerful force for societal change, driving forward the mission of positive transformation on a much larger scale.

Inner Compass: Guiding Questions

As you reflect on the unique role of Sacred Changemakers and how to embody the sacred in business, these guiding questions will help you explore your purpose, challenges, and the impact you're meant to create. Take your time with each question, allowing yourself to dive deep into your journey as a changemaker.

- **What does being a Sacred Changemaker mean to you?** Reflect on your working definition of a changemaker. How do you see your role in transforming business and the world around you?

- **What is the challenge of the sacred in your life and work?** Consider how the concept of the sacred challenges conventional business practices. How comfortable are you with integrating the sacred into your leadership, and what fears or doubts arise when you think about doing so?

- **How do you see changemakers shaping modern business?** Reflect on the current role of changemakers in the business world. How do you believe changemakers can transform traditional business models and drive more ethical, sustainable practices?

- **What does it mean to embody the sacred in your business?** Think about how you can bring more sacredness into your daily business operations, decision-making, and leadership. How can you ensure your actions reflect your values and contribute to the greater good?

- What skills do you need to cultivate as a changemaker? Consider the skills essential for changemaking—strategic thinking, digital proficiency, coaching, etc. Which of these do you feel confident in, and which areas could you develop further to amplify your impact?

- **How will you create a movement around your vision?** Reflect on how you will engage others in your vision for change. What steps can you take to inspire, connect, and bring together people who align with your purpose and are willing to contribute to the movement?

- **How can you develop a changemaker's toolkit for your work?** Think about the tools, resources, and strategies you need to be effective as a changemaker. What should be in your toolkit to help you navigate challenges, lead change, and inspire others to join you?

- **What does collective impact look like for you?** Reflect on the broader vision of collective impact. How can you expand your efforts beyond individual success to create a movement that benefits your community, industry, or the world?

Part 2
CONSCIOUS LEADERSHIP - Becoming Regenerative

4

Regenerative Leadership: Catalyzing Necessary Change

"What you do makes a difference, and you have to decide what kind of difference you want to make." - Jane Goodall.[1]

Leadership as a Sacred Duty

As we have discussed, in this new era of business, leadership is no longer just about guiding a company toward profits. It's about creating resonance—where leaders, employees, and the business are all aligned with a higher purpose. This type of leadership transcends traditional approaches and ventures into **resonant leadership**, where the leader's role is to manage and act as a steward of life, ensuring that every decision and action resonates deeply with all aspects of the world around us.

Resonant leadership naturally aligns with **regenerative leadership**. While resonant leadership works from the inside out, intentionally creating harmony, empathy, and deep connection within ourselves, our relationships, and through our career or business, regenerative leadership takes this further by focusing on also renewing and revitalizing systems, undoing the harm that has been done over decades of consumerism. Leadership moves beyond the tactical and operational to embrace the **sacred duty** of leading in resonance with all life to regenerate what has been lost from a human, community, and planetary perspective.

In regenerative leadership, the leader's role becomes a sacred calling.

It becomes ethical, where it isn't just a strategy for achieving success; it's a way of being that permeates every interaction and decision. This approach calls for a commitment to principles that prioritize the well-being of the human spirit, the communities we serve, and the health of the planet.

It's not simply about what we do but about how we do it—and who we are while doing it. As leaders, we need to embody what matters most.

Leaders who embrace this sacred responsibility understand that their decisions carry far-reaching consequences, influencing the bottom line and the people and ecosystems their business touches. Resonant leadership requires a conscious effort to:

- **Cultivate Transparency**: Open and honest communication is the foundation of trust. It ensures that stakeholders are respected and informed, creating a culture of shared responsibility.

- **Practice Accountability**: Ethical leaders hold themselves and their teams accountable for their actions, ensuring that every business decision aligns with legal standards and a higher ethical purpose.

- **Foster Inclusivity**: Resonant leaders champion diversity and inclusivity, recognizing the power of multiple perspectives and ensuring that every voice has the opportunity to be heard.

- **Champion Sustainability**: In regenerative leadership, sustainability is more than a buzzword—it's a core principle. Leaders must ensure that their businesses preserve and enhance the ecosystems and communities they rely on.

By internalizing these principles, leaders elevate their organizations and contribute to a broader cultural shift towards more ethical, transparent, and sustainable business practices. This is leadership as a sacred duty, where the leader's role is to ensure that the business acts as a force for good, creating positive ripples that extend far beyond the company itself. It's about leading not just a business but a movement that redefines success in today's world.

Our Inner Circle has recorded a powerful conversation on this topic for those looking to explore this concept further. You can listen to *"Sacred Duty: The Role of Spirituality in the Workplace"*[2] by following the link in the Endnotes.

Becoming Regenerative

Regenerative leadership is a transformative approach gaining traction and reshaping today's business landscape. Rooted in the organic principles of renewal, resilience, and holistic success, this leadership model responds to our time's complex, systemic challenges, advocating for practices that sustain and rejuvenate our societies and the natural environment.

In today's world, regenerative leadership is not just desirable—it's urgently needed. While sustainable practices were once seen as the gold standard, we now recognize that sustainability alone is no longer enough. Sustainable practices focus on minimizing harm and maintaining the status quo, ensuring that resources are preserved for future generations.

However, maintaining the status quo is insufficient, given the scale and urgency of our environmental and social challenges. We are in a moment of critical imbalance; climate change, biodiversity loss, resource depletion, and growing social inequalities demand more than just preventing further damage.

This is where regenerative leadership steps in. Unlike sustainability, which aims to *'do no harm,'* regenerative practices actively seek to restore, renew, and regenerate the systems they impact.

It's a forward-thinking approach that goes beyond simply maintaining balance. Regeneration is about creating net positive impacts, leaving ecosystems and communities healthier, more resilient, and more vibrant than before. Restorative practices fall somewhere in between, focusing on repairing the damage done. Regenerative practices push even further, restoring natural and social systems while ensuring they thrive for future generations.

The challenges we face have catalyzed a fast evolution in leadership thinking. Yet many companies remain stuck in the past, believing their corporate sustainability efforts will suffice. They won't. Climate crises and social upheavals have escalated to a point where merely sustaining what we have is inadequate. Businesses must now rethink their role as stewards of economic prosperity and ecological and social well-being.

Regenerative leadership calls for a fundamental shift that requires businesses to integrate regenerative principles at the core of their operations and give them a voice in boardroom strategies. This shift is not just about compliance or reputation management; it's about embedding regeneration into the organization's DNA to influence decision-making from the top down.

In today's rapidly evolving business environment, marked by mounting systemic challenges and an urgent need for sustainable practices, regenerative leadership is fast becoming a necessity. This leadership model is grounded in the understanding that organizations are living systems intricately interconnected with the communities and ecosystems they touch. Just as nature thrives on diversity and interdependence, so do businesses when they embrace their role within these broader systems.

Leaders who adopt this approach recognize that businesses are not isolated entities acting in silos but are integral parts of more extensive, interwoven systems. As such, they create organizational strategies reflecting this deep interconnection, fostering beliefs, attitudes, and values prioritizing sustainability, ethical decision-making, and long-term resilience.

One of the most profound lessons we can learn from nature is the importance of biodiversity. As I have already mentioned, diversity creates resilience in ecosystems. No matter how small, each species plays a unique and vital role in maintaining balance and health. When biodiversity is lost, ecosystems become fragile and more prone to collapse.

The same principle applies to organizations and societies. Regenerative leadership mirrors this insight by emphasizing diversity in nature and people, ideas, and approaches. Leaders who value diversity encourage creative problem-solving, adaptability, and innovation, which are critical in responding to today's complex global challenges.

In learning from nature, regenerative leaders understand that a single force or entity does not dominate thriving ecosystems. Instead, they operate in harmony and coherence, with each part contributing to the whole. This shift from dominance to collaboration is a fundamental principle of regenerative leadership. Rather than trying to control or exploit natural systems, these leaders seek to align with nature's wisdom, working in harmony with it. They recognize that the answers we need are often already present in nature—if we take the time to observe, listen, and learn.

Nature has spent billions of years perfecting systems that regenerate, sustain, and renew themselves. By modeling our businesses on these systems, we can create organizations that are not only sustainable but regenerative, contributing positively to the ecosystems and communities they interact with.

At the core of regenerative leadership is the recognition that the health of our businesses is inseparable from the health of our societies and the natural world. Nature shows us that every action has a ripple effect. Healthy forests, for example, create clean air and water, foster biodiversity, and store carbon—each of these elements reinforcing the entire system's health.

Similarly, regenerative leaders prioritize the well-being of all stakeholders—employees, customers, communities, and the environment—because they understand that these elements are interconnected. When one part of the system thrives, so do the others. This holistic perspective encourages leaders to move away from short-term financial gains and instead focus on creating long-term value. Profit alone is no longer the sole metric of success; instead, success is defined by the ability to thrive within the limits of our planet, regenerating the resources and relationships that sustain us.

Key Principles of Regenerative Leadership:

- **Interconnectedness**: Regenerative leaders recognize that their organizations are living systems intricately linked to the communities, ecosystems, and stakeholders they interact with. They understand that no business operates in isolation, and the health of one part of the system affects the whole.

- **Diversity and Inclusion**: Inspired by nature's biodiversity, regenerative leaders prioritize diversity in all forms—people, ideas, and perspectives. They understand that diversity fosters resilience, creativity, and adaptability, essential for navigating complex challenges.

- **Collaboration over Competition:** Regenerative leaders move away from a mindset of dominance and control and embrace collaboration. They focus on building partnerships and aligning with others to create positive outcomes that benefit the broader system, recognizing that mutual success leads to long-term sustainability.

- **Long-Term Value Creation**: Instead of focusing on short-term profits, regenerative leaders prioritize long-term value creation. They aim to contribute positively to social, environmental, and economic systems, ensuring that their businesses thrive while supporting the well-being of future generations.

- **Holistic Thinking**: Regenerative leaders adopt a systems-thinking approach, viewing their organizations as part of larger ecosystems. They consider the ripple effects of their decisions, understanding that everything is connected and that actions in one area impact others.

- **Restoration and Renewal**: Beyond sustainability, regenerative leaders actively seek to restore and rejuvenate the systems they affect. They adopt regenerative practices that heal ecosystems, rebuild communities, and contribute to the long-term health of people and the planet.

- **Learning from Nature**: Nature is the ultimate teacher. Regenerative leaders study and emulate nature's principles—such as resilience, adaptability, and regeneration—to inform their strategies. They focus on creating businesses that work in harmony with natural cycles and processes.

- **Ethical and Inclusive Decision-Making**: These leaders prioritize fairness, transparency, and inclusivity in their decision-making processes. They consider the well-being of all stakeholders, from employees and customers to local communities and the environment, ensuring that no group is left behind.

- **Thriving within Planetary Boundaries**: Regenerative leaders understand that the planet has finite resources and work to ensure their businesses operate within those limits. They seek to reduce waste, reuse materials, and promote circular economies, ensuring their operations enhance rather than deplete the Earth's resources.

- **Purpose-Driven Leadership**: Finally, regenerative leaders are deeply purpose-driven. They align their organizations with a higher purpose that transcends financial success, focusing on contributing to the greater good and ensuring that their work leaves a lasting, positive impact on society and the planet.

This shift in thinking requires businesses to move beyond conventional growth models, where success is measured by expansion and resource extraction. Instead, regenerative leadership promotes a vision where success is about creating abundance within planetary boundaries.

It's about learning to live within the natural cycles of regeneration, where waste is minimized, and resources are reused or restored. Just as nature has *no waste*, and every element serves a purpose in the broader ecosystem, regenerative businesses aim to create value that also contributes to society's and the environment's well-being.

By adopting this more conscious approach, leaders are fostering more ethical and sustainable practices and positioning their organizations to thrive in a world that increasingly values harmony with nature over domination. They see their organizations as part of a larger ecosystem, aiming to create value that regenerates social and environmental systems.

This requires a significant shift in perspective—moving away from viewing success solely in terms of profit and growth and toward a deeper understanding of success as the ability to contribute positively to the world while thriving within our planet's limits.

As we learn to live in resonance with nature, regenerative leadership offers a pathway to a more resilient, balanced, and ethical future for business—one where we sustain and actively regenerate the natural and social systems that support us all.

This shift is already visible in the marketplace, with several pioneering companies leading the way:

- **Interface**: A global leader in modular flooring, Interface embarked on a journey to eliminate its environmental footprint by 2020 through its Mission Zero® program. Going beyond sustainability, the company has embraced regenerative practices, sourcing natural materials that can be recycled or biodegraded, setting a new standard for industrial companies.
- **Unilever**: Under former CEO Paul Polman, Unilever made a bold commitment to decouple its growth from environmental impact while increasing its positive social contributions. Its Sustainable Living Plan outlines ambitious goals to reduce plastic use, im-

prove health and well-being for billions, and enhance livelihoods for millions, demonstrating the potential of regenerative principles at scale.

- **Tesla, Inc.**: Beyond revolutionizing the automotive industry with electric vehicles, Tesla's mission to accelerate the world's transition to sustainable energy embodies regenerative leadership. By investing in renewable energy solutions and battery technology, Tesla is helping drive a shift toward a more sustainable, regenerative energy system.

However, the transition to regenerative leadership is not without its challenges, particularly in environments where traditional success metrics—like quarterly profit growth and shareholder returns—dominate. Leaders often face pressure to deliver constant growth, sometimes at the expense of long-term sustainability and ethical considerations. This tension creates obstacles for those seeking to adopt a regenerative approach, as it requires navigating difficult trade-offs and redefining success for stakeholders accustomed to conventional measures.

Moreover, regenerative leadership requires a high degree of adaptability and openness to change. It involves continuous learning and evolving in response to the dynamic interplay between an organization and its environment. Leaders must think systemically, recognizing the interconnectedness of various factors and the potential for unintended consequences. This can be a challenge in a business culture that often rewards short-term results and decisiveness over thoughtful reflection and long-term planning.

Despite these hurdles, the movement toward regenerative leadership is expanding, offering a beacon of hope for a more resilient, innovative, and equitable future.

Organizations guided by regenerative principles tend to be more resilient and better equipped to navigate the complexities of the modern world—from climate change and resource scarcity to social inequality and technological advancement. By creating systems that regenerate and renew rather than deplete and destroy, regenerative leaders can drive meaningful change, ensuring their organizations survive and thrive in the face of future challenges.

In essence, regenerative leadership is about reimagining the role of business in society. Organizations guided by regenerative principles are proving that it is possible to thrive by fostering a harmonious balance with the natural world and addressing societal needs. This emerging trend underscores a profound shift in the role of business—from exploiters to nurturers, from contributors to societal problems to catalysts for regeneration and renewal. It's an invitation to businesses to lead with a vision that transcends traditional profit-driven motives, aiming instead to contribute to the flourishing of all life.

As this approach continues gaining momentum, it paves the way for a new era of business that heals, replenishes, and revitalizes, ensuring prosperity for the planet and its people. While this transition may not be easy, the potential rewards—for businesses, society, and the environment—are immense.

As we set the stage for a more sustainable and ethical business model, another critical element comes into focus: *the power of purpose.* Regenerative leaders understand that businesses must operate in harmony with nature and society and have a clear, compelling purpose that resonates deeply with all stakeholders. This shift speaks to the heart of what makes a business thrive from within, shaping its culture, influencing decision-making, and fostering a strong sense of belonging among employees and customers.

This leads us to explore the next crucial concept: unleashing the organization's potential energy. By recognizing their teams' latent creativity, innovation, and commitment, leaders can create the conditions necessary for individuals to convert their potential into impactful efforts.

The key lies in fostering a culture of trust, transparency, and autonomy, where everyone feels empowered to contribute meaningfully. When this potential is unlocked, it transforms into kinetic energy, driving real, sustainable progress.

Unleashing the Potential Energy of the Organization

In physics, potential energy refers to stored energy that, when released, transforms into kinetic energy—energy in motion. Similarly, within every organization lies a wealth of untapped creativity, innovation, and commitment, often lying dormant, waiting to be unlocked. This reservoir of potential energy is not just an abstract concept; it's the living force within your people—their unique talents, their dreams, and their desire to make meaningful contributions. Yet, all too often, this energy remains static, constrained by outdated leadership models, limiting beliefs, and rigid structures.

Imagine the possibilities if every person in your organization felt empowered to bring their whole selves to work—unhindered by fear, judgment, or bureaucracy. The energy stored in each individual, each team, could be set into motion, fueling innovation, collaboration, and growth in ways that ripple across the entire organization.

But this doesn't happen by chance. It requires conscious leadership—leadership that understands the dynamics of potential energy and knows how to create the conditions where this energy can be unleashed.

Unlocking this potential begins with trust. When people feel trusted—when they are given autonomy and the freedom to take risks—they start to tap into their own reservoirs of creativity and passion. Leaders must shift from command-and-control models to creating a culture of empowerment, where transparency, collaboration, and psychological safety reign.

It's about fostering an environment where everyone knows their voice matters, where diverse perspectives are not just welcomed but actively sought. This is where ideas flow, innovation thrives, and people start to see their work as part of something bigger than themselves.

The role of the regenerative leader is to be the catalyst for this energy, much like the sun's role in ecosystems, nurturing growth without controlling every detail. Regenerative leadership is about enabling conditions where people's innate potential can flourish.

By modeling trust, vulnerability, and a willingness to listen deeply, leaders set the stage for teams to connect more authentically with their work and with each other. When this happens, *potential energy* transforms into *kinetic energy*—creative ideas, problem-solving, and collective action begin to flow effortlessly, driving the organization forward.

Mimicking nature's wisdom can guide us here. Just as ecosystems thrive through cooperation, diversity, and the efficient use of resources, businesses can adopt these same principles to create resilient, innovative, and adaptive systems. In nature, nothing is wasted, everything is connected, and energy is continually recycled for the benefit of the whole.

This interconnectedness offers a powerful lesson: businesses, too, can thrive by fostering collaboration, embracing diverse perspectives, and creating systems that are regenerative rather than extractive.

When we look at the natural world, we see that the most resilient ecosystems are those that balance diversity, cooperation, and efficiency. Businesses that take their cues from nature—by valuing the unique strengths and ideas of each person—tap into a wellspring of potential energy that can be harnessed for growth and innovation.

The result is an organization that doesn't just survive but thrives, even in the face of challenges.

In today's rapidly changing landscape, it's clear that old ways of working and leading no longer serve us. Global challenges—from environmental crises to shifting market dynamics—demand a new kind of leadership, one that is attuned to the untapped potential in their teams and knows how to unlock it. Leaders can transform *potential energy* into *kinetic ener-*

gy by cultivating trust, transparency, and autonomy, fueling sustainable growth and collective success.

The opportunity is before us: to embrace regenerative leadership and harness the immense potential energy within our organizations, to lead in ways that reflect nature's principles of resilience, adaptability, and interdependence. This is not just about surviving the future; it's about thriving in it—together.

We also need to recognize that, as leaders, the influence we wield extends far beyond the decisions we make or the strategies we implement. Our influence is woven into the very fabric of how we communicate, the words we choose, and the stories we tell. The language we use, both spoken and unspoken, becomes a powerful tool for conveying what truly matters—our values, our vision, and the message we want to leave behind. It's not just about delivering information; it's about *embodying* the principles and purpose that guide our leadership.

Every word we speak carries potential energy, and as leaders, that energy can either uplift and inspire or create confusion and disconnection. The most effective leaders are conscious of the language they use, recognizing that their words shape the culture of their organization, the mindset of their team, and, ultimately, the outcomes they achieve. When leaders speak from a place of authenticity, clarity, and purpose, their message resonates deeply, touching not just the minds but the hearts of those they lead.

This is where storytelling comes into play as one of the most potent tools in a leader's toolkit. Storytelling goes beyond the transactional nature of communication—it connects people to a larger vision, helping them see the meaning behind their work. It builds bridges between individuals and ideas, creating a shared narrative that inspires change. When we, as leaders, harness the art of storytelling, we unlock the potential to influence others in ways that create lasting transformation and harness the energy of the organization.

Crafting a Narrative That Inspires Change

Storytelling has been a part of human culture for millennia, a powerful vehicle for passing down wisdom, shaping beliefs, and connecting people across generations. As leaders, entrepreneurs, and changemakers, storytelling is not just a tool for communication—it's a way to inspire and create lasting transformation. In the world of leadership, stories go beyond mere anecdotes; they become a bridge between vision and action, fostering connection and motivating others to rise to their potential.

At its core, storytelling is about meaning-making. It's how we make sense of the world and our place in it. When you craft a compelling narrative as a leader, you're not just sharing information—you're helping others connect the dots, understand their role in the bigger picture, and find purpose in their work. Storytelling has the power to break through resistance, align teams, and create movements that drive meaningful change.

A well-crafted story can shift perspectives and ignite action. But in leadership, the goal of storytelling isn't simply to entertain—it's to lead others toward a desired outcome, whether changing behavior, adopting new ideas, or rallying around a shared mission.

To craft a narrative that inspires change, leaders need to ground their story in authenticity. People can sense when a story is being told just for effect. The most powerful stories are the ones that reflect the truth of your own experiences, challenges, and insights. Vulnerability in storytelling allows others to see the leader as human, creating a sense of trust and rapport that is essential for driving change.

When crafting your leadership narrative, consider these elements:

- **Purpose**: Why are you telling this story? What is the purpose-driven message or lesson you want to convey?

- **Challenge**: Every impactful story involves some form of struggle or challenge. What obstacles did you (or your organization) face, and how were they overcome? How did these challenges shape you as a leader?

- **Resolution**: How did you emerge from the experience? What key insights or transformations occurred, and how do they relate to the current situation?

- **Call to Action**: What do you want your listeners to do after hearing the story? How does your narrative invite them to take meaningful action?

By weaving together these elements, you can create a story that doesn't just tell people what to do but inspires them to embrace change. Because they feel personally connected to the journey, the story becomes their own, and they feel compelled to take part in the vision you're leading.

Storytelling is one of the most effective ways to connect with others on a deeper emotional level. Whether you're leading a team, building a movement, or guiding clients through transformation, stories have the power to reach people's hearts and minds in ways that data or directives never can.

When you tell a story, you create a shared experience. Your audience doesn't just hear the words—they begin to see themselves in the narrative. They can relate to the challenges, imagine the possibilities, and feel the emotions embedded in the story. This creates a sense of connection, a bond that transcends logic and reasoning and taps into something far more profound: a shared human experience.

This is crucial in leadership because people aren't just motivated by goals or incentives. They are driven by meaning, purpose, and a sense of belonging. A well-told story can help others see the broader context of their work and understand how their contributions fit into something greater than themselves. This is especially important for Sacred Changemakers, whose work is often deeply personal and rooted in creating positive social or spiritual impact.

When used intentionally, storytelling becomes a tool for transformation. It shifts the focus from what needs to be done to why it matters. It helps others find the courage to step into their power and act toward change. By sharing stories that reflect personal growth, leadership challenges, or moments of awakening, you not only inspire others but invite them to reflect on their own journey, fostering a culture of growth and transformation.

As a Sacred Changemaker, your stories hold immense potential. They can be a catalyst for change, helping you lead with purpose, connect authentically, and inspire others to act. Whether you're speaking to one person or an entire organization, your narrative can shape the future, guiding others on their path to becoming who they need to be to create a better world.

What you say is influenced by what you think. It's time to get practical.

Developing a Sacred Changemaker Mindset

In an era defined by rapid changes and complex challenges, developing your mindset so that it is conscious, regenerative, and resonant is essential. Today's Leaders must manage their businesses' operational aspects and inspire and lead transformative changes that benefit their organizations and the broader society. Here are some proven tools and exercises designed to cultivate these vital leadership qualities:

1. Conscious Self-Assessment

Tool: *Reflective Journaling*

Self-awareness is at the core of resonant leadership. Begin each day with reflective journaling, focusing on your decisions, their outcomes, and whether they align with your core values. This practice helps leaders recognize how their actions resonate within their teams and communities.

Consider the following questions: *"What impact did my decisions today have on my team and the broader community?"* or *"How did I uphold my values in my leadership role today?"* This daily practice grounds you in purpose and helps align your leadership actions with your deeper values.

Action Steps for Conscious Self-Assessment:

1. **Set Aside Daily Reflection Time**: Allocate 10-15 minutes each day, preferably in the morning or evening, to engage in reflective journaling. Choose a quiet space where you won't be interrupted, allowing yourself time to dive deep into your thoughts.

2. **Use a Structured Format**: Start each journal entry with a simple structure to guide your reflections. For example:

    - What decisions did I make today?

    - What were the outcomes of those decisions?

    - Did my actions align with my core values?

3. **Focus on Specific Leadership Moments**: Identify key moments during the day where you made important decisions or interacted with your team. Reflect on how those moments influenced the people around you and whether your choices were aligned with your broader goals or values.

4. **Track Patterns Over Time**: As you journal consistently, begin reviewing your entries weekly or monthly to spot patterns in your leadership behavior. Are there consistent areas where you may not be living up to your values? Where have you successfully aligned your actions with your deeper purpose?

5. **Act on Insights**: Use the patterns and insights from your journaling practice to make conscious adjustments. For example, if you notice a repeated misalignment between your actions and values, take steps to correct that through better communication,

planning, or delegating.

6. **Add a Question to Deepen Your Awareness**: Each week, add a new question that encourages deeper reflection, such as:

    - How did my energy affect my team today?
    - What opportunities did I miss to embody my values?

7. **Be Honest and Compassionate**: Allow yourself the space to be truthful in your reflections, but do so with self-compassion. Growth is a process, and this practice helps you identify both areas for improvement and strengths to celebrate.

By committing to this daily practice, you will begin to see how your leadership evolves in resonance with your purpose, empowering you to become a more conscious and effective leader.

2. Regenerative Thinking Workshops

Exercise: *Scenario Planning*

Due to complexity, leaders need to think beyond short-term gains and develop strategies that consider long-term sustainability. Scenario planning workshops encourage leaders to envision future environmental and social impacts and devise regenerative strategies that actively contribute to healing the systems they rely on rather than depleting them.

By participating in such workshops, leaders cultivate a mindset that seeks to sustain and regenerate, focusing on restoring balance and leaving a positive legacy for future generations.

Action Steps for Regenerative Thinking Workshops:

1. **Organize or Join a Scenario Planning Workshop**: Find or create opportunities to engage in scenario planning specifically focused on regenerative thinking. This could be within your organization or through leadership development programs that emphasize sustainability. If none exist, consider hosting your own workshop.

2. **Define Key Focus Areas**: Begin by identifying the key systems

your business relies on—whether environmental, social, or economic. These could include natural resources, employee well-being, community health, or long-term profitability. Use these as a foundation for your scenario planning.

3. **Explore Multiple Futures**: In the workshop, work through various future scenarios, including:

    - *Best-case scenario*: What does the world look like if everything is aligned with regenerative principles?

    - *Worst-case scenario*: What happens if your business and others continue with extractive practices?

    - *Most likely scenario*: Where are we heading if things continue on their current trajectory?

4. **Identify Regenerative Opportunities**: After mapping out these scenarios, brainstorm ways to shift your business practices toward regenerative strategies in each area. Ask questions like:

    - How can we restore what we take from the environment?

    - How can we ensure our business creates a net positive impact on society?

5. **Prioritize Actionable Strategies**: Focus on the steps your organization can take to move toward regeneration. For example:

    - Invest in renewable energy solutions.

    - Develop community outreach programs that give back more than they take.

    - Implement circular economy principles in product development, focusing on reducing waste and reusing materials.

6. **Embed Regenerative Thinking in Strategic Planning**: Integrate these long-term regenerative strategies into your organization's business plan. Encourage leaders to adopt regenerative goals, such as achieving net-zero emissions, fostering biodiversity, or

advancing social equity initiatives.

7. **Set Measurable Regenerative Goals**: For each strategy, establish clear, measurable goals. For example, *"We will reduce our water consumption by 20% over the next 5 years and invest in reforestation projects."* Monitor progress and make adjustments as necessary.

8. **Foster a Culture of Regenerative Thinking**: After the workshop, encourage ongoing conversations around regenerative strategies. Provide ongoing training and regular updates on your regenerative goals, celebrating milestones and learning from setbacks.

By participating in regenerative thinking workshops, you not only prepare your organization for the future but also contribute to the creation of systems that support the well-being of people and the planet.

3. Resonance Mapping

Tool: *Stakeholder Mapping*

Leaders must understand the needs, values, and expectations of all stakeholders to foster genuine connection and resonance. Stakeholder mapping is an invaluable tool for identifying these key relationships. By understanding who your business impacts—employees, customers, suppliers, or the community—you can design strategies that build trust and create meaningful connections.

This exercise enables leaders to identify where and how to enhance trust, build loyalty, and nurture a community around their business, leading to deeper resonance with all stakeholders.

Action Steps for Resonance Mapping through Stakeholder Mapping:

1. **Identify Key Stakeholders**: Start by listing all the groups or individuals your business impacts. These can include:

    - *Internal stakeholders*: Employees, leadership teams, and shareholders.

- *External stakeholders*: Customers, suppliers, community members, partners, and environmental resources.

2. **Map Out Relationships and Influence**: Create a visual representation of these stakeholders using a stakeholder map. Place your business at the center and arrange stakeholders around it based on their level of influence, interest, and relationship with your organization. Use categories such as:

    - *High influence, high interest*: Those who have significant power over or involvement in your business.

    - *Low influence, high interest*: Those who may not directly affect decision-making but are deeply invested in the outcomes.

    - *High influence, low interest*: Key players who may not be as involved day-to-day but whose support is essential.

3. **Assess Stakeholder Needs and Expectations**: For each group, consider their specific needs, values, and expectations. Ask questions such as:

    - What does this stakeholder group care about?

    - How does our business impact them directly or indirectly?

    - What are their expectations from us, both short- and long-term?

4. **Identify Gaps in Connection and Trust**: Reflect on your current relationships with each stakeholder group. Are there areas where trust is lacking or where relationships could be strengthened? For example:

    - Are employees fully engaged and aligned with your company's mission?

    - Do customers trust your brand beyond the products or services you provide?

5. **Design Strategies for Deeper Resonance**: Once you've mapped

out the key stakeholders and identified gaps, develop strategies that build stronger connections with each group. For example:

- *Employees*: Foster open communication, provide opportunities for growth, and create a culture of recognition and belonging.

- *Customers*: Ensure your offerings align with their evolving values, such as sustainability or ethical sourcing, and prioritize customer service.

- *Community*: Engage in corporate social responsibility (CSR) initiatives that address local needs or environmental sustainability.

6. **Foster Two-Way Communication**: Resonance is built on mutual understanding. Create feedback loops where stakeholders can voice their concerns, share their ideas, and feel heard. Examples include:

   - Employee town halls or surveys.

   - Customer feedback sessions or community roundtables.

   - Regular communication with suppliers about shared goals and expectations.

7. **Set Measurable Goals**: For each strategy, establish measurable outcomes. For example, *"Increase employee engagement by 15% over the next year through quarterly feedback sessions and leadership development programs."* Monitor these goals and adjust as needed to ensure ongoing resonance with each stakeholder group.

8. **Review and Revise Regularly**: Stakeholder needs and expectations can change over time, so make resonance mapping an ongoing practice. Regularly review your stakeholder map and adjust your strategies to stay in tune with evolving dynamics.

By engaging in resonance mapping through stakeholder mapping, you create stronger, more meaningful connections with those your business affects. This practice helps build trust, loyalty, and deeper alignment with the people and communities you serve, making your leadership and business more resonant and impactful.

4. Mindfulness and Meditation

Exercise: *Daily Mindfulness Practice*

Mindfulness is a powerful tool for cultivating emotional intelligence and resonance in leadership. Incorporating daily mindfulness practices, such as meditation or deep breathing exercises, helps leaders stay present and focused. These practices also enhance empathy, allowing leaders to respond thoughtfully to their teams and business environments.

Leaders who practice mindfulness are better equipped to handle stress and complexity, fostering a calm, compassionate leadership style that resonates deeply with their teams.

Action Steps for Daily Mindfulness Practice:

1. **Set a Consistent Time**: Begin by dedicating a specific time each day for mindfulness practice, whether it's in the morning to set the tone for the day or in the evening to reflect. Consistency is key to reaping the benefits, so choose a time that works for you and aim to practice daily for at least 5–10 minutes to start.

2. **Create a Calm Space**: Find a quiet place where you won't be disturbed during your practice. This could be a corner of your office, your home, or even outdoors. The goal is to create a calming environment where you can focus without distractions.

3. **Start with Breathing Exercises**: To begin your practice, focus on your breath. Use deep breathing exercises to center yourself. Inhale deeply through your nose, hold for a few seconds, and exhale slowly through your mouth. As you breathe, bring your awareness to the sensations of each breath—how it feels to fill your lungs and release the air.

4. **Practice Presence**: Once you've centered yourself with your breath, shift your attention to the present moment. This can be done through a body scan (focusing on different areas of your body and releasing any tension) or simply by observing your thoughts without judgment. If your mind wanders, gently bring your focus back to your breath.

5. **Use a Meditation App for Guidance**: For beginners, guided meditations can be helpful. Consider using apps like *Headspace* or *Insight Timer* to help guide your practice. These apps offer a range of mindfulness exercises tailored to different goals, such as reducing stress, enhancing focus, or developing compassion.

6. **Cultivate Self-Awareness**: During your mindfulness practice, reflect on how your thoughts and emotions affect your actions. Ask yourself:

    - How am I feeling at this moment?
    - What emotions or thoughts are influencing my reactions?
    - How can I bring more awareness and calm into my leadership today?

7. **Expand Mindfulness to Daily Interactions**: Mindfulness isn't limited to your meditation sessions. Practice being fully present in your daily interactions—whether it's a meeting, a conversation with a team member, or decision-making. By staying aware and grounded, you can respond thoughtfully rather than react impulsively.

8. **Track Your Progress**: Keep a mindfulness journal to reflect on your practice. Note how you feel before and after each session, and track any changes in your emotional state, focus, or leadership style over time. This will help reinforce the value of your practice and encourage continued growth.

9. **Integrate Mindfulness into Leadership**: As you develop your mindfulness practice, begin to integrate it into your leadership

style. Use mindfulness before meetings to set a calm, focused tone or during moments of tension to manage stress and enhance empathy. Mindful leaders are more emotionally intelligent, making them better equipped to foster a positive, resonant work environment.

By incorporating daily mindfulness practices, leaders can cultivate a greater sense of presence, emotional awareness, and compassion. This not only helps you manage stress and complexity but also creates an environment of calm, clarity, and empathy that resonates deeply with your teams, driving more thoughtful and effective leadership.

5. Ethical Decision-Making Frameworks

Tool: *Ethics Workshops*

In resonant leadership, every decision should be weighed not only for its profitability but also for its ethical implications. Regular ethics workshops provide leaders and teams with frameworks to navigate moral dilemmas with integrity. These sessions reinforce the company's core values, ensuring decisions resonate with a higher purpose and prioritize positive societal impact.

By embedding ethical decision-making into the heart of leadership, businesses build a culture of accountability and transparency that enhances trust and authenticity.

Action Steps for Implementing Ethical Decision-Making Frameworks:

1. **Schedule Regular Ethics Workshops**: Set up quarterly or bi-annual ethics workshops where leaders and teams can explore moral dilemmas and decision-making processes. These sessions provide a structured space for discussing real-world challenges and ensuring that decisions align with company values and societal good.

2. **Define Core Values**: Start each workshop by clearly defining the company's core values. Use these as the foundation for all discussions. Leaders and team members should understand how

these values translate into everyday business decisions. This clarity ensures that everyone is on the same page when it comes to ethical considerations.

3. **Utilize Ethical Decision-Making Models**: Introduce a decision-making framework during the workshops, such as the *Utilitarian Approach (which focuses on the greatest good for the greatest number)* or the *Deontological Approach (which emphasizes duty and adherence to rules and principles)*. Discuss how different frameworks can guide decisions in various scenarios.

4. **Analyze Real-World Case Studies**: Use real-life case studies from your industry or within your company to analyze ethical dilemmas. Encourage participants to evaluate how decisions were made and the ethical implications of those choices. Discuss alternative approaches and how a more ethical path could have been taken.

5. **Create Scenario-Based Exercises**: Design exercises where teams must work through hypothetical scenarios that present ethical challenges. These scenarios could involve conflicts between profitability and social responsibility, environmental impact, or balancing employee well-being with business goals. Encourage open dialogue and have participants use the ethical frameworks discussed to guide their decision-making.

6. **Encourage Cross-Functional Discussions**: Ethical decision-making often involves multiple perspectives. In these workshops, invite leaders from various departments *(e.g., marketing, finance, HR)* to collaborate. This diversity of viewpoints helps uncover potential blind spots and ensures a more holistic approach to ethical dilemmas.

7. **Develop Ethical Action Plans**: At the end of each workshop, encourage teams to create action plans for applying what they've learned to real business situations. These plans should include steps for ethical decision-making, identifying potential challenges, and how to address them. By creating actionable plans,

teams are more likely to incorporate ethical considerations into their daily operations.

8. **Incorporate Ethics into Performance Reviews**: To embed ethical decision-making into your company culture, consider incorporating ethical behavior into leadership and employee performance reviews. This signals that ethical considerations are not just theoretical but a core component of business success and leadership effectiveness.

9. **Foster a Culture of Accountability and Transparency**: Create a system where employees feel empowered to raise concerns about ethical issues without fear of retaliation. Encourage open dialogue and transparency in decision-making processes and ensure there are mechanisms in place for reporting and addressing unethical behavior.

10. **Evaluate and Evolve**: Ethics are not static—what's considered ethical today might change with societal shifts. Encourage leaders to continually reflect on emerging ethical challenges, particularly as new technologies or global issues arise, and adjust frameworks as necessary. The company's ethical standards should evolve to stay relevant and maintain alignment with higher purposes.

By embedding ethical decision-making into leadership through regular workshops, discussions, and frameworks, businesses build a culture that prioritizes integrity, accountability, and transparency. This enhances internal trust and authenticity and positions the organization as a trusted leader in its industry, aligned with the higher purpose of making a positive impact in the world.

6. Leadership Feedback Loops

Exercise: *360-Degree Feedback*

Effective leadership thrives on self-awareness and feedback. Implementing 360-degree feedback systems allows leaders to gather insights from their peers, direct reports, and supervisors. This multi-faceted perspective offers invaluable insights into how others perceive your leadership style, strengths, and areas for growth.

Continuous feedback fosters a culture of openness and improvement, allowing leaders to remain resonant with their teams and to lead with greater clarity and compassion.

Action Steps for Implementing Leadership Feedback Loops:

1. **Introduce 360-Degree Feedback**: Start by explaining the purpose of 360-degree feedback to your leadership team. Highlight that the goal is not to critique but to gather diverse perspectives that help leaders grow in self-awareness, refine their leadership styles, and build stronger relationships with their teams. This process provides a well-rounded view of how others experience their leadership.

2. **Choose the Right Platform**: Implement a digital platform or tool specifically designed for 360-degree feedback. These platforms can facilitate anonymous responses, ensuring that participants feel safe to provide honest and constructive feedback. Ensure the platform is user-friendly and allows for easy data collection and analysis.

3. **Select Feedback Participants**: Choose a diverse group of individuals to provide feedback on each leader. This group should include direct reports, peers, and supervisors to offer a comprehensive view of the leader's impact across different roles. Encourage leaders to seek feedback from team members with whom they frequently collaborate, as well as those outside their immediate circle.

4. **Prepare Leaders for Feedback**: Before the process begins, help leaders understand that feedback is a tool for growth. Address any anxieties they might have and emphasize that the feedback is meant to inspire development and self-awareness, not judgment. Guide leaders on how to interpret and internalize feedback with an open mind.

5. **Create Constructive Feedback Guidelines**: Encourage all participants to give feedback that is constructive and focused on specific behaviors, rather than vague or personal critiques. Provide guidelines on how to deliver actionable insights—what works well and what could be improved, along with suggestions for growth.

6. **Analyze the Feedback**: Once the feedback is collected, provide leaders with a clear and digestible report highlighting key themes. Focus on strengths, areas for improvement, and any gaps between the leader's self-perception and how others perceive their leadership style.

7. **Encourage Reflection**: After receiving their feedback, leaders should take time to reflect on the insights. They can ask themselves questions like, *"What patterns do I see in the feedback?"* or *"Where are my blind spots?"* This reflection phase helps leaders integrate the feedback into their understanding of themselves and their leadership impact.

8. **Create a Development Plan**: Based on the feedback, guide leaders to create a personalized development plan. This plan should include actionable steps for enhancing their leadership skills, such as improving communication, fostering collaboration, or cultivating empathy. It should also include measurable goals to track progress over time.

9. **Incorporate Ongoing Feedback**: 360-degree feedback shouldn't be a one-time event. Encourage leaders to regularly check in with their teams and peers to gather informal feedback. By fostering a continuous feedback culture, leaders can make real-time adjustments to their approach and maintain resonance with their teams.

10. **Celebrate Growth**: After a set period *(e.g., six months)*, revisit the feedback process to measure progress. Leaders should celebrate improvements and acknowledge the feedback contributors for their role in supporting leadership growth. This fosters a culture

of continuous learning and appreciation.

By implementing leadership feedback loops through 360-degree feedback systems, leaders can gain invaluable insights that promote personal growth, enhance their self-awareness, and foster a deeper connection with their teams. This ongoing feedback process strengthens leadership resonance and ensures that leaders remain aligned with the needs of their organizations and teams.

7. Future Visioning

Tool: *Vision Boards*

To lead with resonance and purpose, it is essential to have a clear vision for the future. Vision boards are creative and reflective tools that enable leaders to visualize their company's long-term goals and broader impact. By crafting a visual representation of where you want your business to go, you align daily actions with long-term aspirations.

Vision boards can be revisited and refined, motivating leaders and teams as they work towards a future grounded in purpose and shared success.

By integrating these tools and exercises into your leadership practice, you can cultivate a mindset beyond your business's immediate needs. This conscious, regenerative, and resonant approach to leadership empowers you to thrive in the current marketplace and create lasting, positive change for society and the planet. Through these practices, you're not just leading a business but guiding a movement toward a more ethical, sustainable, and purpose-driven world.

Action Steps for Implementing Future Visioning:

1. **Set the Stage for Creativity**: Begin by dedicating time and space for yourself and your leadership team to focus on long-term goals and aspirations. Create an environment conducive to creativity and reflection—whether it's a quiet retreat, a workshop, or even a digital platform that allows for free expression.

2. **Clarify Your Purpose**: Before starting on the vision board, take a moment to reflect on your core values, purpose, and the broader

impact you want your business to have. Ask yourself: *What kind of world do I want my business to help create?* and *What long-term impact do I want my leadership to have on my team, community, and the planet?*

3. **Gather Materials**: Collect images, words, and symbols that resonate with your vision. These could be cut from magazines, printed from the internet, or hand-drawn. Digital tools such as Canva or Pinterest can also be used to create online vision boards. Encourage your team to use elements that evoke inspiration and align with your company's long-term goals.

4. **Build Your Vision Board**: Start arranging the materials on a board, organizing them in a way that feels intuitive and inspiring. Focus on representing both tangible goals *(e.g., business growth, new product launches)* and intangible aspirations *(e.g., the kind of workplace culture you want to create and your contribution to environmental sustainability)*.

5. **Incorporate Collective Visioning**: If working with your team, have them contribute their ideas and inspirations to the vision board. This fosters a shared sense of purpose and commitment, helping everyone visualize the collective future you're all striving toward. The exercise also promotes team cohesion and ensures everyone's aspirations are considered.

6. **Reflect and Refine**: Once the vision board is complete, take time to reflect on the chosen images and symbols. Discuss the connections between your daily actions and the long-term vision. *Are the steps you're currently taking aligned with this future? What changes need to happen to ensure you're on the right path?*

7. **Keep the Vision Alive**: Place the vision board somewhere prominent where you and your team can regularly see it, or store it digitally in an accessible shared space. Revisit the board during team meetings or personal reflections, using it as a motivational tool to align daily tasks and decisions with your overarching goals.

8. **Refine and Evolve**: As time goes on and your business progress-

es, revisit the vision board and refine it as necessary. Long-term goals can shift, and new insights may arise that must be integrated into your vision. Continuously evolve your board to reflect where your business is headed and to inspire ongoing innovation.

Incorporating vision boards into your leadership practice creates a tangible reminder of your long-term goals and aspirations. This tool allows you to lead intentionally, ensuring that your daily actions and decisions align with your larger purpose. When everyone in your organization shares and contributes to this vision, it fosters a deeper sense of collaboration, commitment, and collective momentum toward achieving meaningful impact.

8. Conscious Communication and Storytelling

Tool: *Storytelling Framework*

Effective communication and storytelling are essential tools for inspiring change and building resonance in leadership. By consciously crafting your message and telling stories that resonate on a deeper level, you can connect with your audience, inspire your team, and drive meaningful action. A storytelling framework helps you shape your narrative in a way that speaks to values, purpose, and the impact you want to create.

Action Steps For Communication And Storytelling:

1. **Identify the Core Message**: Before telling any story, clarify the core message you want to convey. *What is the central idea or value you want your audience to take away?* Whether you're addressing your team or customers, ensure your message aligns with your purpose and the change you wish to inspire.

2. **Connect with Emotions**: People remember stories that evoke emotions. Consider what feelings you want to inspire—hope, urgency, motivation, or empathy. When telling a story, describe real human experiences that reflect those emotions, helping your audience feel a personal connection to the message.

3. **Follow a Structure**: Use a simple storytelling framework like *'The Hero's Journey'* [3] to guide your narrative:

    - **Introduction**: Set the stage. *Who is the hero (your audience, team, or customer)? What challenges are they facing?*

    - **Conflict**: Highlight the obstacles or problems that need to be overcome. This creates tension and draws people in.

    - **Resolution**: Present the solution or transformation. *How did the hero overcome the challenges, and what was the result?*

    - **Call to Action**: End with a clear message or next step. Invite your audience to join in the journey, take action, or adopt a new mindset.

4. **Use Visuals and Analogies**: Stories are more memorable when paired with visuals or analogies that simplify complex ideas. Use metaphors, examples from nature, or real-world scenarios that reflect the change you want to inspire. This helps your audience visualize the message and relate it to their own lives.

5. **Practice Active Listening**: Conscious communication is not just about telling your story; it's about listening to others' stories too. Create space for dialogue and encourage others to share their experiences. This deepens connection and ensures that communication is a two-way street, fostering a culture of collaboration and mutual understanding.

6. **Refine Your Stories Over Time**: As you tell your story, gather feedback and refine it. Pay attention to which stories resonate the most with your audience. Over time, adapt your narrative to reflect better your evolving vision, mission, and the values of those you lead.

7. **Align Stories with Purpose**: Ensure that every story you tell is aligned with your overall purpose and vision as a Sacred Changemaker. Your stories should inspire others to follow your lead and take actions that contribute to a larger cause, whether it's social

equity, environmental stewardship, or collective well-being.

Why It Matters: Conscious communication and storytelling are more than just leadership tools—they are powerful ways to shape your organization's culture, build trust, and inspire others to act. By becoming more intentional in your communication, you ensure that your message resonates deeply and drives the positive change you aim to create.

Redefining Success: New Metrics for Measuring Business Success

As we move toward a more conscious and sustainable way of doing business, it's becoming clearer every day that the old ways of measuring success—mostly by financial performance—just don't cut it anymore. In today's world, where the stakes are high for people and the planet, we need to think bigger. It's time to expand our definition of success to recognize how businesses impact the world, not just through their profits but through how they care for people and the environment.

You've probably heard the saying, *"What doesn't get measured, doesn't get done,"* and there's a lot of truth in that. If we don't start tracking what truly matters, we risk falling into old habits, measuring only what's easy and missing the bigger picture. That's why exploring how we can practically incorporate the triple bottom line—people, planet, and profits—into our everyday business strategy is so important. When we do, we open the door to running a more successful business aligned with values that contribute to the well-being of society and the earth.

Next, we will dive into what this new way of measuring success looks like. We'll talk about how you can redefine success for your business in a way that feels right, grounded, and aligned with the kind of world we all want to live in. Because true success isn't just about growing your bottom line—it's about making sure your growth leaves a positive mark on the world.

People Metrics *(Social Equity and Well-being)*:

Employee Satisfaction and Engagement:

Measured through regular surveys, turnover rates, and participation in professional development programs, high engagement levels indicate a healthy organizational culture that values its members.

- **How to Start:** Implement a regular, anonymous employee satisfaction survey *(e.g., quarterly or biannually)* using tools like Google Forms or specialized platforms like SurveyMonkey or OfficeVibe. Create a few core questions around job satisfaction, work-life balance, opportunities for growth, and alignment with company values. Encourage open-ended feedback for more detailed insights.

- **Take Action:** Review the survey data to spot trends. *Are there departments with higher turnover? Do employees feel heard?* Take immediate, visible actions on the feedback, such as launching new professional development opportunities or creating a more flexible work schedule.

- **Ongoing Strategy:** Follow up regularly. Use the survey results to shape future policies and track how engagement improves over time.

Community Impact:

Evaluate your business's effects on local communities through social initiatives, job creation, and community feedback. Metrics can include the number of local jobs created, investment in community projects, and improvements in local living standards.

- **How to Start:** Identify key community initiatives that align with your company's mission. Partner with local organizations or launch your projects. Set measurable goals, such as how many jobs your business has created locally or how much funding or volunteer hours you've contributed to local causes.

- **Take Action:** Create a community impact report at least once a year. Highlight your initiatives, the outcomes, and feedback from the community. Share it publicly to strengthen your business's connection to the local area.

- **Ongoing Strategy:** Stay in touch with community leaders to continually assess needs and adapt your initiatives accordingly.

Diversity and Inclusion:

Quantify the diversity of your workforce and leadership team. Measure the effectiveness of inclusion programs through employee feedback and the representation of diverse groups at all levels of the organization.

- **How to Start:** Conduct a diversity audit within your company. *How diverse is your workforce regarding gender, race, age, abilities, and other factors?* Develop clear policies that support hiring from underrepresented groups. This could involve posting job openings on diverse job boards or setting up internship programs for marginalized communities.

- **Take Action:** Use employee feedback tools to assess how included people feel. Implement initiatives like diversity training or support groups and ensure diverse representation on leadership teams.

- **Ongoing Strategy:** Continuously monitor diversity metrics at all levels, from entry-level to executive, and regularly adjust your policies based on feedback and performance.

Planet Metrics *(Environmental Sustainability):*

Carbon Footprint:

Calculate your total greenhouse gas emissions to assess and strategize reductions. Implementing renewable energy sources and reducing waste are key strategies.

- **How to Start:** Conduct an audit of your business's carbon emissions using online calculators or third-party sustainability consultants. Focus on energy consumption, travel, waste, and supply chain emissions.

- **Take Action:** Develop a carbon reduction plan with clear, actionable goals. This might involve transitioning to renewable energy, reducing business travel through virtual meetings, or incentivizing employees to carpool.

- **Ongoing Strategy:** Track your progress annually. Publicly commit to carbon reduction goals and share updates on milestones achieved.

Resource Efficiency:

Monitor resource use efficiency, including water, energy, and materials. Setting targets for reducing consumption and transitioning to sustainable materials are actionable measures.

- **How to Start:** Identify key areas where your business consumes resources—water, electricity, and materials—and set measurable goals to reduce waste. Start with simple steps like reducing single-use plastics in the office, upgrading to energy-efficient lighting, and implementing a recycling program.

- **Take Action:** Track monthly usage and celebrate small wins with your team to encourage ongoing participation—for example, measure reductions in paper use by switching to digital alternatives.

- **Ongoing Strategy:** Regularly assess and adjust your targets, aiming for continual improvements. Certifications like ISO 14001 should be considered to enhance credibility.

Biodiversity and Ecosystem Health:

Evaluate the impact of your operations on local ecosystems. This can involve assessments of land use, contributions to conservation efforts, and adopting practices that support biodiversity.

- **How to Start:** Conduct an environmental impact assessment if your business interacts directly with ecosystems *(e.g., agriculture or manufacturing)*. Explore ways your business can support local biodiversity, such as restoring natural habitats or sponsoring conservation efforts.

- **Take Action:** Integrate sustainability into your supply chain by choosing eco-friendly suppliers or partnering with local wildlife preservation projects.

- **Ongoing Strategy:** Regularly monitor your practices and adjust them to ensure they continue supporting biodiversity and ecosystem health.

Profit Metrics *(Economic Viability and Growth)*:

Sustainable Revenue Growth:

Assess the sustainability of your growth beyond traditional revenue metrics. This includes considering the long-term viability of your revenue streams and ethical considerations in generating profits.

- **How to Start:** Analyze your revenue streams and identify the most sustainable ones. *Are you overly reliant on a few customers or short-term projects?* Diversify by creating long-term partnerships, offering subscription-based services, or investing in future-oriented products.

- **Take Action:** Set sustainable growth targets that don't compromise your ethical standards. Measure not just revenue but also the quality of your customer relationships, retention rates, and the social or environmental benefits of your growth.

- **Ongoing Strategy:** Regularly assess your revenue sources to ensure they align with your long-term vision.

Investment in Sustainability:

Track the amount invested in sustainable practices and technologies. This reflects a commitment to long-term success over short-term gains.

- **How to Start:** Set aside a portion of your budget to invest in sustainable practices—whether it's new technologies, waste reduction systems, or employee programs.

- **Take Action:** Track these investments and calculate short-term and long-term returns, including financial savings from energy efficiency or increased brand loyalty.

- **Ongoing Strategy:** Reinvest any savings or additional revenue into sustainability initiatives, ensuring your business grows in a way that supports the future.

Economic Impact:

Measure your business's broader economic impact, including indirect job creation, economic activity stimulated through your supply chain, and contributions to local and national economies.

- **How to Start:** Quantify your business's contribution to the economy, including the number of jobs created, taxes paid, and the ripple effects of your supply chain.

- **Take Action:** Include your broader economic impact in annual reports for transparency and to help stakeholders understand your role in community development.

- **Ongoing Strategy:** Periodically re-assess and report on your economic contributions, focusing on direct and indirect impacts on your local and national economies.

Redefining success in this way requires a shift in how leaders view their business's role in society. It's about expanding the idea of value beyond just financial returns to include how they can make a real, positive difference in the world. But here's the thing—*success isn't a one-size-fits-all concept.*

Each business has its mission, purpose, and unique way of contributing to the world. The real challenge and opportunity is aligning that higher purpose with how success is defined. This inner alignment—between values and action—becomes the foundation for creating meaningful impact.

When businesses personalize their approach to success, they move beyond chasing the usual metrics and instead start to measure what truly matters. They're not just meeting arbitrary goals but making a genuine contribution to a better world in a way that feels authentic and aligned with their core values. By integrating these broader, more conscious measures into their strategic planning and reporting, businesses can lead the way toward a future where success is measured not only by profits but also by their positive impact on people and the planet.

Purpose-Driven Profits: Aligning Business Operations with Your Purpose

By now, it's clear that we're advocating for something more than profit alone—we're embracing purpose-driven profits. This isn't about choosing between financial success and a higher purpose; it's about recognizing how the two can work together in harmony.

When financial success aligns with a meaningful purpose, businesses become more than just profit-generating machines—they become forces for good, driving economic resilience while positively impacting society and the environment. The synergy between purpose and profit strengthens your brand, deepens customer loyalty, and contributes to a more sustainable and equitable world.

For many businesses, especially smaller ones, integrating purpose into daily operations might feel overwhelming. But the truth is, it doesn't have to be. There are practical, accessible tools and partnerships, like B1G1 and 1% for the Planet, that make it easier than ever to weave purpose into your business model.

Whether you're a solo-preneur or the head of a global corporation, simple yet powerful ways exist to create a ripple effect of impact. It's about making conscious choices, with just a little extra effort, that turn everyday business transactions into opportunities to contribute to something bigger.

Here are a few examples of how businesses can align profit with purpose:

Micro-Giving with B1G1:

B1G1.com offers an innovative way for small businesses to embed purpose into their daily operations. This platform allows businesses to support impactful social and environmental projects with every transaction, directly linking routine business activities to positive global change. What makes B1G1 genuinely unique is its alignment with the United Nations Sustainable Development Goals *(UN SDGs)*, making it easy for businesses of all sizes to contribute meaningfully to global progress. Whether it's planting a tree with every sale or providing clean water for each service rendered, B1G1 shows how even small, consistent actions can build up to create significant, lasting change.

Committing to 1% for the Planet:

Another powerful way to align profit with purpose is by joining 1% for the Planet. Businesses that commit to this initiative pledge to donate 1% of their annual sales to environmental causes, reinforcing their dedication to sustainability. This ensures a measurable contribution to the planet's health and resonates with today's consumers, who are increasingly drawn to brands that actively protect the environment. By committing to 1% for the Planet, your business can clearly communicate that it stands for something bigger than profit—helping preserve the world we all share.

Becoming a B-Corp:

The B-Corp certification has become a badge of honor for businesses that meet the highest social and environmental performance standards, accountability, and transparency. Achieving B-Corp status is a powerful way to demonstrate that your business operates with a purpose beyond profit. It's more than just a certification—a movement of companies committed to ethical practices in every area of their operations. Being a B-Corp signals to customers, employees, and investors that your business is dedicated to doing good, ensuring that profit and purpose are seamlessly integrated into your long-term success.

Practical Steps for Aligning Purpose with Profit

Now that we've explored why purpose-driven profits are essential let's understand how to make it happen. Aligning your business operations with a higher purpose doesn't have to be overwhelming—it's about making intentional, meaningful changes that reflect your values while driving sustainable profits.

Here are some practical steps to guide you:

1. **Define Your Purpose:** Start by clearly articulating why your business exists beyond making money. *What social or environmental issues resonate with you?* Get creative about how your business can contribute to addressing these challenges. Whether through your products, services, or partnerships, identifying your unique purpose sets the foundation for everything else.

2. **Integrate Purpose into Your Business Strategy:** Make your purpose central to your operations. This could mean developing products that solve real-world problems, adopting sustainable practices, or ensuring fair labor practices throughout your supply chain. If you're a coach or consultant, this might include additional training to empower your clients to embrace these values. Purpose should be woven into every part of your strategy, driving decisions and actions.

3. **Measure Your Impact:** Develop concrete metrics to track the outcomes of your purpose-driven initiatives. This could include measuring your social or environmental impact, contributions to

local communities, or donations to charitable causes aligned with the UN Sustainable Development Goals *(SDGs)*. By measuring progress, you can see the tangible difference your business is making.

4. **Communicate Transparently:** Share your purpose and the impact you're making with your stakeholders—customers, employees, investors, and the wider community. Transparent reporting and storytelling build trust and inspire others to support your mission. Remember, your employees are a vital part of this journey, too. Help them understand their role in fulfilling the company's purpose, so they feel connected to something bigger.

5. **Leverage Strategic Partnerships:** To amplify your efforts, collaborate with purpose-driven organizations like B1G1 or 1% for the Planet or pursue B-Corp certification. Partnering with these networks extends your reach and demonstrates your commitment to positive change. You can also make a difference locally by supporting community charities or employing underserved communities, ensuring that your business's impact is felt close to home.

By taking these steps, businesses of any size can align their operations with a purpose, driving sustainable profits while contributing to the greater good. Purpose-driven profits aren't just a trend—they're a testament to the power of business as a force for positive change.

In a world where consumers care deeply about values, this approach offers a path to success that resonates with both people and the planet.

We discussed the imperative shift from *'me to we,'* the redefinition of success through new metrics, and the crucial alignment of business operations with purpose-driven profits. These steps not only reconfigure the business landscape but also require well-thought-out, systemic change that can challenge even the most visionary leaders.

While richly rewarding, this change process is not without its complexities and emotional tensions. Systemic change disrupts established patterns, challenges long-held beliefs, and demands a new way of thinking from everyone involved.

As businesses move towards more sustainable and equitable models, they will inevitably encounter resistance from within and outside the organization. The emotional labor involved in this journey is not to be discounted as it requires stakeholders at all levels to reconsider and often radically change their approach to work and collaboration. As I frequently say to my clients, *"If nothing changes on the inside, no sustainable change can happen on the outside."*

Navigating these challenges demands more than a compelling strategy; it requires a profoundly *human* approach to change.

Compassion becomes a critical leadership tool, facilitating smoother transitions and fostering an environment of trust and open communication. Understanding and addressing the human aspects of change management—acknowledging fears, providing clear communication, and offering support—are essential for maintaining morale and commitment during these transformational times.

As a consequence, I want to share some practical techniques for managing business fatigue and staying proactive in the face of continuous change.

Here, the focus is on developing resilience in business structures and within the individuals who power them. Leaders must cultivate environments where compassion for oneself and others is prioritized, ensuring everyone involved is supported through the transitions. This includes creating spaces for dialogue, learning, and emotional support as integral components of the change process.

The strategies we will explore aim to equip you with the tools to survive and thrive in an ever-evolving landscape, turning potential challenges into opportunities for growth and innovation. By embracing a compassionate, human-centered approach to change, your business can navigate the complexities of transformation with greater ease and success, ultimately leading to a more resilient and adaptive business model.

Building a Regenerative Culture

In our quest to build businesses that extend beyond the mere bounds of sustainability to embrace truly regenerative practices, cultivating a regenerative culture within organizations is not just beneficial—*it's essential.*

Regenerative cultures transcend the simple adaptation to change; they welcome and flourish within it, nurturing an environment ripe with continuous learning, innovation, and an unwavering commitment to positive transformation at every level of organizational life. These cultures are built on the foundational understanding that caring for the earth is intrinsically linked to caring for ourselves and our communities. It's a holistic approach that recognizes our interconnectedness with the world around us, insisting that to heal our planet is to heal ourselves.

While critical, sustainability is no longer sufficient to address our complex environmental and social challenges. Sustainability aims to maintain the status quo and prevent problems from worsening, but in a world where degradation has already occurred, we need strategies that can reverse damage and renew. This is where the concept of regenerative cultures comes into play, emphasizing preserving and revitalizing ecosystems, communities, and even the organizational spirit.

The growing need for intimacy, reciprocity, and communion with life underscores a deeper, more existential inquiry into what it means to be human in the 21st century. As we navigate through technological advancements and global crises, the yearning for connection—to each other, our work, and the natural world—becomes more pronounced. Regenerative cultures answer this call by fostering a sense of belonging and purpose, creating spaces where individuals can contribute to something greater than themselves and, in doing so, find more meaning and fulfillment in their work and lives.

Yet, the journey toward cultivating a regenerative culture requires us to ask profound questions about what we need to do differently and who we need to become. It challenges us to reflect on our values, behaviors, and impact on the world. This shift is not merely operational but deeply personal, calling on leaders and individuals within organizations to embody the principles of regeneration in their actions and decisions and potentially even within their lives.

It's about evolving beyond the traditional paradigms of success and progress to embrace a more compassionate, holistic view of growth—one that enriches rather than depletes, restores rather than consumes. By fostering regenerative cultures, businesses can become incubators for this transformation, leading the way toward a future where people and the planet survive and thrive. This section aims to illuminate the path forward, offering practical steps and insights to help businesses navigate this crucial transition, ensuring they play a pivotal role in shaping a more regenerative, resilient, and interconnected world.

Drawing on the insights of Daniel Christian Wahl, whose work on designing regenerative cultures has been influential since its publication in 2016, we can outline ten practical steps to cultivate such a culture within our workplaces.[4]

1. Foster a Shared Vision of Regeneration: Wahl emphasizes the importance of a shared vision that extends beyond the organization to include the well-being of the broader community and the planet. Engage your team in developing a vision statement reflecting these regenerative principles, ensuring every member feels a sense of ownership and responsibility towards this collective goal.

2. Encourage Systems Thinking: A regenerative culture understands that everything is interconnected. Encourage employees to think in systems and understand the broader impact of their actions. This can be fostered through training programs, workshops, and by integrating systems thinking into everyday decision-making processes.

3. Promote Diversity and Inclusion: Regenerative cultures thrive on diversity, recognizing that varied perspectives lead to more resilient and innovative solutions. Make a concerted effort to include voices from different backgrounds, disciplines, and viewpoints. This diversity should be reflected in recruitment policies, team compositions, and the decision-making process.

4. Implement Continuous Learning: Wahl advocates continuous learning as a cornerstone of regenerative cultures. Create opportunities for employees to grow professionally and personally through mentoring programs and professional development courses, and encourage cross-disciplinary learning and collaboration.

5. Create Spaces for Reflection and Creativity: Innovation and creativity are vital for regeneration. Design your workplace to include spaces that encourage reflection and creativity, allowing employees the time and space to think deeply about complex problems and develop innovative solutions.

6. Practice Adaptive Leadership: Leaders in a regenerative culture model adaptability and openness to change. They practice what Wahl describes as *"adaptive leadership,"* leading by example, learning from failures, encouraging experimentation, and being open to feedback and new ideas.

7. Encourage Ownership and Empowerment: Empower employees by giving them ownership of projects that align with the organization's regenerative vision. This not only boosts their motivation but also aligns their personal goals with the organizational mission, fostering a reliable commitment to the culture of regeneration.

8. Measure Success Beyond Financial Metrics: While financial viability is essential, a regenerative culture also measures success in terms of positive impact on the environment, community well-being, and social equity. Implement metrics that reflect these broader goals and celebrate achievements in these areas.

9. Foster Community and Well-being: Wahl highlights the importance of community and well-being in regenerative cultures. Foster a sense of community within your organization through regular team-building activities and community service projects and by supporting employee well-being through comprehensive wellness programs.

10. Embed Regenerative Principles into Everyday Operations: Integrate regenerative principles into your business's daily operations, from resource management to product design and customer interaction. This consistent alignment ensures that the regeneration culture permeates every aspect of the organization.

By embracing the steps inspired by Wahl's visionary work, businesses can cultivate a regenerative culture that secures their long-term resilience and success and significantly contributes to the broader world's healing and flourishing. This approach underscores a profound respect for the emergent nature of regenerative processes, suggesting that at the heart of developing such cultures lies a readiness to make peace with *'not knowing.'* This acceptance opens up a space for exploration and curiosity, emphasizing the importance of asking the right questions over hastily seeking answers.

Implementing regenerative cultures requires a deep commitment to paying attention to relationships—how we interact with one another and collectively contribute to the world's emergence through our actions and being. It is a recognition that the path to regeneration is as much about who we are in the world as it is about what we are doing.

This perspective invites a shift from a focus on immediate solutions to a more patient, attentive approach that *values the process of emergence*—finding and living into new ways of relating to ourselves, others, the community, and life as a whole.

Rather than rushing towards predefined answers, living into these questions together allows for the natural emergence of innovative operating methods that harmonize with regenerative principles. It encourages a culture of continuous learning and adaptation, where the journey becomes a source of inspiration and growth.

Such a culture is marked by a collective endeavor to explore new possibilities for how business can be a force for positive change, fostering environments where creativity and innovation are nurtured and where every individual feels empowered to contribute to the collective vision.

In essence, the journey towards a regenerative culture is an invitation to engage deeply with the complexities and uncertainties of our time, embracing them not as obstacles but as opportunities for genuine human growth and transformation.

It's a call to move beyond the conventional paradigms of business and explore, with openness and curiosity, how we can all play a role in co-creating a world that sustains, regenerates, and thrives. By adopting this approach, businesses pave the way for us all to lead by example, demonstrating that it is possible to thrive economically while positively impacting the world.

It's essential to recognize that our impact must extend beyond the immediate walls of our organizations. This is where our responsibility deepens—to create thriving environments within our businesses, look outward to the communities we are part of, and intentionally consider the ripple effects of our actions. It's time to expand our understanding of who is included in our definition of culture.

Proper regeneration requires us to widen the circle of influence, involving our local and global communities in this transformative process. By broadening our perspective, we can co-create a more inclusive, sustainable future where businesses are agents of positive change for themselves and the wider world.

Inner Compass: Guiding Questions

In this chapter, you've explored the profound role of regenerative leadership in transforming modern business. These guiding questions help you reflect on embodying regenerative leadership, aligning your company with purpose, and redefining success for yourself and your organization. Use them to deepen your connection to your values and your leadership journey.

- **What does leadership as a sacred duty mean to you?** Reflect on how you approach leadership. Do you see it as a responsibility to your organization and the world around you? How can you integrate a sense of sacred duty into your daily leadership practices?

- **How can you embrace regenerative leadership in your work?** Consider what it means to become a regenerative leader who nurtures growth, sustainability, and long-term impact. What steps can you take to ensure your leadership style helps regenerate your team, your organization, and the wider community?

- **How are you unleashing the potential energy of your organization?** Reflect on the untapped potential within your organization. Are you fostering an environment where your team can thrive and contribute their best work? What changes can you make to activate this energy more fully?

- **What is the narrative that inspires change within your organization?** Think about the story your organization is telling, both internally and externally. Is it one that inspires and motivates? How can you craft a narrative that reflects your values and vision, encouraging others to engage with and drive meaningful change?

- **What mindset shifts are required to become a Sacred Changemaker?** Reflect on the changes in mindset that you may need to embrace to fully embody regenerative leadership. How can you shift from a traditional leadership mindset to one that aligns with the principles of sacred changemaking?

- **How are you redefining success within your business?** Consider how you currently measure success. Are your metrics solely focused on financial outcomes, or do they also include social, environmental, and ethical impact? How can you broaden your definition of success to reflect a more holistic and regenerative approach?

- **How aligned are your profits with your purpose?** Reflect on the alignment between your business operations and your purpose. Are your earnings driven by actions that serve both people and the planet? What adjustments can you make to ensure your business generates purpose-driven profits that contribute to the greater good?

- **What steps can you take to build a regenerative culture within your organization?** Consider fostering a regenerative culture that promotes sustainability, collaboration, and long-term impact. What initiatives or practices can you implement to create a work environment that supports growth and well-being for all stakeholders?

5
The Path to Transformation

"People don't resist change. They resist being changed." - Peter Senge[1]

We often think of transformation as something outside of us—hitting those goals, climbing the career ladder, and creating a successful business. *But fundamental, lasting transformation?* It starts on the inside with the urge to change.

It's about understanding who we are at our core and aligning that with what we do in the world. It's peeling back the layers of who we've been told to be and discovering the soul of who we are beneath the layers of social expectation. And that's where the 8 Dimensions of Change come in—they're like a guide, helping us navigate this journey in more expansive ways.

From Me to We: Expanding Consciousness in Business

Embracing a *'we'* mindset is pivotal for businesses transitioning from the old world's focus on individual success to the new era's emphasis on collective well-being. This strategic shift is not merely beneficial from a global perspective; it's fast becoming an imperative for organizations aspiring to thrive in today's complex and interconnected global landscape.

As explored earlier, the evolving business paradigm underscores the importance of sustainability, purpose, and community engagement. Without adopting a mindset that prioritizes the collective good, businesses risk falling behind, unable to fulfill their potential or make a meaningful impact.

The importance of this strategy stems from a fundamental truth that, although not new, has been overshadowed in the rush for competitive advantage: *relationships matter*. The fabric of a successful business has always been woven from the threads of solid, trust-based relationships. However, in pursuing growth and profit, many organizations still need to learn how to cultivate these relationships effectively within the business context.

Today, as societal expectations shift and stakeholders demand greater accountability and ethical conduct from corporations, the *'we'* mindset emerges not just as a moral imperative but also as a strategic one. Businesses that continue to operate with a *'me-first'* attitude risk their reputation, customer loyalty, and long-term viability; in short, they risk losing the trust within their relationships with customers.

In this era, winners and losers will be distinguished not by who can accumulate the most wealth or market share but by who can build the most resilient, inclusive, and purpose-driven organizations. Those who recognize their success is inextricably linked to the well-being of their employees, customers, communities, and the planet will lead the way. This emerging realization prompts a return to the foundational principle that thriving businesses are, at their core, about fostering positive, productive relationships and contributing to the fabric of society.

The following ten action items offer practical steps for embedding the *'we'* mindset into every aspect of organizational life, ensuring that businesses survive and flourish in the new era. They are not a complete list; they are merely a starting point to get you moving in the right direction. By prioritizing collective well-being, you can enhance your business's internal culture, deepen its impact on society, and navigate the path to transformation with integrity and purpose.

1. Develop a Shared Vision

Embracing a *'we'* mindset begins with creating a shared vision that reflects the collective aspirations of everyone involved—employees, stakeholders, and the broader community. This is about moving beyond the traditional focus on individual success and cultivating a shared purpose that aligns everyone's efforts toward common goals. Developing a shared vision enhances engagement and commitment across your organization and fosters a felt sense of belonging and investment in the journey ahead.

Here's a step-by-step guide to developing a shared vision that is inclusive:

Step 1. Initiate Open Dialogue Sessions

Begin by creating spaces for open dialogue. Organize workshops or meetings with key stakeholders, including employees at all levels, community members, customers, and partners. The aim is to ensure everyone feels heard and valued in these conversations. Use facilitation techniques like roundtable discussions, open forums, or structured brainstorming sessions to encourage open communication and active participation. These methods help break down barriers and allow diverse perspectives to surface, creating a solid foundation for a vision that reflects the collective voice.

Step 2. Utilize Collaborative Tools

Leverage collaborative tools and platforms to capture ideas from a wider audience and make the process more accessible. Tools like Google Docs, Miro, or Trello can be invaluable for gathering thoughts and feedback, especially when working across different time zones and schedules. Visual aids, such as mind maps or vision boards, can also be influential in helping participants articulate and align their ideas visually, making abstract concepts more tangible and easier to understand.

Step 3. Conduct Surveys for Broader Input

Not everyone can attend interactive sessions, so extend the opportunity to contribute through surveys or digital polls. This step ensures that you capture the perspectives of a broader audience, including those who might not be present in person. Sharing what you've collected and interpreted from these surveys with the community is crucial. This feedback loop helps validate and refine the responses, ensuring the vision reflects collective input.

Step 4. Facilitate Values Alignment Workshops

Once you have a broad set of ideas and feedback, conduct workshops on aligning personal and organizational values. This step is pivotal in ensuring the shared vision resonates personally with each participant. Activities like the *'Values Auction',* where participants bid on values they believe should be prioritized, can effectively reveal individual and collective priorities. This alignment process strengthens the emotional connection to the vision and fosters a sense of ownership and commitment.

Step 5. Drafting the Vision Statement

With all the insights gathered, the next step is collaboratively drafting the vision statement. Start with a small group to create a preliminary version, then open it up for broader feedback and iteration. The goal is to craft a clear, inspiring vision statement reflecting collective aspirations. It should serve as a rallying cry that motivates and unites everyone involved, a touchstone for all future decisions and actions.

Step 6. Regular Review and Adaptation

Recognize that a shared vision is not static; it should evolve as your organization and its environment change. Schedule regular review sessions to reflect on the vision statement and make adjustments if necessary. Keeping the vision dynamic and relevant helps maintain engagement and ensures it continues to guide your organization's strategic direction.

Step 7. Celebrate and Communicate the Vision

Once the vision is finalized, celebrate this achievement with a launch event. This will energize the team and publicly commit the organization to this shared path. Ensure the vision is integrated into all internal and external communications, becoming a foundational document that guides organizational strategies, decision-making, and operations. Regularly revisiting and reinforcing the vision will keep it alive and active in everyone's mind.

By following these steps, you can ensure that developing a shared vision is inclusive, comprehensive, and effective. This shared vision will be the cornerstone of your organization's strategic direction, strengthening the collective commitment among stakeholders and guiding the transformation from *'Me'* to *'We'*. This is where the inner work of personal alignment meets the outer work of organizational leadership, creating a purpose-driven business that thrives on collaboration and shared purpose.

2. Implement Collaborative Decision-Making

Transforming how decisions are made within your organization is crucial in moving from a top-down, hierarchical model to a more democratic, inclusive approach. When employees feel their voices are heard and valued, they become more engaged and invested in the organization's success. Shifting to a collaborative decision-making process enhances a sense of ownership and helps tap into the collective intelligence of the entire team.

Here's how you can effectively implement this approach in your organization:

Step 1. Establish Clear Guidelines

Before tackling collaborative decision-making, it is important to set clear boundaries and expectations. Not every decision must be made collaboratively, so start by defining the scope. Outline which decisions are open to group input and which should remain within specific roles or management. Communicate the criteria that will guide collaborative decisions, such as alignment with strategic goals, potential stakeholder impact, and financial considerations. This clarity prevents confusion and ensures that the process runs smoothly.

Step 2. Choose the Right Tools and Platforms

Technology can facilitate collaborative decision-making, especially in larger organizations or remote teams. Use digital platforms like Microsoft Teams, Slack, or Asana to gather input, share information, and track the progress of decisions. For voting or consensus-building, consider using tools like Doodle polls for scheduling, which helps groups make decisions online. These tools enable seamless collaboration and keep everyone informed and engaged.

Step 3. Create Cross-Functional Teams

Form cross-functional teams for specific decision-making tasks. These teams should include members from various levels and departments to bring diverse perspectives and expertise to the table. For more significant decisions, consider setting up temporary task forces that work together to solve specific problems or develop recommendations for the leadership team. This diversity enriches the decision-making process and fosters a sense of unity and shared purpose across the organization.

Step 4. Train Employees in Collaborative Techniques

Collaboration doesn't come naturally to everyone, so providing training on effective communication, conflict resolution, and consensus-building is essential. Equip your team with the skills needed for productive collaboration. Additionally, select and train a group of employees in facilitation skills so they can effectively guide group discussions and decision-making sessions. This support helps create a more structured and positive collaborative environment.

Step 5. Implement a Structured Decision-Making Process

Introduce structured workshops for decision-making that follow a transparent process, such as brainstorming, round-robin feedback, group analysis, and collective voting or consensus. This structure ensures that all voices are heard and that the decision-making process is fair and transparent. Include regular feedback loops where decisions are reviewed, and outcomes are evaluated against expectations. This ongoing review helps refine the process and builds trust in the collaborative approach.

Step 6. Foster an Open Culture

A collaborative decision-making process thrives in an open culture where transparency, respect, and inclusivity are the norm. Leaders should model these behaviors by actively seeking input and showing appreciation for team contributions. Encourage an environment where everyone feels safe expressing their opinions without fear of criticism or reprisal. This might involve setting up anonymous feedback channels or ensuring that meetings welcome diverse viewpoints.

Step 7. Review and Iterate

Collaborative decision-making is not a set-it-and-forget-it process. Regularly review the effectiveness of your approach and be open to making adjustments based on feedback. Share success stories where collaborative decision-making has led to positive outcomes, as this reinforces the value of the process and encourages broader participation. Continuous improvement is vital to making this process a natural and effective part of your organizational culture.

Integrating these practices into your organization ensures that decisions are made more democratically, are better informed, and are more likely to be supported by the entire team. This shift from a *me-first to a we-first mindset* is not just a structural change; it's a cultural one that empowers employees and aligns with the principles of inclusive, transformative leadership. It's an essential step in building a collaborative workplace culture where everyone feels invested in the organization's collective success.

3. Promote Diversity and Inclusion

Creating a diverse and inclusive environment is essential for fostering a workplace where all employees feel valued, empowered, and able to contribute their unique perspectives. Diversity and inclusion are more than just buzzwords—foundational elements of a thriving, innovative, and resilient organization. When different voices are heard and respected, it enriches the workplace culture and drives creativity and better decision-making.

Here's how you can effectively promote diversity and inclusion within your organization:

Step 1. Assess Current Diversity and Inclusion Status

Before making any changes, it's crucial to understand where your organization currently stands. Conduct a comprehensive diversity audit to assess the demographic makeup of your workforce. Look beyond just ethnic and gender diversity—consider age, disability, sexual orientation, and diversity of thought. This holistic view will help identify areas where diversity may be lacking. Additionally, inclusion surveys should be distributed regularly to gather feedback on how inclusive employees feel about the workplace. This will highlight any issues or areas that need attention.

Step 2. Revise Hiring Practices

To attract a more diverse range of candidates, start by revising your job descriptions. Ensure they are inclusive and avoid gender-coded language. Focus on essential qualifications to avoid inadvertently excluding qualified candidates. Use diverse recruitment channels to reach underrepresented groups and consider partnering with organizations or job boards catering to these communities. Implement structured interviews and standardized evaluation criteria to minimize biases. You can also use software that anonymizes applications, removing identifiers that could influence hiring decisions based on unconscious biases.

Step 3. Implement Comprehensive Diversity Training

Education is essential to fostering an inclusive culture. Conduct regular training sessions that educate employees about different cultures, identities, and experiences. These sessions should also teach practical skills for creating an inclusive environment, such as effective communication and conflict resolution. Include bystander intervention training to empower employees to address discriminatory behavior when they see it.

This proactive approach supports a workplace culture where everyone feels responsible for maintaining inclusivity and respect.

Step 4. Create Inclusion Committees or Task Forces

Establish structures within your organization that support ongoing diversity and inclusion efforts. Employee Resource Groups *(ERGs)* can provide community support for different demographic groups, advise on diversity issues, and help implement inclusion initiatives. Additionally, a Diversity and Inclusion Task Force should be created that includes diverse members from various levels of the organization. This task force can oversee the implementation of diversity initiatives and ensure they are aligned with the organization's goals and values.

Step 5. Promote Inclusive Policies and Practices

Review and implement policies that support diversity and inclusion, such as flexible working arrangements, remote work options, and family leave policies. These policies accommodate the diverse needs of your workforce, helping everyone thrive. Make sure your workplace is accessible and supportive of people with disabilities. This might include physical modifications, accessible technology, and a supportive culture that respects all abilities.

Step 6. Encourage and Facilitate Open Dialogue

Create opportunities for employees to share their experiences and suggestions openly—host regular forums to discuss diversity and inclusion in a safe and supportive environment. Encourage leaders to participate in these discussions to show their commitment to these values. This open dialogue fosters trust and clarifies that the organization is serious about listening to and acting on feedback.

Step 7. Measure Progress and Hold the Organization Accountable

Set clear, measurable goals for your diversity and inclusion initiatives. Regularly track progress against these goals and share the results with the entire organization to maintain transparency. Include diversity and inclusion metrics in performance reviews and link them to leadership accountability. This ensures that these initiatives are taken seriously and that progress is continuously monitored and improved.

Implementing these steps can create a workplace where every employee feels valued and empowered to contribute fully. A diverse and inclusive environment enhances organizational culture and drives better business outcomes. This is an essential part of the transformation journey: building a business that reflects our diverse world and leads with integrity and purpose.

4. Practice Active Listening

Active listening is more than just hearing words; it's about fully engaging with the speaker, understanding their message, and responding thoughtfully. In an organizational context, practicing active listening is crucial for creating an inclusive and collaborative environment where everyone feels heard and valued. It's a skill that fosters trust, reduces misunderstandings, and improves communication across all levels of the organization.

Here's how you can embed active listening into your company's culture with a step-by-step guide:

Step 1. Educate Your Team on Active Listening

Start by organizing training workshops to educate all employees on the principles and techniques of active listening. It's important to emphasize that active listening involves understanding not just the words being said but also the emotions and intentions behind them. Include role-playing exercises in these sessions to help employees practice their skills in various scenarios, such as during team meetings or one-on-one interactions. This hands-on practice helps employees feel more comfortable applying active listening in real-world situations.

Step 2. Lead by Example

Leadership sets the tone for the entire organization. Ensure that all leaders practice active listening in every interaction, whether during meetings, casual conversations, or when receiving feedback. When leaders demonstrate active listening openly, it sets a standard for the entire team and shows that this behavior is expected and valued. Encourage leaders to actively engage with their teams, showing that they value their input and perspectives.

Step 3. Create a Feedback-Rich Environment

A key component of active listening is creating spaces where feedback flows freely in all directions. Implement regular feedback sessions where employees can give and receive feedback. Use these sessions to practice active listening and ensure all feedback is heard, understood, and respectfully addressed. Additionally, anonymous feedback tools give employees a safe space to express their thoughts and feelings without fear of repercussions. This helps identify any underlying issues that might not be voiced openly.

Step 4. Foster an Open Communication Culture

Encourage open communication across all levels of the organization. Promote an open-door policy where employees feel welcome to speak with their managers and leaders about any concerns, ideas, or feedback. Regular check-ins are also essential. Managers should schedule these sessions to allow team members to share their thoughts and feelings, with the manager practicing active listening and engaging fully with what is shared. This helps build trust and demonstrates that employees' voices matter.

Step 5. Recognize and Reward Good Listening

Recognition is a powerful motivator. Develop programs to recognize and reward individuals who consistently demonstrate excellent active listening skills. This could be through formal recognition during meetings, awards, or even simple acknowledgments. Additionally, consider incorporating active listening as a criterion in performance reviews. Assess how well employees and managers listen to their colleagues and engage with their ideas. This not only reinforces the importance of the skill but also encourages others to develop their listening abilities.

Step 6. Use Technology to Enhance Listening

Leverage collaborative tools to facilitate better communication and active listening. Shared document platforms, forums, and chat tools allow people to articulate their thoughts clearly and enable others to respond thoughtfully. In virtual meetings, use features like hand-raising, questions, and polls to enhance engagement and ensure everyone can be heard. These tools can help bridge the gap between in-person and remote communication, making active listening more accessible.

Step 7. Monitor and Adjust the Listening Practices

Finally, regularly assess how well the organization incorporates active listening into daily operations. Conduct surveys to gather feedback on current listening practices and ask for suggestions for improvement. Commit to continuous improvement based on this feedback and observations, addressing areas where the organization may fall short. Explore new strategies and techniques to enhance active listening, keeping it a dynamic and evolving part of your culture.

By integrating these practices, you can create a workplace where active listening is the norm, not the exception. This will lead to more meaningful interactions, stronger relationships, and a culture where every employee feels respected and heard. Active listening isn't just about improving communication—it's about creating a space where diverse perspectives are welcomed and valued, fostering a truly collaborative and inclusive environment.

5. Create Cross-Functional Teams

Encouraging collaboration across different departments and functional areas is a powerful way to break down silos and promote a more integrated approach to projects and problem-solving. Cross-functional teams bring diverse perspectives and skills together, fostering innovation and enhancing the organization's ability to tackle complex challenges.

Here's how to effectively implement and optimize cross-functional teams in your organization:

Step 1. Define the Purpose and Objectives

Start by clearly defining the purpose and objectives of the cross-functional team. What specific problem are they solving, or what project are they working on? Setting clear goals helps ensure that every team member understands why they're part of the team and what they expect to achieve. Outline the scope of the project or problem area, including the boundaries of what the team should focus on. This clarity helps manage expectations and streamline efforts, ensuring that everyone is aligned from the outset.

Step 2. Select the Right Team Members

Choosing the right people is critical for the success of a cross-functional team. Select team members from different departments or functional areas who can bring diverse skill sets and perspectives. It's essential to ensure that each member's role is clear and that their skills align with the team's objectives. Aim for balanced representation from various departments to promote equality within the team and prevent any single department from dominating the decision-making process.

Step 3. Establish Team Leadership

Assign a team leader who is respected across departments. This person should be capable of motivating the team, managing conflicts, and driving the project forward. For longer-term projects, consider rotating the leadership role among team members. This can enhance engagement, distribute responsibility, and allow different members to develop leadership skills. A strong leader is essential for maintaining focus and cohesion, but rotating the role can foster a more inclusive and dynamic team environment.

Step 4. Foster Effective Communication

Communication is the lifeblood of any successful cross-functional team. Schedule regular meetings with a structured agenda to ensure all team members are updated, aligned, and have the opportunity to contribute their ideas. Use practical communication tools like Slack, Microsoft Teams, or Asana to facilitate easy information exchange and collaboration. These tools help maintain transparency and keep everyone in the loop, no matter where they are located.

Step 5. Encourage Openness and Trust

Building trust within the team is crucial, especially when members don't typically work together. Organize team-building activities to help break the ice and build rapport among team members. Establish a mechanism for conflict resolution within the team to address disagreements constructively. Encourage an environment where members feel safe expressing differing opinions and working through conflicts. This openness and trust are the foundation of effective collaboration and problem-solving.

Step 6. Provide Resources and Support

Ensure the team can access all necessary resources, including data, tools, and technologies, to facilitate effective collaboration and decision-making. Secure support from executives or upper management to give the team the authority and backing they need to execute their tasks effectively. This top-level support empowers the team and signals the organization's commitment to the success of cross-functional collaboration.

Step 7. Measure and Evaluate Performance

Define clear metrics to evaluate the cross-functional team's performance. These should align with the team's overall goals and include team and individual performance indicators. Implement regular feedback loops where team members can assess progress, discuss challenges, and adjust strategies as needed. Include feedback from stakeholders affected by the team's work to gain a broader perspective on the team's impact and areas for improvement.

Step 8. Celebrate Success and Learn from Your Experience

Celebrate successes and milestones to recognize the team's hard work and maintain morale. Acknowledge the contributions of all team members and the value of their collaborative efforts. After a project concludes, conduct a review session to discuss what worked well and what could be improved. Document and use what you have learned to refine the approach for future cross-functional teams. This continuous improvement mindset helps the organization grow and adapt, ensuring that each team builds on the successes and lessons of the past.

Following these steps, you can create effective cross-functional teams that leverage diverse skills and perspectives for better problem-solving and project management. This approach enhances innovation and efficiency and strengthens the organizational culture by promoting inclusivity and collaboration across different business areas. It's a tangible way to move from a siloed, *me-first* mentality to a more integrated, *we-first* approach that aligns with the principles of conscious leadership and collective success.

6. Invest in Community Engagement

Extending the *'we'* mindset beyond your organization to actively engage with the local community is a powerful way to demonstrate your commitment to broader social responsibility. Investing in community engagement contributes to the community's well-being and deepens the connection between your organization and the people it serves. This approach helps create a shared purpose and builds trust and goodwill to benefit everyone involved.

Here's how to develop and implement effective community engagement strategies with a step-by-step guide:

Step 1. Assess Community Needs

Start by understanding the local community's needs. Conduct thorough research or a needs assessment to identify issues and areas where your organization can make a meaningful impact. Engage with community leaders, local government, and other stakeholders in conversations to gain insights into the community's challenges and opportunities. This collaborative approach ensures that your efforts are aligned with real needs and have a greater chance of making a positive difference.

Step 2. Develop a Community Engagement Plan

Based on your research, develop a comprehensive community engagement plan. Define clear objectives for what you aim to achieve through these activities: improving local infrastructure, supporting education, enhancing healthcare, or fostering economic development. Plan specific activities that align with these objectives, such as setting up volunteer programs, initiating community development projects, or organizing community events. A structured plan helps guide your efforts and ensures that your organization's resources are used effectively.

Step 3. Form Strategic Partnerships

Partnerships can amplify your impact and provide mutual benefits. Collaborate with local businesses and nonprofits with similar values or a positive community impact track record. These partnerships can help you leverage resources and expertise, making your efforts more effective. Additionally, consider partnering with educational institutions like schools, colleges, and universities for academic programs, internships, and community service projects. Engaging youth is particularly impactful, fostering a new generation of community-minded individuals.

Step 4. Engage Your Employees

Your employees are a vital part of your community engagement efforts. Develop volunteer programs that encourage employees to participate in community activities during work hours without loss of pay. This could include activities like community clean-ups, teaching, mentoring, or skilled volunteering utilizing their professional skills. Implement a matching gifts program where the company matches employee donations to nonprofits. This not only enhances the personal contributions of your employees but also reinforces a culture of giving within your organization.

Step 5. Communicate and Promote Community Activities

Effective communication is critical to the success of community engagement initiatives. Regularly inform your employees about upcoming opportunities through internal newsletters, meetings, and the company intranet. Externally, use your company's social media platforms and website to promote community events and initiatives. Highlight your commitment to the community and encourage broader participation. Showcasing these activities publicly also helps build your company's reputation as a responsible and engaged community partner.

Step 6. Measure Impact and Gather Feedback

It's essential to assess the impact of your community engagement activities. Develop metrics to evaluate the effectiveness of these initiatives, such as the number of volunteering hours logged, funds raised, or qualitative impacts like improved community relations. Regularly gather feedback from employees and community members to understand what's working well and where there's room for improvement. This feedback helps refine your approach and ensures that your efforts continue to meet community needs effectively.

Step 7. Sustain Engagement

Community engagement shouldn't be a one-time effort. Review your strategies and activities to ensure they align with community needs and your organization's objectives over time. Show a long-term commitment by integrating community engagement into your company's strategic plans and budgeting processes. This ensures that these activities are not just an add-on but a core aspect of your organizational culture and identity.

Step 8. Celebrate and Recognize Contributions

Finally, celebrate the successes and recognize the contributions of those involved. Establish recognition programs to acknowledge and reward outstanding contributions by employees to community projects. Celebrating these efforts can motivate further participation and demonstrate that the company values these contributions. Whether through formal awards, shout-outs in meetings, or spotlight features in newsletters, recognition plays a crucial role in sustaining enthusiasm and commitment.

By investing in community engagement, your organization helps address local issues and builds stronger, more resilient ties within the community. This commitment enhances your company's reputation, attracts like-minded employees and customers, and contributes to a more sustainable and inclusive future. It's about creating a ripple effect of positive change that extends beyond your business, embodying the essence of a *'we-first'* mindset.

7. Adopt Sustainable Practices

Incorporating sustainable practices into your business operations is essential for demonstrating a commitment to collective well-being and environmental stewardship. It's about more than just reducing your carbon footprint; it's about creating a business that is resilient, responsible, and aligned with the values of sustainability. By integrating these practices, you contribute to the planet's health and enhance your company's reputation, operational efficiency, and long-term success.

Here's how to integrate sustainability into your business operations effectively:

Step 1. Conduct an Environmental Impact Audit

Start by assessing your current environmental impact across all business areas. This could include energy usage, waste management, resource utilization, and supply chain operations. An initial assessment helps identify critical areas where improvements can be made. Consider hiring environmental consultants to ensure your audit is thorough and accurate, providing a solid foundation for developing a robust sustainability strategy.

Step 2. Set Clear Environmental Goals

Once you understand your current impact, set specific, measurable, achievable, relevant, and time-bound *(SMART)* goals for reducing your environmental footprint. These goals could include reducing waste by a certain percentage over a set period, achieving carbon neutrality by a specific year, or increasing the use of renewable energy. Publicly committing to these goals holds your business accountable and enhances your corporate social responsibility profile, demonstrating your commitment to stakeholders.

Step 3. Implement Eco-Friendly Operations

To make a meaningful impact, integrate eco-friendly practices into your daily operations. Upgrade to energy-efficient appliances and systems and consider investing in renewable energy sources like solar or wind power for your facilities. Implement comprehensive recycling and composting programs, reduce single-use plastics, and opt for biodegradable packaging materials. Additionally, sustainable sourcing should be prioritized by choosing suppliers who commit to environmentally responsible practices and consider purchasing locally to reduce transportation emissions.

Step 4. Innovate Product Design and Services

Sustainability should be an essential consideration for product design and development. This could involve using recycled materials, designing products for longevity, or ensuring they are recyclable at the end of their life cycle. For service-oriented businesses, consider minimizing your service delivery's environmental impact. This might include reducing travel through virtual meetings, optimizing logistics to cut fuel consumption, or using digital tools to replace paper-based processes.

Step 5. Educate and Engage Employees

Employee engagement is crucial for the success of sustainability initiatives. Develop training programs to educate employees about sustainable practices and how they can contribute at work and home. Encourage involvement in sustainability initiatives, such as forming a *'green team'* or participating in environmental challenges and competitions. When employees are informed and engaged, they can become advocates for sustainability, helping to integrate these values into the company culture.

Step 6. Monitor and Report Progress

Set up systems to track your progress against the environmental goals regularly. This could include monitoring energy consumption, waste production, and recycling rates. Regularly report these outcomes to stakeholders through sustainability reports or updates in your annual reports.

Transparency in your progress helps build trust with stakeholders and shows that your commitment to sustainability is genuine and ongoing.

Step 7. Foster a Sustainable Corporate Culture

Creating a sustainable corporate culture starts with leadership. Ensure that your company's leadership demonstrates a commitment to sustainability, inspiring similar commitments throughout the organization. Integrate sustainability into your core values and make it a part of everyday business decisions. This could include incorporating sustainability into onboarding processes, decision-making frameworks, and regular company communications. When sustainability is a core part of your corporate culture, it becomes a guiding principle for all employees.

Step 8. Engage with the Wider Community and Industry

Sustainability doesn't end within the walls of your business. Participate in or sponsor local environmental projects to increase your visibility as a responsible business and foster good community relationships. Engage with industry groups or consortia to develop sector-wide approaches to sustainability. Collaborative efforts can often lead to more significant impacts than acting alone, and participating in these initiatives can position your business as a leader in sustainability.

By adopting these sustainable practices, your business contributes to the planet's health and positions itself as a leader in corporate responsibility. These efforts can lead to cost savings, improved employee morale, enhanced brand loyalty among consumers, and a competitive edge in your industry. Every step towards sustainability is securing a viable future for the next generations while maintaining profitable and ethical business operations today.

8. Encourage Employee Development

Investing in the growth and development of your employees is one of the most impactful ways to foster a supportive, innovative, and engaged workplace. When employees feel empowered to grow and develop their skills, they are more likely to contribute positively to the organization, take initiative, and remain committed to their roles.

Here's how you can effectively promote and implement employee development initiatives within your organization:

Step 1. Assess Employee Development Needs

Start by identifying your employees' specific development needs. Conduct individual assessments through one-on-one meetings, performance reviews, and employee surveys to understand their skills and knowledge gaps. Additionally, evaluate the needs of different departments or teams to identify common areas where training could enhance performance and productivity. This comprehensive approach ensures that development programs are tailored to individual and organizational needs.

Step 2. Develop Comprehensive Training Programs

Based on the assessments, create customized training plans that address job-specific skills and general professional competencies. These plans should be personalized to enhance each employee's growth in their current role and prepare them for future opportunities. Incorporate diverse learning formats such as workshops, seminars, online courses, and hands-on training to cater to different learning styles and schedules. This flexibility ensures that all employees can participate in the best way for them.

Step 3. Establish Mentorship Programs

Mentorship can be a powerful tool for employee development. Develop a mentorship program that pairs less experienced employees with more experienced ones. Carefully match mentors and mentees based on their skills, interests, and development goals to ensure a productive relationship. Set clear objectives for the mentorship, including what the mentee hopes to learn and achieve, to guide the relationship and make it beneficial for both parties. Mentorship supports skill development and fosters community and belonging within the organization.

Step 4. Support Continuing Education

Show your commitment to employee development by supporting continuing education. Offer tuition reimbursement or financial assistance for courses relevant to the employee's job or career progression. This not only supports their personal growth but also benefits the organization by enhancing the overall skill set of your team. Provide flexible scheduling or time off for employees pursuing further education to show that you value and support their efforts to grow professionally.

Step 5. Encourage Participation in Professional Associations

Professional associations offer valuable networking and learning opportunities. Consider sponsoring memberships for employees in relevant associations or industry groups. This allows them to connect with peers, stay updated on industry trends, and access additional learning resources. Provide time off or financial assistance for travel and registration fees to support and encourage attending relevant conferences, seminars, or workshops. This investment in professional development can bring new ideas and best practices back to your organization.

Step 6. Promote from Within

Show your employees you value their growth by promoting from within whenever possible. Help employees plan their career paths within the organization, identifying potential future positions and the skills and experiences required to achieve these roles. Encourage internal mobility through transfers and promotions, providing opportunities for employees to take on new challenges and responsibilities. This stimulates learning and growth and boosts morale and retention by showing that the organization is invested in their long-term success.

Step 7. Implement a Recognition System

Recognize and reward learning and development achievements regularly. This could be through formal awards, announcements, or features in company communications. Include regular performance review discussions about training and development to highlight accomplishments and set future learning goals. Recognition motivates employees to continue their development efforts and reinforces the importance of continuous learning within the organization.

Step 8. Create a Culture of Continuous Learning

Building a culture that values learning starts with leadership. Ensure that senior leaders advocate for and participate in development activities, setting an example for the entire organization. Make learning resources available to all employees, such as subscriptions to online learning platforms, access to a company library, or regular in-house training sessions. When learning is embedded in the culture, employees are more likely to take advantage of these resources and actively seek out growth opportunities.

By investing in these comprehensive employee development strategies, your organization will enhance the capabilities and satisfaction of its workforce, driving innovation and competitiveness in the market. Employee development is a win-win: it aids in retention and engagement and equips your team to meet current and future challenges. It's about building a skilled, motivated, and prepared workforce to take the organization to new heights.

9. Foster a Culture of Appreciation

A culture of appreciation is more than just saying "thank you" now and then. Creating an environment where employees feel genuinely valued for their contributions and recognition is fundamental to the workplace culture. When people feel appreciated, they are more engaged, motivated, and likely to go above and beyond in their roles.

Here's how to effectively implement and strengthen a culture of appreciation within your organization:

Step 1. Establish Regular Recognition Practices

Implement a structured recognition program that regularly acknowledges employee achievements. This could be during weekly team meetings, monthly company gatherings, or through regular newsletters. A scheduled recognition routine ensures that appreciation becomes a consistent part of the organizational rhythm. Managers and leaders should also be encouraged to recognize and appreciate employees spontaneously whenever they notice commendable efforts. Spontaneous recognition is powerful because it's immediate and reinforces positive behavior on the spot, making employees feel valued in real time.

Step 2. Diversify Recognition Methods

Not everyone prefers to be recognized in the same way, so it's important to offer both public and private forms of appreciation. Use public platforms such as company meetings, bulletin boards, or internal social media channels to acknowledge contributions. Public recognition sets a positive example and highlights the behaviors and achievements the organization values. For those who prefer more personal recognition, offer private acknowledgments through personal notes, emails, or one-on-one meetings where sincere appreciation can be expressed directly and personally. This flexibility ensures that recognition is meaningful and well-received.

Step 3. Incorporate Peer-to-Peer Recognition

Recognition shouldn't just come from the top down. Implement systems where employees can recognize and appreciate their peers. This could be through 'thank you' cards, a dedicated space on the intranet, or tokens that can be given as a sign of appreciation. Peer recognition works because it creates a sense of camaraderie and reinforces a supportive workplace culture. Consider using digital platforms that allow employees to give and receive kudos easily. These platforms can track and display acknowledgments, making it easy to celebrate successes and encouraging a culture where appreciation is shared freely.

Step 4. Link Recognition to Core Values

Align recognition programs with your company's core values. Recognize behaviors that exemplify these values, reinforcing their importance and encouraging others to align with them. For example, if collaboration is a core value, publicly acknowledge a team that worked together exceptionally well on a project. Share stories that highlight how employees' actions embody the organization's values. This celebrates individuals and strengthens the collective understanding and commitment to the company's values, making them a lived experience rather than just words on a wall.

Step 5. Create Awards and Incentives

Develop formal awards programs that recognize outstanding achievements quarterly or annually. Awards could be linked to innovation, customer service, teamwork, leadership, or other categories that reflect your company's priorities. Provide tangible incentives such as bonuses, gift cards, extra days off, or special privileges like preferred parking spaces or office upgrades. These tangible rewards can be a powerful motivator and show the organization's willingness to invest in its employees' well-being and satisfaction.

Step 6. Train Leaders on Effective Appreciation

Ensure your leaders and managers can recognize and communicate appreciation effectively. Provide training on delivering recognition in a way that feels genuine and meaningful. Emphasize the impact of appreciation on employee motivation and retention. Leaders should model appreciation behaviors, as their involvement lends credibility and seriousness to the initiatives. When senior leaders openly participate in these efforts, they set a strong example and encourage a top-down culture of gratitude.

Step 7. Evaluate and Adapt Recognition Efforts

Regularly solicit employee feedback about recognition practices and their impact. Use this feedback to make necessary adjustments to ensure the initiatives remain relevant and valued by employees. Track employee morale and engagement levels through surveys and turnover rates. Analyze trends related to recognition efforts to assess their effectiveness and identify areas for improvement. This continuous evaluation helps keep the recognition program dynamic and responsive to the workforce's needs.

Step 8. Celebrate Team Successes

While individual recognition is important, celebrating team achievements is equally crucial. Organize team outings, luncheons, or small parties to celebrate team milestones or completed projects. These events recognize success, build team solidarity, and reinforce the importance of collective achievement. Make it a practice to formally acknowledge team efforts upon completing significant projects during company-wide meetings or through company communications. Highlighting the team's contribution shows you value collaboration and teamwork, not just individual performance.

By embedding these strategies into your organizational culture, you create an atmosphere where appreciation is not just an occasional act but a fundamental part of the everyday workplace experience. This culture of appreciation can significantly enhance employee satisfaction, loyalty, and performance, creating a more supportive and cohesive work environment. When employees feel valued and recognized, they are more likely to engage fully, contribute creatively, and stay committed to the organization's success.

10. Lead with Empathy And Compassion

Empathetic and compassionate leadership is essential for creating a work environment where people feel valued, supported, and connected. Leaders who genuinely care about the well-being of their teams inspire loyalty, trust, and a strong sense of community. They understand that leading with empathy doesn't just improve individual relationships; it also enhances team dynamics, employee satisfaction, and organizational success.

Here's how to develop and implement empathetic and compassionate leadership within your organization:

Step 1. Understand the Importance of Empathy and Compassion

Begin by educating your leadership team on the importance of empathy and compassion in the workplace. Conduct workshops and training sessions that explore how these qualities can positively impact team dynamics, employee satisfaction, and overall organizational success. Use case studies to illustrate successful examples of empathetic leadership and the positive outcomes it can produce. Helping leaders visualize the practical benefits of empathy and compassion can motivate them to integrate these qualities into their leadership style.

Step 2. Develop Emotional Intelligence (EQ)

Emotional intelligence is a foundational skill for empathetic leadership. Utilize EQ assessments to help leaders identify their strengths and areas for improvement related to empathy and compassion. Based on these assessments, provide personalized training focused on developing self-awareness, emotional regulation, empathy, and social skills. These components of emotional intelligence are crucial for leaders to connect with their teams on a deeper level and respond to their needs effectively.

Step 3. Practice Active Listening

Active listening is another critical element of empathetic leadership. Offer training sessions emphasizing the importance of giving full attention, understanding the speaker's message, and responding thoughtfully. Encourage leaders to hold regular one-on-one or team listening sessions without distractions, focusing solely on understanding employees' perspectives and concerns. When leaders actively listen, they show that they value their team members' voices and are open to their feedback and ideas.

Step 4. Encourage Vulnerability in Leadership

True empathy and compassion require vulnerability. Encourage senior leaders to share their experiences, challenges, and vulnerabilities in appropriate settings. This can help break down barriers and demystify the notion that leaders must always appear strong or infallible. Create a supportive environment where showing vulnerability strengthens and promotes greater connection and trust. When leaders are willing to be open and authentic, it encourages others to do the same, fostering a more connected and supportive workplace culture.

Step 5. Implement Compassionate Policies

Leadership practices are most effective when supported by policies that reflect the organization's values. Advocate for and implement work policies that consider employees' personal lives and challenges, such as flexible working hours, remote work options, and mental health days. Establish support systems like counseling services, mental health resources, and wellness programs that demonstrate a commitment to employees' well-being. Compassionate policies show that the organization values its people beyond their professional contributions.

Step 6. Lead by Example

Empathetic and compassionate leadership starts with daily interactions. Encourage leaders to practice empathy and compassion in their everyday dealings. Simple acts like asking about an employee's day, showing genuine interest in their lives, and providing support during tough times can have a profound impact. Include empathy and compassion as criteria in decision-making processes, encouraging leaders to consider the implications of their decisions on all stakeholders and to minimize negative consequences.

Step 7. Feedback and Continuous Improvement

Create mechanisms for employees to provide feedback on their leaders' performance, particularly regarding how empathetic and compassionate they are. This feedback is invaluable for helping leaders understand how they are perceived and where to improve. Encourage leaders to continually seek ways to enhance their empathetic and compassionate leadership through books, seminars, mentorships, and reflective practices. Continuous learning and self-awareness are vital to maintaining and growing these qualities.

Step 8. Recognize and Reward Empathetic Leadership

Develop programs that recognize and reward leaders who exemplify empathetic and compassionate leadership. Recognition rewards such behavior and sets a benchmark for others to follow. Include empathy and compassion as key criteria for leadership promotions. This sends a clear message about the organization's values and the traits it considers vital in its leaders. Recognizing and rewarding these behaviors creates a culture where empathy and compassion are valued and essential for leadership success.

Implementing these strategies can help your organization cultivate effective, empathetic, and compassionate leaders. Such leaders build stronger teams, inspire greater loyalty, and create a more inclusive and supportive workplace culture. Empathetic leadership is not just about understanding others' perspectives; it's about taking action to support and uplift those around you, creating a work environment where everyone feels valued and connected.

By embracing and implementing these strategies, we're not just tweaking business as usual—*we're reshaping it from the ground up.* This isn't just about hitting targets or meeting quotas; it's about shifting our approach to how we lead, work, and engage with the world around us. We're moving from a narrow focus on individual success to a much more expansive vision of prioritizing collective well-being and making a real difference.

When we step into this new way of being, our impact ripples out far beyond the walls of our organizations. We start building inclusive, collaborative, and sustainably driven environments. We become part of something bigger, a network that's actively contributing to the health of our communities and the planet. And it's not just good for the world—it's good for business, too.

This shift attracts people who are looking for more than just a paycheck. It brings in those who want their work to align with their values and care about equity, sustainability, and making a meaningful impact. It deepens the loyalty of customers and partners drawn to businesses that stand for something more than profit.

When we lead with empathy, inclusivity, and a commitment to the greater good, we set a new standard that others will be inspired to follow.

The transformation we're talking about here is more than just a strategy—*it's a call to action.* It asks us to keep learning, stay open, and challenge the old ways of doing things. It asks for courage to not just think differently but to act differently, boldly and intentionally.

And the rewards? They're not just in the form of business growth but in creating a legacy of positive impact that goes well beyond the bottom line.

This is just the beginning. We're laying the groundwork for a more conscious, purpose-driven approach to business and leadership. It's time to move from imagining a better future to actively creating it, using every tool, insight, and ounce of inspiration. The steps we take now to shift from 'me' to 'we' and to build a culture rooted in appreciation, empathy, sustainability, and inclusivity are the steps that lead us to a future where businesses aren't just successful—they're a force for good, strengthening our communities and helping to heal the planet.

Let's not just dream about what's possible; remember, we have the power to make it happen.

Inner Compass: Guiding Questions

This chapter invites you to explore the transformative power of expanding consciousness in business—from shifting from "me" to "we" to fostering collaboration, empathy, and sustainability within your organization. Use these guiding questions to reflect on how you can contribute to a collective vision that drives meaningful change.

- **How can you expand your leadership from "me" to "we"?** Reflect on how your current leadership approach might still be focused on individual success. How can you broaden your perspective to prioritize collective well-being and expand your leadership to serve the greater good?

- **What does a shared vision look like for your organization?** Consider the role of a shared vision in your business. How aligned are your team members with your organization's mission? What steps can you take to develop a clear, collective vision that everyone can contribute to and believe in?

- **How are you implementing collaborative decision-making?** Reflect on how decisions are made within your organization. Are there opportunities to include more voices in the process? What changes could you implement to ensure a more inclusive and collaborative decision-making structure?

- **How are you promoting diversity and inclusion in your workplace?** Consider the diversity of your team and the inclusivity of your leadership practices. Are all voices being heard and valued? What additional steps can you take to foster a culture actively promoting diversity and inclusion?

- **How are you practicing active listening in your leadership?** Reflect on your listening habits when engaging with your team or stakeholders. Do you listen to understand, or are you focused on responding? How can you practice active listening to build stronger connections and improve communication?

- **How can you invest more in community engagement?** Reflect on your organization's relationship with the community. Are you actively contributing to the well-being of the communities you serve? What initiatives can you take to invest more deeply in community engagement and create a positive impact?

- **How aligned are your business practices with sustainability?** Consider how your organization is adopting sustainable practices. Are there areas where you can be more intentional in reducing your environmental impact and fostering long-term sustainability?

- **How are you fostering a culture of appreciation and empathy?** Reflect on how you show appreciation for your team and lead with empathy. What steps can you take to create a culture where everyone feels valued and supported, leading with compassion in your leadership style?

6

From The Individual To The Collective

"Business can no longer be a bystander in a system that gives it life in the first place. We have to be a part of the solution." – **Paul Polman.**[1]

As we've discussed, this new era of business is not just about adjusting strategies to become more purpose-driven or responding to market demands; it's about fundamentally rethinking the role of leadership and business in society. It's about aligning with practices that widen the circle of our influence from individuals to the collective, to ensure sustainability, resilience, and a deeper connection to our collective humanity and the planet.

This chapter explores three foundational principles that define this shift and invite us to go beyond purpose to lead in alignment with the world around us:

1. Integrating Indigenous and Sacred Wisdom

The timeless practices of indigenous cultures and sacred traditions offer an abundance of wisdom. Often overlooked in the fast-paced corporate world, these cultures hold the keys to living in balance with the earth, community, and spirit. They possess an intrinsic understanding of the interconnectedness of all life and a profound respect for the planet—a perspective that's becoming increasingly critical as we face environmental, social, and economic crises.

Indigenous wisdom teaches us about stewardship, community-centric leadership, and long-term thinking—principles that can transform today's leadership styles and decision-making processes. Imagine if corporate leaders embraced the concept of making decisions for the benefit of the next seven generations, a principle found in many indigenous cultures. This long-term thinking naturally leads to more ethical, sustainable business practices that drive profit, uplift communities, and protect the planet.

Incorporating these values into modern business means creating organizational cultures that value collective well-being over short-term gains, balancing growth with stewardship, and fostering relationships built on reciprocity and respect. This section examines how integrating Indigenous and sacred wisdom can inspire leaders to make decisions that encourage business to thrive economically while promoting social justice and environmental sustainability.

2. Learning from Nature

A natural progression from indigenous wisdom bring us to our relationship with the natural world. Nature has long been a teacher, offering unmatched balance, regeneration, and interconnectedness strategies. Natural systems thrive through cycles of growth, decay, and renewal. We will explore these in greater detail because nature's principles are more than mere inspiration—they are critical frameworks for how businesses can thrive in the future.

In nature, everything has a purpose, and nothing is wasted. Every part of an ecosystem contributes to the health of the whole, and this is where businesses have the most to learn. Moving beyond sustainability to regeneration means adopting practices that don't just maintain the status quo but actively contribute to the restoration and renewal of ecosystems and communities.

Nature's cycles show us how to operate in ways that sustain life and enhance it, making regeneration a fundamental principle for businesses to adopt in the face of today's environmental and social challenges.

Why does this matter more than ever now?

The systemic challenges we face require solutions that mirror nature's inherent ability to adapt, thrive, and regenerate. Sustainable practices may have been enough in the past, but the scale and urgency of these issues now demand more. Nature shows us that diversity leads to resilience, and businesses must mirror this by embracing diversity in thought, people, and operations to stay agile and innovative.

It's time to move beyond simply reducing harm and instead design business models that restore and replenish the ecosystems they affect, creating value for shareholders and the world.

The lessons nature teaches us—interdependence, adaptability, and resilience—are precisely what businesses need to navigate today's complexities. Just as ecosystems rely on diverse species to maintain balance, companies can learn that fostering diversity within their teams and supply chains is not just beneficial—it's essential for long-term survival.

Companies can also mimic nature's circular processes by creating supply chains that eliminate waste, close resource loops, and contribute positively to the communities they engage with. This shift requires businesses to operate more like ecosystems, where collaboration and interconnection lead to greater strength and resilience. It's a power move from *'power over'* to *'power with'*.

By learning from nature, businesses can adopt a regenerative mindset that helps them survive and thrive—building adaptive, resilient systems designed for long-term impact. In this next stage of business evolution, it's not just about reacting to environmental pressures; it's about proactively creating systems that regenerate the natural and social environments damaged by us.

It's not enough to create sustainability; we must restore the damage we have done. In this way, businesses can ensure they're not just sustaining themselves but actively contributing to the well-being of the planet and future generations.

3. Becoming a Conscious Citizen

In today's world, so many of us are naturally shifting toward thoughts about the collective and what it means to be human and alive in the world today. In our search for meaning and purpose in our lives, we are open to the possibility that our lives can have a bigger impact than we originally thought. We know we have a purpose, a sacred calling to be, and do so much more to contribute to a better future, and we're doing our best to understand the challenges we're facing.

We now know how the required changes must extend beyond our inner journeys to shift outwards in our lives, shaping our actions, decisions, and interactions. Our work to align ourselves with higher levels of consciousness is vital; our inner journey defines us. However, actual change only happens when we apply that inner work to the outer world. This is where leadership begins to ripple out, creating an impact that moves beyond ourselves to benefit our communities, businesses, and society as a whole.

To do this, we introduce *the Five-Step Continuum*, a framework that helps leaders translate their inner transformation into actionable steps. Moving through these five stages, we can lead with greater purpose, building businesses that balance profit with purpose, care, and contribution. This continuum serves as a guide for leading consciously, allowing us to create more cohesive, purpose-driven teams and organizations.

The *Five-Step Continuum* encourages collective well-being. Each step elevates consciousness and invites us to expand our impact in ways aligned with our deepest values. Whether you're redefining your business success, fostering stronger relationships, or contributing to a greater cause, this continuum will guide you toward actions that resonate on a higher level and serve your individual growth and the greater good.

Throughout this chapter, we consider how these guiding principles are already shaping the practices of forward-thinking leaders around the globe. By integrating purpose and blending ancient wisdom with modern insights, leaders are finding new pathways to success, ensuring longevity and profitability while contributing to a more equitable, sustainable, and flourishing world.

As we navigate these principles, it becomes clear that this shift toward a new era of business isn't just a passing trend—it's a profound evolution already in motion. Leaders who embrace these principles are pioneering the charge, demonstrating that purpose is not one-dimensional and that integrating Indigenous wisdom, learning from nature, and building resonant relationships are viable and essential for thriving in today's complex and interconnected world.

It's time to reflect on our role in this transformational movement. *How can we lead more consciously, create financially successful businesses, and enrich the planet and all its inhabitants?* The answers lie in embracing resonance, leading with purpose, and aligning our strategies with the collective well-being of people and the earth.

These principles are not just theoretical—they come from deep wells of wisdom that have guided humanity for generations. As we look ahead, we must also look back, drawing from the profound insights of those who have lived in harmony with the earth for centuries. But first, let's begin with purpose.

The Power of Purpose

In today's rapidly evolving business landscape, purpose has become a pivotal force, driving innovation, employee engagement, and customer loyalty. But we're not talking about surface-level, purpose-driven branding.

Genuine purpose is more than a marketing message—it's embedded into the very fabric of an organization's daily operations, shaping its culture, influencing decision-making processes, and creating systems that allow every employee to thrive. When purpose is deeply integrated into the organizational culture, it's not just a label; it becomes a lived experience that guides how organizations engage with their employees, customers, and broader communities.

To embody purpose and walk the talk requires more than public declarations or campaigns—it means creating an empowering environment where employees feel encouraged to bring their whole selves to work. This kind of culture fosters openness and trust, where giving and receiving feedback, being heard, and feeling supported are foundational elements.

In this way, employees feel safe to make mistakes, learn from them, and grow in their roles. In such settings, every role and job function is aligned with the company's mission and goals, which enables individuals to see where they belong, the value they add and how their contributions directly support the broader purpose. This, in turn, fuels motivation, innovation, and long-term commitment.

Purpose-driven companies are no longer outliers—they are becoming mainstream, catalyzed by consumers and employees demanding more from businesses. People want meaning and vote with their money, choosing to support companies that align with their values. What started as a small movement years ago has gained tremendous momentum, catching many leaders off guard when they initially didn't realize this shift's positive impact on profitability.

At first, purpose-driven business was seen as an idealistic trend, a *'nice-to-have.'* It was thought that a company could not be purpose-driven and profitable. It was considered a choice, but today we have overwhelming evidence that proves the opposite is true. We now know it's not only the future of business—it's essential for survival in a rapidly changing marketplace.

Consumers are increasingly drawn to brands that stand for something beyond profits. They want companies to contribute positively to society or the environment and are willing to pay a premium for brands they trust. Data shows that purpose-driven companies outperform their competitors on multiple fronts, including financial performance.

According to a 2020 study by Deloitte, purpose-oriented companies had 30% higher levels of innovation and 40% higher levels of workforce retention than their peers.[2] Another study by Cone/Porter Novelli found that 78% of Americans believe companies must do more than make money—they must also positively impact society.[3] These numbers illustrate that purpose isn't just good for people and the planet but also for business.

We're entering an era of *'purpose-driven profits'*, which are becoming the new standard. It's not just about maximizing financial returns; it's about balancing profitability with making a meaningful difference in the world.

Purpose is defined not by shareholders alone but by the people who work for and buy from these companies—employees, customers, and the communities they serve. This is a profound shift in the marketplace. Companies aligning with this new reality will thrive; those clinging to old models risk being left behind.

The Impact of Purpose on Business

The integration of a clear, altruistic purpose within an organization significantly elevates its potential by:

- **Fueling Innovation**: When a common purpose unites employees, it creates a sense of shared mission that inspires them to think outside the box. Knowing the 'why' behind their work drives them to find new, creative solutions that further the organizational mission.

- **Boosting Engagement**: A shared sense of purpose transforms a job from a set of tasks into something more meaningful. When employees see how their work contributes to a larger vision, they become deeply engaged and invested in the company's success.

- **Enhancing Loyalty**: Customers are increasingly drawn to brands that stand for something bigger than profits. When companies practice what they preach—making genuine efforts to contribute positively to society or the environment—they cultivate deep loyalty. This goes beyond transactional relationships; it fosters a connection rooted in shared values.

To illustrate the diversity and impact of purpose in today's business world, here are five purpose statements from companies across different industries. These examples demonstrate a genuine commitment to embodying purpose in every aspect of their operation:

- **Airbnb**: "To create a world where anyone can belong anywhere, providing healthy travel that is local, authentic, diverse, inclusive, and sustainable."

- **LinkedIn**: "To connect the world's professionals to make them more productive and successful and to transform the way companies hire, market, and sell."

- **Lego**: "To inspire and develop the builders of tomorrow, fostering creativity and learning through play."

- **Salesforce**: "To empower companies to connect with their customers in a whole new way, leveraging our technology for social good."

- **IKEA**: "To create a better everyday life for many people, making sustainable, high-quality home furnishings accessible to as many people as possible."

These statements are not mere aspirations; they reflect how these companies weave their purpose into every layer of their structure and culture. By doing so, these organizations ensure that their purpose-driven brand isn't just a facade but a genuine representation of their operations, strategies, and the daily experiences of their employees and customers. This alignment between purpose and practice fosters environments where innovation flourishes, employee engagement deepens, and customer loyalty endures.

Integrating a clear and altruistic purpose into an organization's operational and cultural fabric is not simply an aspirational trend—it's a growing reality in today's business world. More companies are awakening to the fact that customers increasingly demand authenticity, responsibility, and a commitment to societal and environmental well-being.

Purpose has shifted from being a *'nice-to-have'* to becoming a critical pillar of future business success. This shift is driven by a collective consumer consciousness that values the quality and price of products and services and the ethos and impact of the companies behind them.

Purpose becomes a key differentiator in this landscape—a beacon that attracts loyal customers and passionate employees, creating a virtuous cycle of engagement, innovation, and growth. The movement towards purpose-driven business is gaining momentum, underscoring that the future of business success is inextricably linked to an organization's meaningful contributions to the world. Embracing this reality is beneficial—it's essential for companies aiming to thrive in tomorrow's competitive, ever-evolving marketplace.

Future-Proofing Your Business with Purpose

Purpose is here to stay, and as this shift gains momentum, there will be winners and losers. Companies that fail to adapt will find themselves at a disadvantage, while those that integrate purpose into their core will thrive. Purpose-driven businesses not only future-proof themselves but also create a lasting, positive impact on the world.

This isn't just about doing what's profitable—it's about doing what's right. And in today's world, the two are more connected than ever. By aligning your business with a clear purpose, you can ensure long-term success while contributing to a more just, sustainable, and meaningful future.

Purpose is also a natural emergence of regenerative leadership. Just as regenerative leaders seek to restore and rejuvenate the systems their businesses impact—social, environmental, and economic—purpose-driven organizations align with a higher mission that transcends profits.

Purpose is the guiding force, directing businesses to operate with integrity, consider long-term impacts, and create value that benefits everyone, not just a few. When purpose is integrated into regenerative leadership, businesses naturally thrive because they foster environments where people are inspired, connected, and working towards a common goal that serves humanity and the planet. This alignment between purpose and regenerative leadership is the key to business resilience and the foundation for a future where businesses are potent agents of positive change.

The message is clear: if you want to future-proof your business, align with purpose now—for all the right reasons. Not only is it the ethical choice, but it's also the path to long-term profitability. Purpose-driven profits are the future, and those who embrace this shift will lead the way forward.

Purpose is a guiding force and a gateway to deeper alignment with the natural world and collective well-being. As businesses shift from profit-centric models to purpose-driven missions, we are invited to broaden our understanding of leadership and impact.

This is where ancient wisdom becomes invaluable. Indigenous cultures and sacred traditions offer insights into sustainability, interconnectedness, and balance that modern business practices often overlook. They remind us that regenerative leadership and purpose are not abstract ideals—they are grounded in real, lived experiences of harmony with nature and respect for all life.

Before we explore the profound lessons these traditions offer business, I want to share a recent experience from the Amazon Rainforest that reshaped my perspective on life, leadership, and purpose.

Integrating Indigenous and Sacred Wisdom into Modern Business

In October 2023, I had the incredible privilege of traveling to Ecuador with the Pachamama Alliance. There, I was immersed in the heart of the Amazon jungle, living alongside the Achuar and Sapara peoples. This experience shifted something fundamental in me—my relationship with life itself. It unveiled a stark contrast between our fast-paced, disjointed world and the profound simplicity of life deeply rooted in the natural world.

The jungle was alive in ways that were almost overwhelming. The air buzzed with energy—the calls of monkeys, the hum of insects, the vibrant songs of birds. Everywhere I looked, life was flourishing. It was unlike any forest I had ever known, teeming with life, diversity, and an unspoken harmony.

But what struck me most wasn't just the physical abundance of life; it was the spirit that infused everything. The Achuar and Sapara people see the world in a way that most of us in the modern world have forgotten. They understand that every living thing has a spirit, that we are not separate from the world but part of it, woven into the same fabric. They live this truth daily, moving through their world with reverence and respect, taking only what is needed and giving thanks in return. It's a life lived in balance, deeply connected to the earth, each other, and themselves.

I remember standing in the jungle one morning, surrounded by the lush, green canopy, and feeling something I had never felt before—a sense of safety and belonging, not just to the place or the people, but to life itself. It wasn't based on anything material. It was a spiritual bond, a recognition that I was part of something much bigger than myself. For the first time in my life, I felt genuinely connected—not only to the earth but also to my soul. The forest was alive, overflowing with life, and I felt myself as a part of the world for the first time.

The Achuar and Sapara live with an acute awareness of the interconnectedness of all life. They know, without needing to be told, that everything we do creates ripples in the world around us. Though simple by modern standards, their lives are rich with knowledge and wisdom. They understand that life is sacred and that understanding shapes everything they do—how they walk through the forest, care for their families, and treat the land. It's a beautiful and wise way of living, reminding me that the quality of our lives is defined by the relationships we cultivate—with ourselves, our communities, and the earth.

But as beautiful as it was, this way of life is threatened. The relentless march of modernity—driven by our insatiable hunger for resources—is encroaching on their world, just as it has everywhere else. I listened as the people spoke about how the Ecuadorian government is pushing to build more roads through the forest, which will inevitably lead to the destruction of the ecosystem they depend on. They asked for help to protect the forest and to keep their way of life alive. It was heartbreaking to hear of the continued destruction that has already forced many tribes deeper into the jungle. The Elders are fighting to preserve their wisdom, but the allure of the cities tempts the younger generations, and the ancient ways are slipping away.

When I returned to the modern world, the contrast hit me harder than I ever anticipated. Flying back into Pujo on a small jungle plane, I looked out at the endless expanse of concrete replacing the green canopy of trees, and I felt tears well up in my eyes. Stepping off the plane, I was confronted with gray, lifeless, and suffocating concrete everywhere. The vibrant symphony of the jungle was gone, replaced by the harsh sounds of modern life.

It made me question everything—*why do we, as humans, believe this is a better way to live? Why do we isolate ourselves in concrete boxes, disconnected from the earth and each other? How did we stray so far from our natural roots?*

This journey was a wake-up call for me.

It reminded me that we have forgotten something essential about who we are. We've convinced ourselves that we have dominion over the natural world, but now, we are paying the price for that hubris. This experience in the Amazon reminded me that it's time to remember our origins, to reconnect with the sacredness of life—for all our sakes.

I learned in the Amazon that we are all interconnected, part of a delicate web of life stretching to its breaking point. We can no longer afford to stand by and watch. As leaders, as businesses—powerful forces in the world—we must become part of the solution. The wisdom of the indigenous cultures I met is invaluable, offering us a roadmap for living and working in harmony with the earth. They know what we are only beginning to realize: that life itself is sacred and that our survival depends on remembering this truth.

It's time for us to listen. We have much to learn from these cultures, the earth, and each other. But to learn, we must be willing to open our minds, see the world differently, and build a future that honors both the planet and its inhabitants.

As we move forward, let this journey be our guiding light—a reminder of the delicate balance we must strive for between progress and preservation, between our ambitions and the needs of our planet. We are all in this together. The future of business, humanity, and the Earth depends on our choices today.

And yes, that *'we'* includes you.

Personal Reflections

My time in the Amazon left me with a deep well of personal reflections, shaping how I now view life, business, and my role as a Sacred Changemaker. I want to share some of these reflections with you, hoping they resonate and inspire you to reflect on your path.

- **It's not about what you have or don't have.** The things you buy and the possessions you collect won't define who you are or who you're becoming. Who you are is something that comes from within. It's the interior journey that shapes you, not the external world.

- **Fear creates resistance, but surrender creates flow.** We often resist life out of fear, but in surrender, we begin to flow and resonate with the world around us.

- **The journey won't change you**—it's your purpose and your choices that do. How I respond to what is triggered inside me and the truth that resonates with my soul will determine whether I come home to myself. It's all in how I choose to engage with life.

- **"Be humble** *as though you can't afford to buy a crust of bread when, in fact, you own the whole bakery."* I came across this quote from Kris Jenner on the plane to Ecuador, which struck me deeply. It's about humility, holding success lightly, and always staying grounded.[4]

- **The power of presence.** I can't honestly remember or understand anything if I don't first remember myself—my presence in body, mind, emotion, and spirit. This is where my energy, my life force, lies.

- **The four sacred gifts:** The power to forgive the unforgivable, the power of unity, the power of healing, and the power of hope. These are the energies that sustain life.

- **We are never without light.** Light is the source of all things, even when we feel enveloped by darkness.

- **I once believed teachers were awakened beings with credibility and experience,** but I've realized that we are all interconnected. We all have access to the same knowledge and the same wisdom. The path to wisdom is like a mirror, reflecting the different parts of ourselves we meet along the way. We have more wisdom within that we know. We can be our own teachers.

- **The balance of masculine and feminine.** Women are the river; men are the banks. Together, they create the flow of life. Both are needed in harmony for the river to thrive.

- **More life happens at the edges.** In nature, biodiversity flourishes where two ecosystems meet. The same is true for us—when we approach the edges of our comfort zones, we create more energy and life force.

- **Everything is medicine.** Every interaction and experience is an opportunity for healing. How can I become good medicine for others, helping to heal their disconnection from the divine, from nature, and themselves?

- **What we eat affects how we connect.** Genetically modified food severs our natural connection to the universe's guidance. Eating fresh, natural foods, especially those from our local environment, helps our bodies adapt to the changes we need to make to thrive. Nature send us important wisdom through our food. As one wise Elder asked me, *"If you don't eat from where you live, how can the Earth speak to you and tell you what it needs?"*.

- **Intuition is nature speaking to our body.** What lives within us? Naked ambition? Greed? The will to make a difference? The universe itself? Likely, all of these. Our task is to listen deeply and choose wisely.

- **Living in harmony with creation means listening to all energies.** To be in resonance with the world, we must learn to respect and work with all the energies around us. It requires seeing beyond physical reality and connecting with the unseen world within and around us.

- **Guardians of the earth.** If we are to protect the planet, we need more people who truly "own" themselves—people who understand their rights, responsibilities, and the power they hold as guardians of nature.

- **Darkness is an illusion.** It only serves to amplify the light.

- **Neutrality of the forest.** There is a spirit in nature that lies beyond judgment, a presence that connects us all. It reminds me of Rumi's words: "Out beyond the field of right and wrong, there is a field. I will meet you there."

- **Prayer is about relationships.** It's not just about asking for help but about creating a relationship with the sacred, cultivating resonance with the divine, and offering gratitude for what we have received.

- **The single note of a bird in the jungle** struck me as one of the most beautiful sounds I've ever heard. This bird sings just one clear, proud note among all the noise and melodic birdsong. It's a reminder that we each have our unique song to sing, and we must sing it boldly.

- **Fierce protection of life means using my body as an instrument.** When I align with nature, my body naturally knows what needs to be done and finds the strength to do it.

- **We must be like water.** Water touches and changes everything it encounters. What if we flowed through life the same way?

- **We are interdependent, not independent.** Energy flows between us, and that energy needs to circulate freely for life to thrive. Relationships are at the core of who we are. Individualism is an illusion.

- **The extinction of life on Earth continues even in plain view of those with the most resources.** We've become hyper-individualistic, and the imbalance in power, particularly among traumatized men in leadership, continues to harm us all.

- **Consciousness is continually expanding.** We are constantly invited to elevate our awareness and nourish life through spiritual practice, presence, and prayer.

- **Generosity and invitation.** How can I make myself an invitation for the well-being of all life? How can I be generous in every aspect of my life? What is the invitation my life is standing for?

- **Sacred moments elevate our reality.** In these moments, we are lifted to higher frequencies, where possibilities beyond the ordinary exist—where we can truly hear, heal, understand, and forgive.

- **How do we activate the sacred potential within each of us?** To move from energy consumers to producers, we must integrate all parts of ourselves into a unified whole, resonating with clear intention.

- **Energy management is a collective effort.** It's not just about individual energy but about how we, as communities, circulate and elevate the energy around us.

- **Conviction happens when all parts of ourselves resonate.** When our energy aligns into a singular, clear vibration, we move forward with purpose and intention.

- **Don't wait until you're dead to emerge from the darkness.** The universe is full of beauty and wonder, and we are meant to see it while we are here on Earth.

- **I don't want to invest in a way of life that is ending.** What if my life were not just an invitation but a prayer? A melody that inspires others to sing and dance with joy? A Sacred Invitation to elevate our way of life?

- **Our purpose as humans is to serve the well-being of all life.** It's why we're here. I aim to help us all live in resonance with ourselves, each other, and the Earth.

I hope that something in these reflections resonates with you, encouraging you to pause, reflect, and deepen your own experience of life and work.

Reflecting on the profound lessons from my journey and the depth of connection I felt with the earth and its people, one thing becomes clear: we cannot separate ourselves from the wisdom that has guided humanity for thousands of years. In our quest for progress, we often overlook the essential truths that remind us of our interconnectedness, our responsibility to the planet, and our role as stewards of life.

Now more than ever, as businesses face unprecedented challenges, it's time to turn to the ancient wisdom that has always been with us. The question is...

What does Indigenous Wisdom have to offer modern business?

In short, a LOT.

Today's business world is increasingly defined by rapid change and complexity. Yet, the timeless wisdom of indigenous cultures and sacred traditions offers profound insights into how we can navigate these turbulent times. Rooted in millennia of lived experience and a deep connection to the natural world, indigenous wisdom teaches us about harmony, balance, and the interconnectedness of all life. These principles, often overlooked in today's fast-paced corporate environment, hold the key to transforming businesses into forces for good—economically viable, environmentally sustainable, and socially equitable.

Although I could write an entire book on this topic alone *(and maybe I will in the future)*, I want to highlight a few threads of understanding that can inspire you to dive deeper:

- **Community and Connection:** At the heart of Indigenous cultures is the understanding that individual well-being is intimately connected to the health and prosperity of the community. In these cultures, no one thrives in isolation—the well-being of the whole is what measures success. Modern businesses can draw from this insight by fostering a culture prioritizing collaboration, mutual support, and a sense of belonging among employees, stakeholders, and the broader society. When companies nurture this communal spirit, it enhances employee engagement and satisfaction and strengthens the social fabric that holds everything together. This solid foundation creates sustainable business growth based on profit, meaningful relationships, and shared purpose.

- **Stewardship of the Earth:** Indigenous wisdom reminds us that we are not separate from nature but an integral part of it. This profound respect for the earth guides their principle of stewardship, where the natural world is seen as a source of life, not merely a resource to exploit. Businesses that embrace this principle adopt sustainable practices that protect and regenerate the environment, from reducing waste and carbon footprints to supporting biodiversity and ecosystem health. By honoring this relationship with the earth, businesses ensure their long-term viability and actively contribute to the well-being of society and the planet.

- **Long-term Thinking:** One of the most striking differences between indigenous perspectives and modern business practices is the timescale. In contrast to the short-term focus so prevalent in today's business world, indigenous cultures advocate for long-term thinking, where decisions are made with future generations in mind. This fosters a sense of responsibility and foresight that many businesses today desperately need. When leaders think beyond quarterly profits and consider the long-term impact of their actions, they create more resilient organizations capable of navigating sustainability challenges while building a lasting legacy for future generations.

Many businesses already incorporate these sacred principles into their operations, and the results are remarkable. For example, a company that integrates community values into its model might implement profit-sharing schemes or support local initiatives that benefit the community. Similarly, businesses embracing stewardship principles might ethically source materials, reduce their environmental footprint, and contribute to conservation efforts. Long-term thinking manifests in investments in renewable energy, sustainable innovations, or programs that develop future leaders and employees.

By weaving the rich tapestry of indigenous and sacred wisdom into the fabric of modern business practices, we can create business models that achieve financial success and align deeply with ecological balance and social justice. This integration is a pathway for businesses ready to lead in this new era—championing a model of commerce that honors the past, thrives in the present, and safeguards the future.

Isn't this the natural, human-centric way of doing business we long for?

This brings us seamlessly to another invaluable teacher: *nature itself.*

Learning from Nature: Embracing the Wisdom of Living Systems

With its intricate tapestry of life, the natural world has operated on principles that have ensured survival and flourishing for millennia. These principles—balance, regeneration, interconnectedness, growth, decay, and renewal cycles—are a masterclass in resilience and sustainability.

As we look to nature for inspiration, we uncover a blueprint for building businesses that are not merely sustainable but regenerative—businesses that contribute to the health of the ecosystems and communities they touch rather than depleting them. For companies that want to survive and thrive, nature's lessons provide profound insights into creating resilient, adaptable, and regenerative business models.

At the heart of this is adopting a living systems mindset. To fully harness nature's wisdom, businesses must see themselves not as isolated entities but as interconnected parts of a much larger ecosystem. This shift in perspective—simple yet revolutionary—fosters an understanding of how organizations can thrive in harmony with the natural world rather than in opposition to it.

In nature, everything is part of a cycle. Nothing is wasted; what one organism discards, another uses for nourishment. This closed-loop system ensures that resources circulate, supporting growth, regeneration, and balance. In the same way, businesses can adopt models where waste is minimized, outputs from one process become inputs for another, and the cycle of resources is seamlessly integrated into every facet of operation.

This kind of holistic thinking shifts the mindset from businesses as independent, competitive entities to businesses as integral players within an interconnected ecosystem. When we embrace this approach, we move toward the kind of resilience and adaptability that nature has demonstrated for billions of years.

Every organism in nature contributes to the larger ecosystem through the cyclical use of resources. Nothing is wasted. This principle ensures the sustainability and balance of ecosystems and is a critical lesson for businesses looking to reduce their environmental impact and boost economic efficiency.

By designing business processes where waste is minimized, and the output from one stage feeds the next, companies can create closed-loop systems—just like nature. It's a model of efficiency that reduces waste and fosters innovation and economic growth through more intelligent use of resources.

For example, manufacturing companies that recycle materials back into production or food businesses that repurpose organic waste into compost or bioenergy are all tapping into this regeneration cycle. They embody nature's circular wisdom, turning potential waste into value while minimizing environmental impact.

However, adopting nature's principles requires more than operational adjustments—it demands a fundamental shift in how business leadership thinks about systems. To truly thrive, today's leaders must embrace a living systems mindset, understanding that their organizations—like all living things—exist within a web of interconnections. The health and success of the business are inseparable from the well-being of the environment, communities, and stakeholders it interacts with.

Why Leadership Needs a Living Systems Mindset

In today's complex and interconnected world, adopting a living systems mindset is no longer just about ecological responsibility—it's a strategic imperative. Nature offers us powerful metaphors and models for operating in a world of constant change and increasing complexity.

Let's look at how human physiology offers profound lessons for organizational adaptability and resilience.

- **Neural Networks: Enhancing Interconnections.** In the human brain, neural networks enhance learning and decision-making by creating complex interconnections. Similarly, businesses can thrive by increasing connectivity—within their teams, across departments, and with external stakeholders. The more connected a company is, the better it can process information, innovate, and solve problems efficiently. Just as the brain strengthens with use, an organization becomes more adaptable, innovative, and resilient when it fosters meaningful connections and exchanges of information.

- **Endocrine Feedback Loops: Responsive Adaptation.** The endocrine system in our bodies uses feedback loops to maintain balance and adjust functions in response to external and internal changes. Establishing effective feedback mechanisms is essential for businesses to remain adaptive. Continuous feedback allows companies to fine-tune their processes and strategies based on performance and market shifts, ensuring they stay aligned with long-term goals while remaining responsive to immediate needs. It's about dynamically adjusting to maintain balance and progress—just like the body does.

- **Immunologic Memory and Innovation: Learning from Experience.** The immune system's ability to remember pathogens and adapt to new ones teaches us the importance of learning from experience and applying that knowledge across an organization. Similarly, businesses must continually evolve by learning from past challenges and integrating those lessons into future strategies. This 'memory' allows organizations to innovate, embrace new ideas, and stay resilient. Like the immune system, businesses must maintain a clear sense of their core identity while allowing for necessary adaptations that strengthen the whole.

- **Cellular Turnover: Embracing Change.** Just as cells in the body are constantly rejuvenated and replaced, businesses must embrace ongoing transformation. Stagnation is the enemy of growth, and the most resilient organizations regularly review and update their practices, products, and strategies. This commitment to renewal—whether it's through fostering innovation, adopting new technologies, or responding to evolving customer needs—keeps businesses relevant and vibrant, just like nature's constant cycles of renewal and regeneration.

- **Cellular Communication: Effective Messaging.** Communication between cells is essential for health and survival in living organisms. The same is true in business. Clear, effective communication within and between the company and its external stakeholders is crucial for success. Leaders must foster a culture where information flows freely, ensuring that every part of the organization stays connected, engaged, and aligned with the larger mission. Effective communication keeps the organization healthy, agile, and able to adapt to environmental changes.

These natural metaphors show that businesses, like living organisms, must be adaptable, connected, and in constant dialogue with their environment to thrive. A living systems mindset encourages companies to embrace change, foster innovation, and operate with a long-term perspective, all while maintaining a deep respect for the natural world and the people they serve. This gives us a pathway to sustainable success.

Adopting a living systems mindset isn't just an ecological necessity; it's a pathway to long-term, sustainable success. By understanding and integrating these biological principles into business practices, leaders can unlock new levels of adaptability and resilience. Aligning with nature's processes strengthens the organization's foundation and offers a strategic advantage in an ever-evolving world. Businesses that operate as living systems—dynamic, interconnected, and adaptive—are better positioned to thrive amidst uncertainty.

As we begin to recognize the profound benefits of this mindset, it becomes clear how interconnected these concepts are with broader strategies derived from nature. Enhanced interconnections, responsive adaptation, and continuous learning—rooted in natural systems like neural networks and immunologic responses—become the building blocks for businesses that survive and excel. These organic strategies, emphasizing cooperation, resilience through diversity, and sustainable growth cycles, offer invaluable wisdom for companies seeking to lead in a rapidly changing environment.

This transition requires a shift in internal culture and external operations, translating these biological insights into practical, scalable strategies.

Nature shows us how to do it.

Nature's genius lies in its ability to regenerate, adapt, and thrive over millennia. It has mastered survival through strategies prioritizing cooperation, interconnectedness, and resilience. For businesses, this offers a powerful template.

One of the core principles is cooperation over competition—nature shows us that collaboration often leads to greater survival rates and thriving ecosystems. For businesses, this means shifting from cutthroat competition to a model that values partnership, teamwork, and shared resources to achieve mutual benefits:

- **The Power of Cooperation and Collaboration:** In the natural world, symbiotic relationships are everywhere—different species benefit from each other's existence in ways that ensure survival. Consider the mutual relationship between trees and fungi, where nutrients are exchanged through a vast underground network that benefits both. Businesses can draw inspiration from this interconnectedness by forming strategic partnerships that leverage diverse strengths and resources. For example, technology firms might collaborate with environmental organizations to create sustainable innovations, or companies might forge alliances with competitors to enter new markets or develop breakthrough technologies. This isn't just about altruism; cooperation creates more robust and resilient organizations primed for long-term success.

- **Leveraging Diversity for Resilience:** Nature thrives on biodiversity. The more diverse an ecosystem, the more resilient it is to change. In business, diversity in people, ideas, and approaches functions similarly—it builds adaptability and strengthens the organization's ability to weather external pressures. When businesses foster diverse teams and encourage different perspectives, they unleash creativity and innovation. Diverse ideas can lead to novel solutions, making the company more agile and better equipped to respond to shifting market conditions. This diversity should be visible in workforce demographics and reflected in how problems are approached and solved, driving the company's ability to evolve.

- **Harnessing Human Dynamics, Power from the Source:** Businesses, like ecosystems, rely on the energy and contributions of every individual. Just as ecosystems maintain vitality through the balance of all elements, a business thrives when each employee feels empowered to contribute their full potential. Leaders who embrace this human dynamic—who recognize the intrinsic power and energy within their teams—are better equipped to cultivate innovation and growth. By fostering a culture of empowerment and creativity, leaders can harness the collective intelligence of their workforce, turning that energy into a driving force for progress.

- **Networked Power for Resilience and Sustainability:** Just as ecosystems depend on vast networks of interconnections, businesses thrive when they build strong internal and external networks. These networks share information, resources, and capabilities, enhancing resilience. When businesses are well-networked, they can quickly adapt to external changes, leveraging partnerships, knowledge-sharing, and collaboration to stay agile. It's a principle seen in nature repeatedly: resilience comes from connection, not isolation.

- **Self-Regulating Systems and Interconnectedness in Business:** In nature, ecosystems are self-regulating. Feedback loops constantly monitor changes and adjust to maintain balance. Businesses can learn from this by creating internal mechanisms that continuously assess and adapt their environmental and social impact. By embedding feedback processes that monitor sustainability metrics, organizations can ensure they're reactive and proactive, making adjustments supporting long-term viability. This self-regulation ensures that the business continually evolves in response to internal and external shifts.

This principle of interconnectedness—where every action influences the whole—reminds us that businesses, like natural systems, must consider their broader impact. Every decision, from sourcing materials to product disposal, ripples outward. Adopting sustainable practices at every stage of the business lifecycle aligns the organization with nature's wisdom, creating a more balanced and thriving operation.

By integrating these principles, businesses can move toward models like the circular economy, where waste is virtually eliminated. Products are designed for reuse, recycling, or safe reintegration into the environment, drastically reducing environmental impact. This shift enhances sustainability and opens new avenues for innovation and cost-saving. Renewable energy sources, like solar or wind, mirror nature's regenerative capabilities, allowing businesses to tap into an endless supply of clean energy while decreasing dependence on finite resources.

Internally, fostering a culture of collaboration and cooperation creates the fertile ground for innovation and resilience. Externally, building diverse teams and cultivating partnerships across industries ensures that businesses can navigate challenges and seize new opportunities. It's not just about surviving change but thriving because of it.

By looking to nature's wisdom, businesses can create models that are not only economically successful but ecologically harmonious. This approach—where waste becomes a resource, abundance flows naturally, and cooperation fuels growth—is the future of sustainable business. It's about building systems that thrive, not by dominating their environment, but by integrating with it.

As we move forward, adopting these principles becomes critical for developing business models where life flourishes for all—*human, ecological, and economic.*

As we have seen, nature operates remarkably efficiently, maximizing energy use while ensuring nothing is wasted. Every organism, system, and process in the natural world contributes to the cycle of life, using just enough energy to thrive without depleting resources. This principle of optimized energy use offers a powerful lesson for businesses, reminding us that there is often untapped potential lying dormant within organizations, waiting to be unleashed.

Just as nature harnesses its energy to sustain growth and renewal, organizations must find ways to unlock the potential energy within their people, converting it into meaningful action.

We can see this journey as a continuum, from focusing solely on *'Me'* to embracing the collective *'We.'*

Next, I want to share a five-step journey that reflects an elevation in consciousness—a path where individual success is no longer the end goal but a gateway to collective impact and global well-being. To thrive in this new era, businesses and leaders must first become who they need to be—fully aligned in mind, heart, and spirit—to create the change they wish to see in the world.

From Me to We in Action

As we've explored, the inner journey of transformation is essential for leaders and changemakers to align with higher levels of consciousness. The shift from *'Me'* to *'We'* requires deep self-awareness, healing of old narratives, and resonance with new ways of thinking and being. This journey begins within each of us, shaping the way we lead, make decisions, and interact with the world.

The Resonance Codes revealed how, as we evolve in consciousness, our thoughts, behaviors, and decisions naturally align with a broader, more inclusive view of success. But how do we apply this inner work to create practical change in business and leadership?

This is where the five-step continuum offers a pathway for leaders and businesses to operate with greater consciousness and purpose, moving beyond personal interests toward collective impact. Each step represents an opportunity to elevate our engagement with others, from trust-building to contributing to something greater than ourselves.

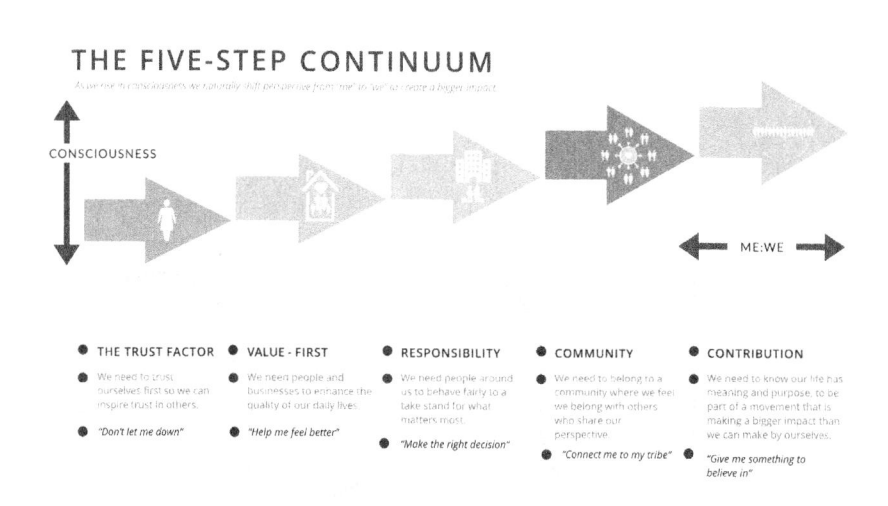

THE FIVE-STEP CONTINUUM

- **THE TRUST FACTOR**
  - We need to trust ourselves first so we can inspire trust in others.
  - *"Don't let me down"*

- **VALUE - FIRST**
  - We need people and businesses to enhance the quality of our daily lives.
  - *"Help me feel better"*

- **RESPONSIBILITY**
  - We need people around us to behave fairly to take stand for what matters most.
  - *"Make the right decision"*

- **COMMUNITY**
  - We need to belong to a community where we feel we belong with others who share our perspective.
  - *"Connect me to my tribe"*

- **CONTRIBUTION**
  - We need to know our life has meaning and purpose, to be part of a movement that is making a bigger impact than we can make by ourselves.
  - *"Give me something to believe in"*

The Five-Step Continuum: As we rise in consciousness we naturally shift perspective from "me" to "we" and in doing so create a bigger impact

Step 1: The Trust Factor

At the beginning of any relationship—personal or professional—people think, *"Don't let me down."* This reflects the most basic but essential human need: trust. Trust forms the foundation for any meaningful connection. Without it, relationships can't grow or thrive. In business, customers want to know they can rely on you to deliver on your promises.

You can't inspire trust in others unless you trust yourself first, underscoring the need for doing your own inner work. We must first align our actions with our values, ensuring we show up authentically. This requires integrity, transparency, and consistent follow-through. Trust is fragile—once broken, it's difficult to rebuild—so cultivating inner integrity and personal resonance is critical for long-term relationships with others in our lives and customers, as well as employees in our work.

Step 2: Value-First

Once trust is established, we ask, *"Help me feel better."* This step moves beyond basic needs into the realm of value creation. Businesses that understand this focus on delivering experiences that resonate with customers help them overcome their challenges, and improve their well-being. This could mean reducing stress, solving problems, or simply creating moments of joy.

The key to success for leaders is creating environments where people feel valued and empowered. However, this requires inner awareness—leaders must first feel fulfilled within themselves to consistently provide value to others. The inner journey fosters this awareness and empathy, allowing us as leaders to connect with people on a deeper level, both personally and professionally.

Step 3: Responsibility

As relationships deepen, our expectation shifts to *"Make the right decisions."* This is about personal responsibility that goes beyond individual actions—it's about taking accountability for the broader impact of those actions. In business, this step asks leaders to consider profit, people, and the planet. It's a call for holistic and ethical decision-making that serves all stakeholders, not just the financial responsibility to shareholders.

This step reflects an elevated level of consciousness, where leaders operate from an integrated perspective—balancing short-term needs with long-term sustainability. Leaders who embody this step understand that their choices shape the future and take responsibility for creating outcomes that benefit society as a whole.

Step 4: Community

Once trust, value, and responsibility are established, people seek deeper connections, asking, *"Connect me to my tribe."* At this stage, both personal and professional relationships become about belonging. In business, this means creating inclusive cultures where employees and customers feel part of something larger than themselves.

True community emerges when people connect with other like-minded people and feel seen, valued, and understood. Leaders must cultivate environments where collaboration and connection can flourish. As individuals and organizations align with higher resonance levels, they naturally attract communities that reflect shared values and support collective growth. The inner work of belonging—first feeling connected within—allows leaders to foster meaningful connections outwardly in the community.

Step 5: Contribution

At the highest level of the continuum, the focus becomes, *"Give me something to believe in."* This is where the search for purpose and meaning takes center stage. Once people feel secure, valued, and connected, they naturally want to contribute to something greater than themselves.

This step is about aligning with purpose-driven missions and becoming a force for good, whether advocating for social justice, environmental sustainability, or community well-being. Leaders at this level inspire others to contribute their talents and energy to shared goals that positively impact the world. Everyone benefits.

True fulfillment comes from knowing that our lives and actions make a difference. This sense of contribution reflects the highest level of resonance, where individuals and businesses operate from a place of alignment, purpose, and service to the collective in unity consciousness.

This five-step continuum reflects the expansion of consciousness required to move from *'Me'* to *'We.'* As we progress along this path, we raise our self-awareness and align our actions with a sense of purpose and connection. We recognize that personal growth and leadership are intertwined—as we evolve individually, we naturally create a ripple effect that inspires collective change.

This evolution invites us all, particularly businesses and leaders, to redefine success—moving beyond personal or financial gain toward collective well-being and long-term sustainability. It's a shift from working solely for individual achievement to embracing a broader role—one where we act in service to the greater good. This journey calls for purpose-driven impact: balancing profit with contribution, responsibility, and care for all stakeholders.

At its core, this shift reflects the essence of a Sacred Changemaker—someone who integrates inner transformation with outer action, leads with authenticity, and is aligned with a higher mission. By becoming more self-aware, we expand our role and influence, allowing us to step into leadership that transforms not just our individual businesses but extends outwards into the community and society. We live with the understanding that what we do matters and that we are constantly having an impact, whether intentional or not.

The question is, *are we having the impact we want to have?*

In the next section, we'll explore *regenerative leadership* and dive deeper into the mindset, values, and practices that define this path. This journey is about creating external change and becoming who we need to be—leaders and changemakers capable of weaving purpose, resonance, and consciousness into everything we do.

Inner Compass: Guiding Questions

In this chapter, you've explored the deep connection between purpose, indigenous wisdom, and what we can learn from nature. These guiding questions invite you to reflect on how purpose fuels your business, the role of sacred wisdom in your leadership, and how your place on the conscious continuum shapes your impact. Use them to further align your leadership with the vision of creating meaningful change and a future rooted in sustainability and trust.

- **How clear is your sense of purpose in your leadership and business?** Reflect on how well your leadership and business are aligned with a larger sense of purpose. What does your purpose mean, and how does it shape your day-to-day actions?

- **What impact does your purpose have on your business decisions?** Consider how purpose influences your choices and strategy. Are there areas where your purpose isn't fully integrated? How can you embed purpose into your business operations to ensure long-term success?

- **How are you future-proofing your business with purpose?** Reflect on whether your business is prepared for future challenges by aligning with a mission beyond profit. What actions can you take to ensure your business thrives while contributing positively to society and the environment?

- **What can you learn from indigenous and sacred wisdom to inform your leadership?** Consider the principles of interconnectedness, respect for life, and balance found in indigenous and sacred wisdom traditions. How can you integrate these values into your leadership style and business practices?

- **How can you apply the wisdom of living systems to your organization?** Consider nature's lessons about collaboration, balance, and regeneration. How can these insights shape your business, fostering resilience and sustainability in your operations and leadership approach?

- **Why is it important for leadership to adopt a living system mindset?** Reflect on how a living system mindset that embraces complexity, adaptability, and interdependence can enhance your leadership. How can shifting to this mindset create more coherence and resonance within your team and organization?

- **How can you expand your impact from 'me' to 'we'?** As you explore the continuum from personal to collective well-being, consider how your individual growth and actions contribute to the greater good. What steps can you take to move from self-centered focus to collaboration?

- **How can you embody collective well-being in your leadership and actions?** Think about expanding your leadership to benefit your organization or business, the broader community, and the planet. What shifts can you make to prioritize collective well-being in your decisions?

Part 3
REIMAGINING BUSINESS - A Force For Good

7
Transformational Business Models

"The best way to predict the future is to create it" – Peter Drucker.[1]

As the business world undergoes a profound transformation, we can see how success is no longer measured solely by financial gain. Today, businesses are being recognized for the positive contributions they make to society and the planet. Consumers seek more than just products and services—they want to support companies that embody responsible practices, align with their values, and actively contribute to the common good.

This shift represents a redefinition of business success, where the integration of profitability and social impact is desirable and necessary for long-term relevance and growth.

Innovative business models seamlessly combining profit with purpose have become essential for organizations wishing to thrive. Companies that embrace this approach are positioning themselves as leaders in a new era—one that demands more than financial success and places a strong emphasis on social responsibility and environmental stewardship.

In this chapter, we explore three powerful business models that challenge traditional operating models and offer new opportunities for companies to make a meaningful impact.

From social enterprises that reinvest their profits into community projects to B Corporations that balance purpose with profit to the Buy-One-Give-One model that turns every transaction into a charitable act, these frameworks demonstrate how businesses can drive positive change.

By weaving together practical insights, theory, and compelling case studies, we will uncover how these transformational business models can reshape a company's bottom line and its role in the world. This will prove that profitability and purpose can coexist and even enhance one another.

One of the most accessible and compelling ways to blend purpose with profit is through the Buy-One-Give-One *(B1G1)* model. This approach has become widely recognized for its simplicity and profound impact, allowing businesses to integrate philanthropy into their daily operations seamlessly.

The premise is straightforward: for every product sold, the company donates a similar product—or a portion of profits—to those in need. This model helps address pressing social challenges and resonates deeply with consumers, who appreciate the transparency and the direct, tangible impact of their purchases.

1. Buy-One-Give-One (B1G1) Model

At its heart, the B1G1 model is a simple yet transformative business practice. By connecting every customer transaction with a direct act of giving, businesses invite their customers into a shared mission of creating positive change. This model speaks to the human desire for meaning and purpose, where purchases express care and compassion for others. This approach is especially effective for small businesses and solopreneurs, offering a clear, transferable benefit that customers can instantly relate to and value.

Example: TOMS Shoes

TOMS Shoes is a pioneering example of how the B1G1 model can redefine what it means to succeed in business. With a mission to improve lives through commerce, TOMS took the simple act of buying a pair of shoes and turned it into a powerful catalyst for social change. Initially, for every pair of shoes purchased, TOMS donated a pair to a child in need. This addressed an immediate need and created a ripple effect—providing children with the shoes they needed to attend school, stay healthy, and seize new opportunities for their future.

As TOMS grew, so did its vision. It expanded its giving to include eyewear, restoring sight to individuals through surgeries, prescription glasses, and medical treatment. Later, it added clean water initiatives, recognizing the profound impact that access to safe water has on health, education, and economic development. TOMS demonstrated how the B1G1 model could evolve, scale, and adapt to address the community's most critical needs worldwide.

The genius of TOMS' model lies not just in its generosity but also in its ability to meaningfully engage customers. Consumers could see the direct impact of their purchases, making them active participants in the company's mission. This sense of shared purpose fueled both sales and brand loyalty, positioning TOMS as a leader in the movement toward businesses that do good while doing well.

In conclusion, the B1G1 model offers a powerful pathway for businesses looking to integrate social good into their core operations. By actively allowing customers to participate in the company's mission, businesses can foster deeper connections, build loyalty, and stand out in an increasingly crowded marketplace. Whether you're a small business owner or a solopreneur, the B1G1 model provides a scalable and adaptable framework for driving commercial success and meaningful impact, proving that even the smallest businesses can be a force for global change.

To further amplify the impact of the B1G1 model, we're proud to announce our partnership with **B1G1**. This not-for-profit organization empowers small businesses to make a significant difference through micro-giving. B1G1 makes it incredibly easy for companies of any size to embed meaningful giving into their everyday operations by aligning each act of giving with the ***United Nations Sustainable Development Goals (SDGs)***. Using simple technology, you can embed your contributions onto your website, communicating transparently to your customers.

It's a simple yet powerful way to ensure that your business creates positive ripples worldwide. We've partnered with B1G1 at **Sacred Changemakers** because we believe that we can drive transformative change together.[2]

2. B-Corporations

B Corporations *(or B-Corps)* are at the forefront of a global movement redefining the role of business in shaping a more sustainable and inclusive world. B-Corps are held to high social and environmental performance standards, transparency, and accountability, as defined by **B-Lab**, the nonprofit that certifies these businesses. To become a B-Corp, companies comprehensively assess their impact on workers, customers, the community, and the environment. What sets B-Corps apart is their legal commitment to balance profit and purpose, ensuring that their business decisions benefit a broad range of stakeholders, not just shareholders.

The benefits of running a B-Corp go beyond just certification. B-Corps is part of a vibrant and growing global community that offers access to a wealth of resources, conferences, and peer support networks. These resources help businesses continually improve their impact and scale their social and environmental efforts. Being a B-Corp is not just about certification; it's about becoming part of a movement that connects purpose-driven businesses, empowering them to make a meaningful difference in the world.

Example: Patagonia

Patagonia, a trailblazer in environmental responsibility, exemplifies the power of the B-Corp movement. As a certified B-Corporation, Patagonia has built its brand around its mission: *"We're in business to save our home planet."* From using organic cotton and recycled materials in its products to taking a stand against overconsumption with campaigns like *"Don't Buy This Jacket,"* Patagonia consistently proves that a company can achieve financial success while deeply committed to environmental activism and sustainability.

One of Patagonia's critical contributions as a B-Corp is its relentless transparency. It provides detailed insights into its supply chain and labor practices, ensuring fair labor conditions while advocating for improvements across the industry. Patagonia also dedicates a significant portion of its resources to environmental causes, donating millions to grassroots conservation efforts. Its status as a B-Corp amplifies its leadership in the industry and pushes other companies to rethink their business practices.

Patagonia is not alone—hundreds of other businesses are joining the B-Corp movement, leveraging the certification to demonstrate their commitment to building a more equitable and sustainable economy. B-Corps represents a broad spectrum of industries and businesses, from technology startups to established retail giants. For companies considering the journey, the B-Corp community offers extensive guidance through the certification process, making aligning business success with social good easier.

Why B Corp?

Becoming a B-Corp is more than a badge; it's a declaration of intent—a public commitment to doing business in a way that benefits all. Businesses that become B-Corps differentiate themselves in the market, attracting customers, employees, and investors drawn to purposeful leadership. B-Corp certification also offers a robust framework for continuous improvement, encouraging businesses to assess and improve their social and environmental impact over time.

We encourage you to explore the B-Corp movement and see if it resonates with your business values. It's a powerful way to ensure that your company is profitable and a force for good in the world; whether a small startup or an established company, the tools and resources available through B-Lab and the B-Corp community will support you on this transformative journey.

To learn more, visit **bcorporation.net**[3] and consider if this powerful movement could fit your business, driving purpose and profit hand-in-hand toward a better future.

If the B-Corp movement inspires you and you want to dive deeper into its potential for your business, I invite you to listen to a special episode of the **Sacred Changemakers Podcast** titled *"To B Or Not To B – Is B-Corp The Future Of Your Business?"* featuring **Tim Jones**, also known as *"That B-Corp Bloke."*[4] In our conversation, Tim, the CEO and Founder of Grow Good, shares his deeply personal journey from corporate disillusionment to leading a global consulting firm dedicated to helping businesses become B-Corp certified. He unpacks the rigorous certification process, highlights its benefits and challenges, and offers invaluable advice for anyone considering this transformative path.

Together, we explore how businesses can not only balance purpose and profit but thrive by aligning with the B-Corp ethos. Tim's insights are filled with wisdom, practical steps, and a heartfelt call to action for any leader seeking to make a meaningful impact. This is a must-listen for changemakers ready to step into a new way of doing business.

3. Social Enterprises

Let's explore another emerging business model integrating financial success with meaningful social impact—**Social Enterprises**. These businesses are built on the foundation of creating positive change, with societal and environmental objectives woven into the very fabric of their operations.

For social enterprises, the mission is not an afterthought; it's the driving force that shapes every decision, every strategy, and every product they bring to market. By reinvesting a significant portion of their profits back into addressing pressing social issues—whether it's improving community well-being, enhancing education, or safeguarding our planet—social enterprises offer a powerful blueprint for businesses that want to contribute to societal welfare while remaining competitive.

Example: Thank You Group

A shining example of a social enterprise in action is the **Thank You Group**, an Australian-based company with a bold vision to end extreme poverty. The Thank You Group offers a range of consumer goods such as water, food, and body care items, but what sets them apart is their commitment to donating 100% of their profits to life-changing global projects. Their model is simple and impactful: with each purchase, consumers directly contribute to essential initiatives, such as providing clean drinking water, health services, and education in impoverished communities worldwide.

What makes the Thank You Group so compelling is the scale of its mission and how it turns everyday consumers into active participants in a global movement. By choosing their products, customers are no longer passive buyers—they're empowered changemakers contributing to a larger purpose. This deepens the connection between the brand and its customers, creating loyalty built on shared values.

The Thank You Group's success serves as an inspiring testament to the viability of the social enterprise model. They've shown that businesses don't have to sacrifice profitability for impact—on the contrary, social enterprises can thrive by aligning their operations with the values of today's increasingly conscious consumers. By proving that social impact and financial success can go hand in hand, they challenge conventional business norms and encourage others to rethink what's possible.

In essence, social enterprises like the Thank You Group are redefining what it means to be successful in business. They demonstrate that a company's honest value can be measured not just by financial performance but by its lasting, positive impact on the world. As more consumers, employees, and investors seek to align their choices with their values, the demand for businesses like these continues to grow, pushing the boundaries of what it means to do good through business.

If this resonates with you, I encourage you to explore the growing world of social enterprises and discover how this model could align with your vision for creating lasting change.

Let's now explore how we can redefine giving and trust within the modern landscape of business and philanthropy.

Redefining Giving and Trust

Traditionally, giving has been synonymous with charity, a term that often carries both admiration and skepticism. The digital age has amplified this association, with charities typically seen as the ultimate representation of giving. However, this view has become increasingly polarized, especially after scandals or mismanagement that shake public confidence. These events often cast a shadow over the entire nonprofit sector, causing widespread doubt about the integrity of charitable efforts.

Interestingly, when similar breaches of trust occur in the business world—through corporate fraud or financial mismanagement—the blame tends to focus on individuals rather than the industry as a whole. This stark contrast in public perception creates a curious dichotomy:

charities are often held to an unrealistic operating standard without significant administrative costs, while businesses are expected to invest heavily in growth, marketing, and innovation. This double standard limits the potential impact of charitable organizations and underestimates their contribution to societal well-being.

Charities do far more than provide aid; they offer people the profound experience of being part of something larger than themselves, contributing directly to the betterment of society. In this sense, the value charities deliver is not dissimilar to that of businesses. Yet, while businesses have traditionally focused solely on generating profit, many are now embracing socially conscious goals, moving towards the triple bottom line: people, planet, and profit. This shift demonstrates how the lines between charity and business are becoming blurred, with both sectors increasingly overlapping in their objectives and operations.

Social business is a potent hybrid model championed by Nobel laureate Professor Muhammad Yunus that bridges this gap. Social businesses operate intending to solve social problems while maintaining profitability and reinvesting their earnings to further their mission. This model proves that financial viability and social impact are not mutually exclusive; they complement each other, creating a sustainable pathway to positive societal change.

Effective giving in today's world transcends the limitations of traditional charity. It requires a more strategic, long-term investment approach akin to how businesses build sustainability and growth. By adopting business-like efficiency, charities can magnify their impact, while companies inspired by the charity sector can integrate a mission of social good at their core. This hybrid approach fosters a more holistic view of how we can improve the world.

Companies like **Warby Parker** and **Whole Foods** are leading this charge by embedding social missions directly into their business models, much like innovative charitable organizations such as **Charity Water** and **Kiva** are redefining what charitable impact looks like. This evolving paradigm shows us that the lines between profit-making and philanthropy are not rigid but fluid, inviting a new era where purpose and profit coexist harmoniously.

As we dive deeper into the potential of blending business efficiency with charitable intentions, it becomes clear that implementing these ideas requires a practical, grounded approach.

The next section will explore concrete methods and innovative tools to help you implement these concepts. Whether refining an existing business or launching a new initiative, this section will offer essential steps to build a business model that drives profit while amplifying social impact.

Get ready to operationalize these insights into sustainable, purpose-driven projects that resonate with your growing vision for this new era.

Community as the Way Forward

In a world that often prioritizes individual achievement and competition, the power of community is becoming increasingly evident. While individual effort is valuable, the most significant and lasting change happens collectively.

As leaders, entrepreneurs, and changemakers, we are being called to embrace a new way forward—one that recognizes the profound impact of collaboration and peer support. Community is more than a network; it's a shared space where people come together to create a more significant impact than anyone could achieve alone.

In our work as Sacred Changemakers, the challenges we face—*social, environmental, and systemic*—are too vast for any single individual or organization to tackle on their own. To truly inspire change for good, we must move beyond the limits of individualism and embrace the strength that comes from working together.

This shift toward community is a practical solution and a profoundly spiritual one. It acknowledges that we are all interconnected, and our actions ripple out to affect the collective whole.

When we unite around a shared vision, we create movements that have the power to transform the world. Whether you're leading a company, a nonprofit, or a grassroots initiative, the key to sustainable change lies in building strong, resilient communities where people feel connected, supported, and empowered to contribute their unique gifts.

Collaboration is the foundation of a thriving community. When we work together, we leverage our collective wisdom, talents, and resources, making us far more effective than we would be as individuals. The same holds true for peer support. It's not enough to gather people together; we must also foster environments of mutual care where everyone feels valued, heard, and empowered to contribute.

In leadership, collaboration means moving away from top-down decision-making and embracing shared leadership models where all voices are respected and diverse perspectives are celebrated. It means recognizing that each person brings something valuable to the table and that we are stronger when we work together toward a common goal.

This collaborative approach strengthens both innovation and resilience within organizations and movements, as it ensures that solutions are more inclusive, creative, and adaptable.

Peer support, on the other hand, is about creating networks where people can learn from and uplift each other. In many ways, it's the antidote to the isolation that so many leaders feel. Sacred Changemakers know that the journey of transformation can be challenging.

Still, it becomes lighter when we can lean on a community of like-minded individuals who are walking a similar path. In these spaces of support, we can share our struggles, celebrate our wins, and receive guidance from those who understand the journey.

How to Build Movements and Strengthen Community Connections

Building a movement isn't about amassing followers—it's about creating a shared vision that resonates deeply with people and inspires them to take action. It starts with a clear purpose that aligns with the community's values and needs. Movements that thrive are those that invite participation, creating a sense of ownership for everyone involved.

Here are critical steps to building and strengthening community connections:

1. **Create a Compelling Vision:** People are drawn to a cause when they see a clear and inspiring vision of what's possible. Your vision should reflect not just your own goals but the hopes and dreams of the broader community. It should speak to the collective desire for a better world and invite others to join you in creating it.

2. **Foster Meaningful Relationships:** At the heart of every strong community is a network of genuine relationships. Take time to get to know the people in your community on a personal level. This goes beyond transactional interactions—build trust by being present, showing empathy, and offering support when it's needed.

3. **Encourage Participation:** Movements succeed when people feel like they are part of something larger than themselves. Encourage active participation by creating opportunities for people to contribute in ways that align with their strengths and passions. Whether it's through events, volunteer efforts, or online engagement, give people a way to feel connected to the cause.

4. **Provide Resources and Support:** For any movement or community to thrive, its members need resources and support to help them along the way. This could mean offering educational content, organizing peer mentorship opportunities, or simply creating spaces where people can exchange ideas and learn from each other. Empower your community with the tools they need

to succeed.

5. **Celebrate Collective Wins:** Acknowledge and celebrate the progress of the community as a whole. Whether big or small, each achievement represents a step forward toward the collective vision. These celebrations reinforce a sense of shared purpose and keep the momentum going.

The path forward is clear: community is the way. Through collaboration, shared purpose, and peer support, we will build movements capable of transforming the world.

As Sacred Changemakers, we are not meant to walk this path alone. By coming together, we multiply our impact, strengthen our resolve, and ensure that the change we seek is lasting, meaningful, and aligned with the highest good for all.

But community alone is not enough. To truly create sustainable change, we must also ensure that our business models reflect these values. It's not just about connecting with others; it's about reshaping the way we do business to balance purpose and profit.

This is where conscious business models come into play—offering a path to integrate our mission for a better world with the practicalities of economic success. By building businesses that prioritize both financial health and societal impact, we can lead the way forward, ensuring that purpose-driven organizations not only survive but thrive.

Conscious Business Models: Balancing Purpose and Profit

The evolution towards conscious business models represents a significant shift in the corporate world, where the pursuit of profit becomes harmoniously integrated with the mission to make a meaningful impact on society and the environment. This approach enriches the company's value proposition and resonates deeply with consumers, employees, and stakeholders who are increasingly looking for businesses that contribute positively to the world.

This shift signals a departure from traditional business practices, spotlighting companies that have ingeniously embedded social and environmental consciousness into their operations.

Here, we want to share some examples of businesses embodying this shift, inspiring how value can extend beyond financial gain to foster societal and environmental well-being. Below are real-life examples of companies embodying this balance, demonstrating that it is possible to thrive economically while being a force for good.

1. Etsy: A global online marketplace for handmade and vintage items, Etsy champions small businesses and craftspeople worldwide. It operates under a B Corp certification, emphasizing its commitment to social responsibility, environmental practices, and transparency. Etsy's platform supports thousands of independent creators and promotes a more sustainable and human-centered approach to commerce.

2. Seventh Generation: As a leading producer of eco-friendly household products, Seventh Generation bases its business model on the principle of sustainability. By prioritizing products made from plant-based ingredients and advocating for chemical safety laws, the company demonstrates that environmental responsibility can go hand-in-hand with profitability.

3. Greyston Bakery: Renowned for its open hiring policy, Greyston Bakery offers jobs to anyone willing to work, regardless of their background or work history. This innovative approach produces delicious baked goods and addresses unemployment and social exclusion issues. By prioritizing community well-being alongside its business operations, Greyston is a compelling example of how companies can contribute positively to society while remaining profitable.

4. Who Gives A Crap: Selling environmentally friendly toilet paper, Who Gives A Crap donates 50% of its profits to build toilets and improve sanitation in the developing world. Their business model is a prime example of how products we use daily can be transformed into vehicles for change, proving that businesses can be both profitable and a force for global betterment.

5. Bombas: Driven by a mission to address homelessness, Bombas sells high-quality socks and apparel, adopting a one-for-one giving model similar to TOMS Shoes. For each item purchased, Bombas donates an item to someone affected by homelessness, integrating product quality with a reliable commitment to social impact.

6. Allbirds: As a footwear company, Allbirds integrates sustainability into every aspect of its product design and supply chain, using natural materials to create comfortable shoes. Beyond its product, Allbirds invests in regenerative agricultural practices and projects to reduce its carbon footprint, embodying how businesses can innovate towards sustainability and profitability simultaneously.

These companies beautifully illustrate that integrating purpose with profit is feasible and increasingly offers a competitive advantage in today's market. They demonstrate that the journey towards a conscious business model is as varied as it is impactful, offering unique pathways for companies to contribute to a more equitable and sustainable world.

As businesses, large and small, embrace this paradigm, they pave the way for their own success and the prosperity of the communities and environments they touch. This shift towards purpose-driven business models reiterates the fundamental truth that success in the modern era is not solely measured by financial returns but by the positive legacy a company leaves behind.

Creating a Regenerative Business

The concept of a regenerative business goes beyond the traditional approach to sustainability as this is no longer enough. We need to adopt a proactive approach to business that contributes positively to the renewal of environmental and social systems. This section explores how you can embed regenerative practices into the core of your business operations, ensuring that your enterprise acts as a catalyst for proper regeneration.

Principles of Regenerative Business

1. **Holistic Thinking:** Start with adopting a holistic approach to your business processes. Recognize that all business components are interconnected with the broader ecological and social systems. This perspective will help you identify and implement practices that benefit your business, the environment, and the community.

2. **Resource Renewal:** Focus on creating systems that replenish and enhance the resources they use. For instance, if your business relies on natural resources, invest in technologies or practices that restore these resources at a rate faster than they are consumed. This might mean supporting reforestation, engaging in sustainable sourcing practices, or investing in renewable energy sources.

3. **Waste Reduction and Upcycling:** Aim to minimize waste in all forms and find innovative ways to repurpose or upcycle waste products. This can be achieved through designing products with their end-of-life in mind, promoting circular economy principles within your industry, or partnering with other businesses to utilize each other's waste products creatively and effectively.

Implementing Regenerative Practices

1. **Community Engagement:** Actively involve the community in your regenerative efforts. This can be done by supporting local initiatives, providing education and resources, or creating

employment opportunities that contribute to regional economic resilience.

2. **Building Resilience:** Equip your business and its surrounding community to withstand environmental and economic challenges. This involves not only preparing for potential disruptions but also building systems that are flexible and adaptable to change.

3. **Innovative Collaboration:** Seek partnerships with organizations, nonprofits, and businesses aligning with your regenerative goals. Collaborative efforts can amplify your impact, pooling resources and knowledge to tackle more significant systemic issues more effectively.

Measuring Impact

1. **Develop Impact Metrics:** Establish clear metrics to measure the effectiveness of your regenerative practices. This could include tracking improvements in resource efficiency, waste reduction, community well-being enhancements, and other environmental and social impact indicators.

2. **Regular Reporting:** Commit to transparency by regularly reporting on these metrics. Share your successes and challenges with stakeholders, inviting feedback and fostering a culture of continuous improvement.

3. **Adapt and Innovate:** Use the insights gained from these measurements to refine your approaches continually. Innovation should be at the heart of your regenerative practices, ensuring your business remains responsive to new information and changing conditions.

Creating a regenerative business is one of the most profound ways to ensure your legacy has a lasting, positive impact on the world. By integrating these principles into your business model, you contribute to our planet's sustainability and set a standard for ethical and impactful business practices. This journey towards regeneration is not just about what you leave behind; it's about setting a pathway for future generations to build upon, ensuring that the legacy of innovation, responsibility, and regeneration continues to flourish.

Scaling with Integrity: Conscious Expansion in Business

Growth, universally pursued by businesses as a hallmark of success, often carries an unspoken implication: to expand continuously is to thrive, while to remain static is to falter. Over my almost 30-year career as a leadership consultant, I have heard this repeated so many times in boardrooms across the world: *"If we're not growing, we're not static; we're falling behind our competitors."* And although there is some truth in that statement, it comes at a high cost.

This relentless pursuit of growth, deeply ingrained in the fabric of modern business practices, is seldom questioned, reflecting an unconscious bias towards expansion as the only path forward. This unchecked growth comes with significant costs, not only to the businesses themselves but also to society and the environment at large.

The essence of how growth is pursued can profoundly impact a business's future, determining its legacy as either a force for positive change or a contributor to ongoing societal and environmental challenges.

Scaling with integrity challenges this conventional narrative, proposing a more conscious approach to growth that keeps sight of the core values and mission that initially define a business.

By integrating principles of ethical operation, social responsibility, and environmental stewardship into the scaling process, businesses can ensure their expansion contributes positively to the world. It represents a nuanced balance, recognizing when growth enhances the company's mission and when it merely serves as an unsustainable *(and maybe even dangerous)* pursuit of more. This approach questions the endemic belief that continuous expansion is synonymous with success, highlighting the dangers of a growth-at-all-costs mentality.

The relentless drive for growth without reflection or restraint is increasingly recognized as unsustainable. It contributes to the depletion of natural resources, exacerbates social inequalities, and pushes our planet to its environmental limits.

This unexamined expectation—that a company must constantly grow to be successful—overlooks the possibility of sustainable success through thoughtful, mission-aligned expansion. The real challenge comes back to redefining success not by the sheer scale of a business but by its ability to make a meaningful, positive impact.

In a world where the consequences of unchecked growth are becoming ever more apparent, from climate change to widespread social disparities, the call for a shift in business paradigms grows louder. Scaling with integrity invites businesses to grow in ways that enrich rather than dilute their contributions to society.

It encourages us all to cultivate a deep awareness of the impact of our growth strategies and make conscious choices that align with a sustainable vision for the future. This approach ensures the long-term viability of the business and supports the well-being of our communities and the health of our planet.

Here are some of the common mistakes I've seen business leaders make when scaling solutions with conscious intention and integrity:

Mistake #1: Sacrificing Quality for Quantity

- **Solution**: Maintain rigorous standards for product and service quality, even as production increases. Implement scalable quality control processes that grow with your business, ensuring your commitment to excellence remains uncompromised.

Mistake #2: Overlooking Environmental Impact

- **Solution**: As you scale, integrate sustainable practices into every level of operation. From sourcing materials to waste management, ensure that your growth strategy includes clear environmental guidelines that align with your mission.

Mistake #3: Neglecting Company Culture

- **Solution**: Preserve your company culture by embedding your core values into hiring, onboarding, and employee development programs. As your team grows, foster a sense of community and shared purpose that reflects your business's original ethos.

Mistake #4: Compromising on Social Responsibility

- **Solution**: Keep social responsibility at the forefront of your scaling strategy. This might involve expanding your social impact programs in proportion to your growth, ensuring that as your business benefits, so does the community.

Mistake #5: Diluting Mission Focus

- **Solution**: Regularly revisit and reaffirm your mission statement. Ensure that all new ventures, products, or market expansions align with your overarching goals. Use your mission as a guiding star for decision-making at all levels.

Mistake #6: Disregarding Ethical Supply Chains

- **Solution**: Commit to transparency and ethics in your supply chain. As you scale, vet suppliers and partners for their labor practices, environmental impact, and business ethics to ensure alignment with your values.

Mistake #7: Prioritizing Short-term Gains Over Long-term Vision

- **Solution**: Develop a long-term strategic plan that balances immediate business needs with your mission and vision for the future. Make decisions that support sustainable growth, even if they require a greater initial investment or a longer timeframe to see returns.

Mistake #8: Losing Personal Connection with Customers

- **Solution**: Implement systems and practices that maintain a close relationship with your customers even as your business grows. Personalized communication, feedback loops, and community engagement initiatives can strengthen this connection.

Scaling with integrity requires mindfulness, dedication, and a willingness sometimes to make the hard choice over the easy gain. It's a nuanced balance between growing and recognizing when enough is enough, ensuring that success does not come at the expense of the company's foundational ethics.

By avoiding these common pitfalls and adhering to solutions grounded in conscious intention and integrity, businesses can grow in a manner that advances their economic interests and upholds their commitment to positively impacting the world. This more balanced approach to scaling ensures that success is measured by the company's size and the depth of its contributions to society and the environment.

Of course, when we implement change, we want it to be a positive force for good. I don't believe any of us set out to do intentional harm. Unfortunately, we now know that our current business practices are not always turning out to be the force for good we might have wished.

The good news is that we can and will do better.

Now, we have explored business's vital role in driving meaningful and sustainable change across society. We have highlighted the necessity of evolving business practices to ensure both survival and profitability and generate positive social and environmental outcomes.

This chapter encourages all as business leaders, to act as catalysts for positive change, advocating for a paradigm shift in which companies adapt to changing landscapes and actively contribute to crafting a future where humanity and the planet can thrive. By offering practical guidance and inspiring examples, I hope you feel inspired to spearhead your changemaking movement, ensuring wherever your business inspires change it does so for the greater good.

Tools and Strategies: How to Map Your Business Ecosystem

Integrating transformational business models, whether through social enterprises, B Corporations, or the Buy-One-Give-One *(B1G1)* approach, requires more than just a noble mission. It demands planning, strategic execution, and long-term commitment.

Below, I've outlined practical tools and strategies to help you embed these models effectively and sustainably within your business operations, ensuring your impact is profound and scalable.

1. **Define Your Core Mission and Impact Goals**
   Tool: Impact Mapping
   Start by clearly defining your company's social or environmental mission. Use impact mapping to outline specific goals, strategies to achieve them, and metrics to measure your progress. This roadmap will help you stay aligned with your mission and communicate your purpose more effectively.
   Example: *For a B1G1 model, you might determine whether you're donating a product, service, or a percentage of profits and how each transaction will directly impact individuals or communities.*

2. **Assess and Align Business Operations**
   Strategy: Sustainability Audits
   Conduct a sustainability audit to evaluate your current operations, supply chain management, production processes, and labor practices. The goal is to identify areas where you can better align business practices with your mission and impact objectives.
   Example: *A social enterprise might adjust its production methods to maximize financial returns and social benefits, ensuring that every aspect of the business supports the mission.*

3. **Engage StakeholdersTool**
   Stakeholder Engagement Workshops
   Building authentic relationships with stakeholders—*employees, customers, suppliers, and community members*—is essential to long-term success. Use stakeholder engagement workshops to gather input, build support, and ensure everyone involved understands and contributes to the business's mission.
   Example: B-Corporations thrive on transparency, where clear communication about impact goals creates better connections and trust among all parties involved.

4. **Legal Structure and Certification**
   Strategy: Legal Re-structuring
   If you're pursuing B-Corp certification or launching a social enterprise, you may need to restructure your business legally. This might include altering corporate governance structures to reflect accountability standards that align with your social mission.
   Example: Engage with legal experts specializing in corporate responsibility to ensure your business structure aligns with your goals and is legally compliant.

5. **Measure and Report Impact**
   Tool: Impact Reporting Software
   Regularly measuring and reporting your social and environmental impact is vital to building stakeholder trust and transparency. Using specialized software to track your progress ensures that your initiatives deliver the intended results.
   Example: Whether you're running a social enterprise or a B1G1 business, transparent reporting on the number of donations, individuals helped, or environmental impact creates accountability and builds credibility.

6. **Marketing and Consumer Engagement**
   Strategy: Storytelling and Impact Communication
   Storytelling is a powerful tool to communicate your impact and mission to consumers. Make your marketing about more than just the product; share the stories behind your social mission and the lives being changed because of their purchases.

Example: For a B1G1 business, create content that connects consumers with the tangible impact they make through their purchases, sharing stories of individuals or communities directly benefiting.

7. **Build a Supportive NetworkTool**
   Partnerships and Collaborations
   Form strategic partnerships with organizations or businesses that can amplify your social impact. Collaboration with like-minded entities can expand your mission's reach and create a more meaningful impact.
   Example: Social enterprises can partner with local NGOs to facilitate ground operations or with other businesses to co-create products that support their mission.

8. **Scale ResponsiblyStrategy**
   Scalable Impact Models
   As your business grows, ensure your social impact scales with it. This requires thoughtful planning to maintain your mission's integrity while reaching more people or addressing larger problems.
   Example: A B1G1 company might scale by diversifying its product offerings or expanding its geographical footprint to create more impact without sacrificing quality.

By applying these tools and strategies, businesses can effectively integrate and sustain transformational models over time. These practices serve the company's mission and create a brand that resonates deeply with consumers, fosters loyalty, and stands out in a crowded market. Transformational business models drive real-world impact while ensuring long-term financial success—a powerful combination that defines the future of business.

Navigating Challenges: Techniques for Managing Business Fatigue

As businesses undergo systemic changes, addressing the inevitable business fatigue that can arise from continuous adaptation and the pressure to remain proactive is essential. Managing this fatigue and staying ahead of change requires a comprehensive strategy that builds resilience within the organization's structure and people.

Here, we explore the often-overlooked practical advice and techniques that enable leaders and their teams to maintain momentum and effectively navigate the complexities of transformation.

Creating Supportive Environments

- **Regular Check-Ins:** Implement regular check-in meetings focusing on project updates and the team members' well-being. This practice helps leaders gauge the team's stress levels and allows them to address concerns before they escalate.

- **Transparent Communication:** Maintain open lines of communication about organizational changes. Transparency helps reduce uncertainty, which is a significant contributor to stress and fatigue. Use clear, consistent messaging to explain why changes are happening, how they are implemented, and what benefits they are expected to bring.

- **Foster a Culture of Feedback:** Encourage a culture where feedback is seen as a constructive part of growth. Create formal and informal opportunities for feedback, ensuring that all team members feel their voices are heard and valued.

Developing Individual and Organizational Resilience

- **Training and Development:** Offer training programs focused on developing skills that enhance personal resilience, such as stress management, effective communication, and adaptive thinking. Equipping employees with these skills helps them manage change more effectively.

- **Promote Work-Life Balance:** Encourage practices that promote a healthy work-life balance. This could include flexible working hours, remote working options, and ensuring realistic and manageable workloads. A balanced team is less likely to experience burnout and more likely to maintain productivity through change.

- **Wellness Programs:** Implement wellness programs that include activities like mindfulness sessions, exercise classes, and mental health workshops. These initiatives can mitigate the effects of stress and build a stronger, more focused team.

Staying Ahead of Change

- **Scenario Planning:** Engage in regular scenario planning exercises to anticipate potential industry changes and challenges. This proactive approach allows the company to adapt quickly to external changes and maintain a competitive edge.

- **Innovative Thinking Workshops:** Organize workshops that encourage innovative thinking and problem-solving. These sessions aim to harness employees' creative potential, inviting them to contribute ideas that can improve operations, products, or services.

- **Leverage Technology:** Utilize technology to streamline processes, enhance communication, and facilitate change management. Digital tools can help teams stay connected and efficient, especially when navigating complex changes.

- **Build a Change-Ready Culture:** Cultivate an organizational culture that views change as an opportunity for growth rather than a threat. Celebrate successes, even small ones, during the transformation process to boost morale and reinforce the positive aspects of change.

By implementing these strategies, businesses can manage fatigue effectively and remain agile in a dynamic business environment. A compassionate, human-centered approach ensures that while the organization strives for innovation and adaptability, it also supports the well-being and development of every team member. This balance is crucial for sustainable growth and long-term success in today's ever-evolving marketplace.

Navigating the path to transformation has laid the groundwork for a profound shift in the business paradigm—from the traditional pursuit of individual success to a holistic approach that emphasizes collective well-being, environmental stewardship, and equitable growth. By exploring strategies for embracing a 'we' mindset, redefining success with new metrics, and aligning operations with a purpose that transcends profit, businesses are invited to reimagine their role in society and their potential to contribute positively to the world.

From 'Me' to 'We' has underscored the need to foster a culture of inclusivity, collaboration, and mutual support. By prioritizing the collective over the individual, organizations can create environments where innovation is nurtured, employees feel valued and empowered, and the business can also catalyze societal change.

When we redefine success and become intentional about the broader impact our business can have on the world, we are challenged to look beyond traditional financial metrics and consider the wider impact of our operations on the community, the environment, and social equity.

By adopting measures that reflect these dimensions, we can align our strategies with sustainable and equitable growth principles, ensuring their success contributes to a healthier and more just world. Running a business like this just *feels* better too!

Purpose-driven profits demonstrate that businesses can be successful AND purpose-driven; the two are not diametrically opposed. Aligning business operations with a clear, altruistic purpose is not only feasible but essential for achieving sustainable profits and long-term success.

As we conclude this chapter, it's clear that the path to inspiring the human spirit in business is complex and multifaceted, requiring a deep commitment to change at both the individual and organizational levels. Yet, the promise of this new era of business is one of immense potential—a world in which companies thrive economically and contribute to the flourishing of all life.

By weaving the threads of community focus, redefined success, and purpose-driven profits into the fabric of our business operations, we can navigate the path to transformation with confidence, integrity, and a vision for a better future.

And that is a business worth creating.

Inner Compass: Guiding Questions

As you reflect on business's potential to be a transformative force in society, these guiding questions are designed to help you explore how to align your business model with purpose, integrity, and positive impact. Use them to consider how your organization can be a catalyst for change, driving both profitability and social good.

- **How aligned is your business model with a purpose-driven mission?** Reflect on your current business model. Does it prioritize purpose as much as profit? What shifts can you make to ensure your business contributes meaningfully to societal and environmental well-being?

- **What can you learn from transformational models like B1G1 and B Corporations?** Consider the impact of business models such as Buy-One-Give-One (B1G1) and B Corporations. How can these approaches inspire change in your business? What elements could you adapt to align your business with giving and sustainability?

- **How does your organization foster trust within its community?** Reflect on how your business builds trust with customers, employees, and stakeholders. What actions can you take to deepen trust through transparency, consistency, and genuine engagement?

- **How can you build community as part of your business model?** Consider how your business currently engages with and supports the broader community. What steps can you take to cultivate stronger connections and create a business that thrives through collaboration and collective well-being?

- **How well are you balancing purpose and profit in your business decisions?** Reflect on how you navigate the balance between purpose and profit. Are there areas where you may be compromising one for the other? What strategies can you use to ensure both are equally prioritized?

- **How are you integrating regenerative practices into your business?** Consider how your business can not only be sustainable but regenerative, giving back more than it takes. What practices can you implement to create a company that contributes to the regeneration of both people and the planet?

- **What strategies will help you scale your business with integrity?** Reflect on your plans for growth. How can you ensure that as your business scales, it maintains integrity and stays true to its purpose? What processes can you put in place to support conscious expansion?

- **How are you managing business fatigue and staying resilient?** Consider the challenges you face in managing business fatigue. How do you maintain energy and momentum, both personally and within your organization? What techniques can you adopt to sustain resilience and well-being as you navigate these challenges?

8
Conclusion: Now You Know What Will You Do?

"Never doubt that a small group of thoughtful, committed citizens can change the world. Indeed, it is the only thing that ever has." - Margaret Mead.[1]

As we close this book, we must pause and reflect on our profound journey together. From understanding the essence of what it means to be a Sacred Changemaker to envisioning a legacy that transcends traditional metrics of success, each chapter has built upon the last, creating a roadmap for transforming your business and the world around you.

Key Takeaways

- **The Sacred Changemaker's Path**: Becoming a Sacred Changemaker is about far more than achieving business success. It is a profound, personal transformation that aligns your actions with your values, the community, and the planet. This journey begins within, with self-reflection, mindfulness, and a commitment to personal growth.

- **Conscious Business Practices**: We've explored how integrating conscious, regenerative business models can drive economic success while addressing the social and environmental challenges we face. These practices are not just ethical but also practical, fostering long-term sustainability, resilience, and a deeper sense of purpose.

- **Community and Collaboration**: No changemaker works in isolation. The strength of your impact is magnified when you actively engage with a community of like-minded individuals. Building and nurturing these connections is essential for sparking innovation, fostering support, and driving collective action toward shared goals.

- **Legacy and Impact**: Ultimately, the legacy you leave—both through your business and your personal life—reflects your commitment to these principles. We've discussed how to define, measure, and expand your impact, ensuring it aligns with your vision for a better world.

The Call to Action

Reflection is only the first step. Real change happens when we transform those inner shifts into outer action. The world is ready for you to lead change in more regenerative ways, and now is the time to step into your role as a Sacred Changemaker.

The world is waiting.

Here are a few *(more!)* practical steps to guide you as you move from contemplation to action:

1. **Reflect and Plan**: Take some time to revisit the insights from this book. *Which ideas resonated most deeply with you?* Begin planning to integrate these concepts into your daily life and business practices.

2. **Set Concrete Goals**: Based on your reflections, set specific, measurable goals that align with the changes you want to implement. Whether it's adopting new business practices, starting a community initiative, or enhancing your leadership skills, define what success looks like for each goal.

3. **Engage with the Community**: Reach out to the Sacred Changemakers community or similar networks. Participate in discussions, attend events, and seek mentorship or collaborative op-

portunities to deepen your engagement and broaden your impact.

4. **Take the First Step**: Identify one small action you can take today that aligns with your new goals. Even a small step can create momentum, leading you toward greater transformation.

5. **Commit to Continuous Learning**: The path of a changemaker is one of lifelong learning. Continue seeking new knowledge, challenging your assumptions, and refining your approach as you grow.

As we come full circle, it's time to reflect on your legacy—not just for today or tomorrow, but for generations yet to come.

The question to ask yourself is: **Will you be a good ancestor?**

In Ecuador, I learned from indigenous wisdom about the importance of looking seven generations into the past to honor the lives and lessons of those who came before. Equally, for balance, they also look seven generations into the future to ensure that any choices made today will benefit those yet to be born and, at a very minimum, will not cause any harm.

What seeds are you planting today that will blossom long after you are gone? Your choices now—how you live, lead, and conduct your business—directly shape the world that future generations will inherit.

We are here for only a short time, but our impact ripples through time. We are not only humans and business leaders but stewards of the Earth, caretakers of its resources, and guardians of the human spirit.

Imagine what would happen if we transformed our thinking about who we are becoming as humans and as leaders—if our way of doing business was fueled by the human spirit and elevated toward human flourishing.

Imagine how this would transform the physical, emotional, mental, and spiritual well-being of people in the workplace and beyond. The ripple effects would be profound, touching families, communities, and ultimately the Earth itself.

The greatest legacy we can leave is a life lived with intention, one that honors the planet and all living things.

As more of us embrace the path of Sacred Changemaking, I believe that many of today's challenges—*division, disconnection, and environmental degradation*—will begin to ease. As we elevate our consciousness, we will heal the fractures that divide us when we recognize the shared values that unite us.

Rates of depression, anxiety, addiction, and suicide will decline as people understand they are not alone—that they are part of something much more significant, something deeply connected. We will begin to show up fully in our lives, bringing our whole selves to work and embodying our purpose in all that we do.

A Vision for the Future

Before you take your next step, take a moment to envision the world you want to help create. *What impact will your life and leadership have? How will the work you do now influence future generations?*

The journey ahead is a challenge but also a profound opportunity. Each step you take, with intention and heart, can transform the future. The seeds you plant today will one day grow into something extraordinary—a legacy that transcends generations and fosters a world where people and the planet can thrive.

Thank you for stepping forward and choosing this path. Your courage and commitment make the world a better place.

Let's embark on this journey together, creating a future that resonates with our highest aspirations and values. It's time for us to live in harmony—with ourselves, each other, and all living things.

The time for Sacred Changemaking is now.

Legacy And Impact

> *"What counts in life is not the mere fact that we have lived. It is what difference we have made to the lives of others that will determine the significance of the life we lead."* - Nelson Mandela.[2]

As we look towards the horizon, our focus naturally extends beyond the immediacy of daily tasks to the profound, long-term impact of how we live our lives on society and the planet. This moment invites you to think deeply about the legacy you wish to leave behind. It's an invitation to consider the success you aim to achieve in your lifetime and the enduring mark you want to leave behind as an imprint on the world. Perhaps, like me, you will consider your life itself an invitation to change.

In every chapter, this book challenges you to look at the world with a broader perspective, recognize the ripple effects of your actions, and make conscious choices that will lead to a sustainable and equitable future.

The time is now for us to fall in love with the emergence of life and understand how it is a co-creation of value between us. We must pay attention to the relationships in between and realize that we need to feel more inspired by what you and I, what we, the collective, can co-create together, than whatever we can each do alone.

We need to prepare ourselves to move beyond what we know and let go of the old ways to become and be better. We need to fall in love with relationships, not of people, but the space in between.

Take a moment now to reflect on what would make this life truly worthwhile for you. Now consider what kind of world you want to help co-create for our grandchildren. The relationship between your two answers is where the emergence of life begins to flow.

What is your Sacred Invitation?

Ask yourself about your sacred calling and what you came here to do in this lifetime. These questions aren't just philosophical musings; they touch on the true essence of your existence and the legacy you're yearning to build.

Far from esoteric, research suggests that these inquiries are most often expressed by the dying, who regret not following what felt most natural and meaningful to them. If you want to live a life without regrets, it's worth taking time to figure out what matters most to you.

Passion is the quintessential fuel for legacy. It lights up your path with purpose and propels you toward creating something genuinely significant. Your passion will sustain you through challenges, push you beyond conventional limits, and inspire you to make contributions that deeply resonate with who you are.

As we walk the path of becoming Sacred Changemakers together, remember that every day is an opportunity to author your life story—one that you'd be proud to recount to future generations.

So, consider the narrative you wish to craft.

What stories do you want to share with your grandchildren about your choices, the values you stood for, and your impact on the world?

These reflections are potent catalysts for intentional living, ensuring that the legacy you build is one of purpose, integrity, and positive transformation.

It also needs to be YOUR legacy, your song of significance, the thing you can NOT do.

The cost of not pursuing this path isn't measured in missed opportunities for financial gain or professional recognition but in the profound sense of what could have been, of potential left unfulfilled and contributions not made.

The true price we will pay for apathy is beyond our comprehension. Maybe it will be realizing that you could have contributed to creating a better world but chose instead to stand on the sidelines.

As you contemplate your legacy and impact, allow the wisdom of indigenous cultures to illuminate your path. These cultures speak of dreaming of a new future for humanity—one harmonious with the Earth and all its inhabitants. This profound concept of dreaming is a sacred practice of envisioning and actively creating a future that aligns with the deepest truths of our existence.

As you reflect on the legacy you wish to leave behind, consider how your dreams and sacred calling can contribute to this collective vision for humanity.

Let your sacred calling guide and propel you forward, fueled by your deepest passions. It's about making choices—every single day—that move you closer to your aspirations and contribute to the broader tapestry of a future we all yearn for. This journey of creating a legacy is deeply personal yet universally impactful. It's about aligning your actions with values that resonate with you and echo the aspirations of those who dream of a better world.

Indigenous wisdom teaches us that each individual's dreams are threads in the larger fabric of our collective future. By honoring your dreams and taking concrete steps to realize them, you participate in this ancient tradition of dreaming a new existence for humanity.

Envision a legacy that celebrates your achievements and embodies the principles you hold dear, leaving a mark on the world that inspires future generations to dream even bigger.

This is the story you are called to write, not someday in the future, but one day at a time, starting today. Each decision and action you take is a sentence, paragraph, or chapter in this unfolding narrative.

- *What story do you choose to tell?*
- *How do your dreams contribute to the collective dreaming of a new future?*
- *And what will be the cost of not pursuing this path, not just for yourself but for the world that eagerly awaits your contribution?*

Your journey as a Sacred Changemaker is not merely about personal fulfillment; it's a vital part of a significant movement toward personal healing, business sustainability, and equity for all. By daring to dream and act on those dreams, you join a lineage of visionaries who understand that creating a better future begins with the courage to imagine it and the resolve to bring it to life.

Defining your legacy becomes fundamental as you ponder the narrative you want to craft and the mark you wish to leave on the world. This section guides you through the process of envisioning the long-term impact you aim to achieve, helping you shape a legacy that aligns with your deepest values and aspirations.

Understanding Your Core Values

Before you can define your legacy, it's crucial to have a clear understanding of your core values. These principles guide your decisions and actions and should serve as the foundation of the legacy you aspire to leave.

1. **Identify Your Values:** List the values that resonate deeply with you. These include integrity, compassion, innovation, stewardship, and community. Reflect on how these values have influenced your choices and how they can shape your future actions.

2. **Evaluate Alignment:** Consider how well your current actions and career align with these values. Are there discrepancies between what you value and how you live or work? Identifying these gaps can provide crucial insights into the adjustments needed to forge a more authentic path.

Articulating Your Vision For Good

Once you fully understand your values, you can begin to articulate a vision for your desired impact. This vision should encompass your personal and professional goals and the broader influence you hope to have on society and the environment.

1. **Life Vision Statement:** Craft a vision statement that encapsulates the impact you wish to make. This should be a concise and inspiring expression of your aspirations, such as *"To empower and uplift through education"* or *"To lead innovation for environmental sustainability."*

2. **Goal Setting:** Break down your vision into actionable goals. *What specific achievements would contribute to your legacy?* Setting clear, measurable goals will help you track progress and focus on your long-term vision.

Creating a Plan for Impact

With your values and vision defined, the next step is to create a strategic plan that outlines how you will achieve your legacy. This plan should include both short-term actions and long-term strategies.

1. **Short-Term Actions:** Identify what you can do now to build your legacy. These might be small steps, like volunteering, starting a blog, or leading a project at work that aligns with your values.

2. **Long-Term Strategies:** Develop long-term strategies that will scale your impact over time. This might involve advancing your education, changing career paths, starting a business, or establishing a non-profit organization.

Reflecting on the Ripple Effects

Every action you take has the potential to create ripple effects, influencing others and the world in ways you might not immediately see. Reflect on the potential ripple effects of your actions.

1. **Community Influence:** Consider how your actions might influence your community. *How will your work, ideas, or leadership inspire or support others?*

2. **Environmental Stewardship:** Reflect on how your legacy could impact the environment. *What steps can you take to ensure your actions contribute positively to ecological health?*

3. **Global Impact:** Think about the global implications of your legacy. *In what ways can your contributions extend beyond your immediate community or country?*

Embracing Flexibility and Resilience

As you work towards your legacy, be prepared to embrace flexibility and resilience. Your path may not always be straightforward, and obstacles are inevitable.

1. **Adaptability:** Be open to adjusting your plans as circumstances change. Staying adaptable will help you navigate challenges while maintaining sight of your ultimate goals.

2. **Resilience:** Cultivate resilience by developing a solid support network and maintaining a positive outlook. Resilience will empower you to overcome setbacks and continue pursuing your legacy with determination.

Defining your legacy is more than just setting goals; it's about creating a life that reflects your deepest desires and longings. By thoughtfully considering the long-term impact you wish to have, you can ensure that your legacy is meaningful to you and contributes significantly to the well-being of others and the planet's health. This process is integral to your journey as a Sacred Changemaker, empowering you to leave a lasting imprint on the world.

As you contemplate the legacy you wish to leave behind, it becomes evident that the impact of your business operations will need to extend far beyond the financial bottom line. Your work can be a powerful vehicle for your legacy, embodying the principles you cherish by sustaining and regenerating resources and communities.

This realization guides us into the next crucial aspect of crafting your legacy, for we are writing our collective history in every moment and every action. Your legacy is a part of that.

What will future generations say about our time in human history?

Will You Be A Good Ancestor?

As we come full circle in this journey, it's time to reflect beyond our lifetime and into our place in the history books. We live in a world often focused on short-term goals—quarterly profits, immediate results, quick wins. *What if we shifted our perspective? What if we extended our timeline beyond our lives and began thinking about the impact we're making on the generations yet to come?*

In Ecuador, I learned from indigenous traditions about looking seven generations back, honoring the ancestors who came before us, and acknowledging that we are standing on their shoulders. Their wisdom, decisions, and sacrifices shape the lives we live today. It's humbling to realize how deeply we are connected to the past—and, just as importantly, to the future. This brings us to an essential question:

What kind of ancestor will you be?

What seeds will you plant during your lifetime that will blossom long after you're gone?

As leaders, entrepreneurs, and changemakers, we are not just shaping the present—we are shaping the future. The choices we make, the businesses we build, and the communities we nurture are the foundation upon which future generations will stand.

Some of us have children, grandchildren, or students, while others may not. However, we are all future ancestors. We all have a responsibility to nurture, protect, and restore balance to the Earth—our shared home, Mother Earth, Gaia, Pachamama. She gives us life, sustains us, and provides our needed resources.

The most incredible legacy we can leave is to live in a way that honors her and all life.

We don't need anyone to tell us that the world must change. The current way of life is unsustainable. But now you have the tools to walk forward in a new way. The real question is:

- **What will you do with them?**
- **Will you become a Sacred Changemaker, a force for good in your life and the world?**
- **Will you take action, face reality, and hold the space for others to inspire and create a ripple effect of change across the globe?**

When I look up at the night sky, I imagine the ancestors watching over us. I feel their presence with every breath. They remind me that the choices we make today will echo into the future.

- **Will you be a good ancestor?**
- **Will you honor the legacy of those who came before by leaving behind a world that is more sustainable, compassionate, and just?**
- **Can those yet-to-be-born depend on you?**

This isn't just about leaving a legacy of material wealth or personal achievement. It's about leaving behind something far more meaningful—*a world where future generations can thrive.* It's about being the kind of ancestor who planted seeds of change and tended them with care, ensuring they would flourish long after we are gone.

The universe moves in perfect synchronicity, and we are part of that rhythm. We need to decide how we want to move within it. *Will we continue to try to dominate it, or will we learn to live in a relationship with it?* Our choices will either create harmony and coherence or dissonance and destruction. If we genuinely seek balance, we must align ourselves with the rhythm of life, just as the universe does.

So take a moment to step outside, look up at the stars, and reflect on your place in humanity's great lineage. You are part of a vast web of life, connected to all who came before and will come after. One day, you will be an ancestor, watching over the future generations who walk this Earth.

What legacy will you leave behind?

Throughout this book, I hope I have inspired you to embrace change—not just the change you anticipated, but a more expansive vision of transformation. We must shift from short-term thinking to a long-term view of our potential as human beings and as stewards of this planet. We each have a part to play in this great dance of life. It is up to each of us to decide whether we will take responsibility for our home, for the future, and the well-being of all life.

To be good ancestors, we must heal ourselves, love from our center, and bring that love into our leadership and business. We must honor everyone's stories, tell the truth, and create spaces where healing can take place. We must challenge injustice, embrace diversity, and respect all living things. We must learn to live regeneratively, give back more than we take, and honor the sacredness of life in all we do.

Will you be a good ancestor?

The choice is yours.

Inner Compass: Guiding Questions

This chapter invites you to reflect on the deeper aspects of your legacy and the impact you want to leave behind. These guiding questions help you connect with your sacred calling, clarify your core values, and consider the legacy you are building. Take your time with each question, allowing yourself to explore your influence on the future, personally and through your work.

- **What is your sacred calling, and how are you living it?** Reflect on the unique purpose that calls to you at the deepest level. How are you currently embodying this calling in your life and leadership? What steps can you take to fully align your actions with your sacred mission?

- **How clear are you on your core values?** Consider the core values that guide your decisions and shape your leadership. Are these values consistently reflected in your actions and business practices? How can you ensure that your values remain at the forefront of your life and work?

- **What kind of ancestor do you want to be?** Reflect on the long-term impact of your choices, not just for the present but for future generations. What legacy do you hope to leave behind, and how can you start planting the seeds for that legacy now?

- **How does your business contribute to your legacy?** Consider the impact your business is having on the world. How aligned is your business model with the legacy you want to create? What changes can you make to ensure that your business contributes to the well-being of future generations?

- **What are the seeds of change you are planting today?** Reflect on your actions now—whether in your personal life, business, or community. Are these actions aligned with the future you want to create? How can you nurture these seeds to ensure they grow and flourish over time?

- **How can you honor the ancestors who came before you?** Reflect on the wisdom, strength, and sacrifices of those who came before you. How can you honor their legacy by continuing the work they started or by forging a new path that reflects the values they passed down?

- **What does it mean for you to build a legacy of impact?** Consider the ways in which your personal and professional life contribute to the broader world. How can you expand your influence to create a lasting, positive impact on your community, industry, or the planet?

- **How will you ensure that your life's work continues after you're gone?** Reflect on the systems, structures, or mentorship you can put in place to ensure that the values, mission, and purpose you've embodied continue to influence others long after you've left. What can you do today to create a lasting, sustainable impact?

Epilogue

"If success or failure of this planet and of human beings depended on how I am and what I do... HOW WOULD I BE? WHAT WOULD I DO?" – R. Buckminster Fuller[1]

As I sit here reflecting on our journey together through this book, I feel an overwhelming sense of gratitude. Writing *Beyond Profit* has been one of my life's most important and personal missions. It has come from the deepest part of me, my passion for change, and my belief that each one of us holds the power to make a profound difference in this world.

This book is more than words on a page—*it's an invitation, a call to action,* and *a heartfelt plea* for you to join me in something much bigger than ourselves.

I've shared stories, insights, and strategies with you, but what truly matters now is what you do with them. This is your invitation to step into a new way of being, one that doesn't just lead a business but transforms it—and, through that, transforms our world.

You don't have to be perfect, and you don't have to have all the answers right now. All that's required is a willingness to take that first step, to embrace the calling that has brought you here, and to trust that together, we can create something extraordinary.

I still remember standing in rooms full of leaders, from the highest-ranking executives to the most passionate entrepreneurs, and asking, *"Who here sees themselves as a leader?"* The hesitation in those rooms often surprised me, and it became clear that leadership is often seen as something for *"others,"* for those with titles and authority. But the truth is, we are all leading, whether we recognize it or not. We lead ourselves, we lead our families, and, most importantly, we lead by the example we set every single day.

Leadership is not a role we step into—it's who we are at our core.

As we reach the end of this book, I want to extend my deepest gratitude to you. Thank you for investing your time, energy, and heart into these pages. Thank you for embracing the concepts, challenges, and visions laid out before you. Most importantly, thank you for the difference you are committed to making in the world. Your intentions and efforts to create positive change and reshape how we do business are essential to us all.

Sink or swim, we are in this together.

You've been invited to join us in transforming yourself so we can all become who we need to be to help others do the same. This movement goes beyond personal success; it is about creating a meaningful and lasting impact on the world.

Your willingness to embark on this journey, challenge the status quo, and envision a different way of doing business speaks volumes about your leadership and commitment to something far greater than any one of us can achieve alone.

It's important to recognize that our future, both as individuals and as a collective, will be shaped by the actions we take today. We stand at a pivotal moment in history—*one where our decisions and actions will determine the course of humanity's survival.* This is a monumental responsibility and an unparalleled challenge. The stakes could not be higher, but the potential for transformation is within us all.

We already have what we need to make a lasting, positive difference.

The truth is, the world doesn't just need business leaders—it needs people who care deeply, who act with purpose, and who are willing to be brave enough to step forward and say, *"I will make a difference."* Those who recognize that all life is sacred and that inspiring change, *the right kind of change,* is necessary now.

I know that if you've made it to the end of this book, something in you resonates with this message. Maybe it's a whisper, maybe it's a roar, but it's there—the desire to make a meaningful impact and to be part of the change our world so desperately needs.

As we learn to live in resonance with ourselves, each other, and all living things, we unlock the potential for profound change. This book is my personal invitation for you to join me and step into that potential, to become a Sacred Changemaker, and to contribute to a future that honors life in all its forms.

But remember, this path of transformation is not one we walk alone. We are a community of leaders, visionaries, and changemakers—each playing our part in weaving a new tapestry of business and society that reflects our highest aspirations.

The journey to becoming a Sacred Changemaker is about more than just business; it's about us, the lives we touch, the systems we help transform, and the legacy we leave behind. It's about how we learn to love ourselves, each other, and all living things, not forgetting the relational field that gives us our place in the web of life.

Thank you for walking this path with me. Let's make our journey one that future generations will look back on and say, *"They didn't just talk about change—they lived it."* Together, we can and will make a difference. I hope this is not the end of the journey for you but merely the beginning, and I am honored to walk this path with you.

With love, resonance, and an unwavering belief in us,

Jayne xo

Next Steps: Join Our Sacred Changemakers Inner Circle

As you close this book, know that your journey as a Sacred Changemaker is just beginning. You've gained new insights, inspiration, and a call to create meaningful change within yourself and the world around you. Now it's time to put those aspirations into action, and the good news is—you don't have to do it alone.

We invite you to continue this life-affirming journey with our community at Sacred Changemakers. Here, you'll find a space to grow, learn, and make a lasting impact alongside like-minded individuals equally committed to creating positive change in the world.

- **Visit Our Website**: Start by exploring more at SacredChangemakers.com[2]. This is your portal to a wealth of resources, tools, and insights that can support your ongoing journey toward growth and impact.

- **Take the Resonance Codes Evaluation** a powerful tool for personal and relational growth. Discover your home frequency and learn how to navigate your energetic development. The Resonance Codes provide deep insights into how you engage with others, how you face challenges, and how to move into a state of resonance and flow. It's a powerful tool for personal and relational growth. Learn more here[3]

- **Sign Up for Our Newsletter**: Stay connected with us by subscribing to our newsletter. You'll receive curated content, the latest updates, and inspiring stories delivered directly to your inbox. It's an easy way to stay plugged into our community and keep the momentum going. Sign up on our website[4]

- **Listen to Our Podcast**: Dive deeper into the stories and ideas shaping our mission by tuning into the Sacred Changemakers podcast[5]. Each episode is designed to inspire and challenge you, offering insights from trailblazers in conscious business and community leadership who are redefining what it means to create change.

- **Join Our Inner Circle:** If you are ready to commit to the next level, we invite you to apply to our exclusive, invitation-only Sacred Changemakers Inner Circle[6]. This carefully curated community offers personalized support, deeper collaboration, and unique networking opportunities to help you accelerate your growth and maximize your impact.

The world needs more than leaders; it needs Sacred Changemakers—individuals like you ready to step up and make a difference. By joining our community, you're committing to your own personal evolution and to being part of a larger movement. Together, we can turn individual actions into collective power, creating a future that reflects our highest values and aspirations.

Thank you for embarking on this journey with us. We are truly grateful to have you as part of the Sacred Changemakers community, and we look forward to witnessing the incredible impact you will make. The path ahead is full of possibility, and every step you take moves us toward a more just, sustainable, and compassionate world.

Let's make this journey unforgettable—creating a legacy of lasting change for generations.

Visit us today and take the next step toward transforming your passion into action. Your story matters, your impact is needed, and this is just the beginning.

Together, let's create a world where every action contributes to a brighter future for us all.

Acknowledgements

Beyond Profit is a reflection of the evolution in my work, inspired by a powerful shift I see in so many leaders today—a shift toward purpose, inclusion, and the belief that business can be a force for good.

My clients and colleagues have profoundly shaped this book, from business leaders responding to the UN SDGs and the Inner Development Goals to those integrating Diversity, Equity, and Inclusion and prioritizing purpose-driven profits. Witnessing their efforts to build more conscious businesses has been humbling, and Sacred Changemakers' mission is to support this growing wave of change. This moment of human evolution is gaining ground, and I'm honored to be part of it.

I must thank my spirit guides, the Elders, whose wisdom and encouragement continue to be my compass throughout this journey.

To the late Joan King, a brilliant mentor during my early days in the U.S. who helped me deepen my thinking about resonance—your insights and our conversations continue to inspire me.

To Laurie Benson and the Pachamama Alliance for inviting me to participate in an unforgettable journey into the Amazon rainforest in Ecuador – I am forever changed.

To my private clients, thank you for your trust and for pioneering new paths in business—you bring essential light to this work.

To my podcast guests, thank you for sharing your insights and paving the way toward a more conscious future—your support means so much.

My Sacred Changemakers Inner Circle members, who courageously bring these ideas to life every day, are a continual source of inspiration. Your commitment, resilience, and the impact you're making in the world move me deeply. Our community calls are often the highlight of my week, and I am humbled and honored to share this journey with each of you. Thank you for embodying this work with such grace and dedication.

To my husband, Nick, for his unwavering belief in my work, his proofreading skills, and his willingness to handle life while I was deep in the writing process.

To my family, thank you for your understanding when I was immersed in creating and missed out on precious moments.

And to my sacred circles of women, who have supported me every step of the way, pushing me to keep going even when the path wasn't clear—you know who you are (!) I honestly don't know where I'd be without you.

A special thank you to Kym Ellis for her invaluable feedback on the early draft—your honesty and insights helped shape this book in meaningful ways.

To Steven Morris, I am deeply grateful for your unwavering support and for lending your voice to the Foreword—your belief in this work means more than words can convey.

To all of my colleagues who read the book pre-launch and offered feedback and testimonials, your encouragement has been invaluable.

Finally, my wish is that *Beyond Profit* serves as a catalyst for readers to reimagine the future of leadership and business. I hope this book inspires you to expand your approach to change, to move beyond traditional models, and to pioneer a path where purpose and profit align in harmony.

To the coaches, consultants, and leaders committed to making a difference, may this work encourage you to inspire change for good. We have the power to create a future where business thrives and uplifts us all, and I hope you now also have a compass to help you move into action. We can be the guides that humanity needs.

Endnotes

Introduction

1. *"Citizenship in a Republic"* speech delivered at the Sorbonne in Paris, France, on April 23, 1910 by Theodore Roosevelt. More recently come to be known as "The Man In The Arena".

2. *The Sacred Changemakers Podcast*: https://SacredChangemakers.com/podcast

3. Paul Polman, *SDG Business Forum*, October 2019

4. Jayne Warrilow, *The Secret Language Of Resonance*, 2014

5. Charles Eisenstein, *"Sacred Economics: Money, Gift & Society in the Age of Transition"*, North Atlantic Books, Berkeley California, 2021

6. Paul Polman, CEO of Unilever, speaking at the SDG Business Forum 2019

7. Zeno, *"Strength of Purpose Study"*, June 17, 2020: https://www.zenogroup.com/insights/2020-zeno-strength-purpose

8. Jordan Bar Am, Vinit Doshi, Anadi Malik, Steve Noble McKinsey & Company, and Sherry Frey, NielsenIQ *"Consumers Care About Sustainability – and Back It Up with their Wallets"*, February 6, 2023

9. Diana O'Brien, Andy Main, Suzanne Kounkel and Anthony R, Stephan, Deloitte, *"Purpose is Everything: How brands that authentically lead with purpose are changing the nature of business today"*, article 15 October 2019

10. UN Secretary-General António Guterres, *"We do have a choice: Creating tipping points for climate progress – or careening to tipping points for climate disaster."*, May 2024 – https://www.un.org/sg/en/content/secretary-general/speeches/2024-06-05/discurso-especial-sobre-la-acci%C3%B3n-clim%C3%A1tica-%E2%80%9Cla-hora-de-la-verdad%E2%80%9D

11. SHRM Foundation, *Mental Health in America, A 2022 Workplace Report*, 2022: https://www.workplacementalhealth.shrm.org/wp-content/uploads/2022/04/Mental-Health-in-America-A-2022-Workplace-Report.pdf

12. The Federal Reserve Bank of St. Louis, Institue For Economic Equity, The State Of US Wealth Inequality, 2024: https://www.stlouisfed.org/institute-for-economic-equity/the-state-of-us-wealth-inequality

13. Gallup, State Of The Global Workplace Annual report, 2024: https://www.gallup.com/workplace/349484/state-of-the-global-workplace.aspx

14. Rasmus Hougaard, Angela Gest McCall, Harvard Business Review, Idea Brief "Compassionate Leadership: How to Do Hard Things in a Human Way" 2021: https://www.harvardbusiness.org/wp-content/uploads/2021/12/Compassionate-Leadership-How-to-Do-Hard-Things-in-a-Human-Way-Idea-Brief.pdf

15. Jakob Trollbäck, Episode 144, Sacred Changemakers Podcast, *The Intersection of Design And Sustainability,* 2024: https://sacredchangemakers.com/144-the-intersection-of-design-and-sustainability-with-jakob-trollback/

16. © Jayne Warrilow International, LLC

17. Dr Manto Gotsi, Bayes Business School, University of London, *"A Paradox Approach to Organizational Tensions During the Pandemic Crisis," Journal Of Management Inquiry, Volume 30, 2021*

18. Edelman, *Brand Trust Barometer* 2023: https;//edelman.com/trust/2023/trust-barometer

19. Dawn Heiberg, FirstUp, *Key statistics about Millennials in the workplace:* May 2024 https://firstup.io/blog/key-statistics-millennials-in-the-workplace/

20. Pew Research Center, *Majority of workers who quit a job in 2021 cite low pay, no opportunities for advancement, feeling disrespected,* March 2022: https://www.pewresearch.org/short-reads/2022/03/09/majority-of-workers-who-quit-a-job-in-2021-cite-low-pay-no-opportunities-for-advancement-feeling-disrespected/

21. Hans Rosling, *The Worldview Upgrader – Gapminder launches a groundbreaking new service to fight misconceptions,* November 2020: https://www.gapminder.org/news/the-worldview-upgrader-gapminder-launches-a-groundbreaking-new-service-to-fight-misconceptions/

22. The Internal Development Goals, https://www.idg.com/

23. Jerry Colonna, *Reunion: Leadership and the Longing to Belong*, Harper Collins, 2023

24. About Sacred Changemakers Vision: https://sacredchangemakers.com/about/

The Leader Within

1. Howard Zinn, *"You Can't Be Neutral on a Moving Train: A Personal History of Our Times.",* Beacon press, Boston, 2018

2. David Whyte, the poem *Working Together* in *"River Flow: New & Selected Poems.",* Many Rivers Press, 2007

3. Insight Timer is a free meditation app offering a vast library of guided meditations, music tracks, and talks led by experts. It's available for both iOS and Android devices. https://insighttimer.com/

4. *Happier Me App for Teens & Adults:* https://happierme.app/

5. Jack Kornfield, *"Buddha's Little Instruction Book"*, Bantam, May 1, 1994

A New Way Of Being

1. Jayne Warrilow, *"The Secret Language of Resonance: The Incredible Truth About Life and Well-being"*, JWI, 2024

From The Individual To The Collective

1. Paul Polman, Andrew Winston, *"Net Positive: How Courageous Companies Thrive by Giving More Than They Take"*, Harvard Business Review Press, 2022

2. Deloitte, 2020 Global Marketing Trends: https://www2.deloitte.com/us/en/insights/topics/marketing-and-sales-operations/global-marketing-trends/2020/purpose-driven-companies.html

3. Cone/Porter Novelli Purpose Study 2018, Engage For Good: https://engageforgood.com/2018-cone-porter-novelli-purpose-study/

4. Kris Jenner, *"The Power of Personal Branding"* on Masterclass.com

Regenerative Leadership: Catalyzing Necessary Change

1. Jane Goodall, Jane Goodall Institute Canada: https://janegoodall.ca/what-we-do/

2. Dr. Al Spicer, Lynn Rousseau, Angela Nesbitt, Crina Ancuta, Jo Meadwell, Tess Cox, Episode 133. Sacred Duty: The Role Of Spirituality In The Workplace, Sacred Changemakers Podcast – https://sacredchangemakers.com/133-sacred-duty-the-role-of-spirituality-in-the-workplace/

3. **Campbell, Joseph** – The Hero's Journey, Joseph Campbell on His Life and Work (The Collected Works of Joseph Campbell) November 2018, Published by Joseph Campbell Foundation

4. Daniel Christian Wahl, *Designing Regenerative Cultures,* Triarchy Press, 2016

The Path to Transformation

1. Peter M. Senge, *The Fifth Discipline: The Art & Practice of The Learning Organization,* Crown Currency; Revised & Updated edition (March 25, 2010)

Transformational Business Models

1. Peter F Drucker, *Management Cases*, Revised Edition by Joseph A. Maciarello, Harper Collins, 2009

2. We encourage you to join us on this journey. Integrating B1G1's model into your business will enhance your social impact and inspire your customers and community to participate in something extraordinary. Every transaction can make a real difference. Visit **B1G1.com** for more details. When you use our referral code **BM13056**, B1G1 will make even more impact on our behalf. Let's create a better world, one purposeful act at a time.

3. If you want to find out more about becoming a B-Corp, go here https://bcorporation.net

4. Tim Jones, Episode 137 "*To B or not to B?*" Sacred Changemakers Podcast https://sacredchangemakers.com/137-to-b-or-not-to-b-is-b-corp-the-future-of-your-business-with-tim-jones137/

Conclusion: Now You Know What Will You Do?

1. Margaret Mead, https://en.wikiquote.org/wiki/Margaret_Mead

2. Nelson Mandela speaking at the *90th birthday celebration of Walter Sisulu* at the Walter Sisulu Hall in Randburg, Johannesburg, South Africa, on May 18, 2002.

Epilogue

1. R. Buckminster Fuller, as quoted on https://www.goodreads.com/quotes/105761-if-success-or-failure-of-this-planet-and-of-human

2. https://sacredchangemakers.com

3. https:/quiz.sacredchangemakers.com

4. https://sacredchangemakers.com

5. https://sacredchangemakers.com

6. https://sacredchangemakers.com/community

Publisher's note: Every possible effort has been made to ensure that the information contained in this book is accurate when going to press, and the publishers and author cannot accept responsibility for any errors or omissions, however caused. No responsibility for loss or damage occasioned by any person acting or refraining from action as a result of this publication can be accepted by the editor, the publisher, or the author.

Copyright © 2024 by Jayne Warrilow

All rights reserved.

No portion of this book may be reproduced in any form without written permission from the publisher or author except as permitted by U.S. copyright law.

This publication is designed to provide accurate and authoritative information in regard to the subject matter covered. It is sold with the understanding that neither the author nor the publisher is engaged in rendering legal, investment, accounting, or other professional services. While the publisher and author have used their best efforts in preparing this book, they make no representations or warranties with respect to the accuracy or completeness of the contents of this book and specifically disclaim any implied warranties of merchantability or fitness for a particular purpose. No warranty may be created or extended by sales representatives or written sales materials. The advice and strategies contained herein may not be suitable for your situation. You should consult with a professional when appropriate. Neither the publisher nor the author shall be liable for any loss of profit or any other commercial damages, including but not limited to special, incidental, consequential, personal, or other damages.

Published by Changemaker Press, Sacred Changemakers LLC

Book Design by Jayne Warrilow

First edition 2024

ISBNs

ISBN 978-1-947285-02-6 (eBook)

ISBN 978-1-947285-03-3 (Hardcover)

ISBN 978-1-947285-04-0 (Paperback)

Printed in Great Britain
by Amazon